Reading and the Elementary School Child

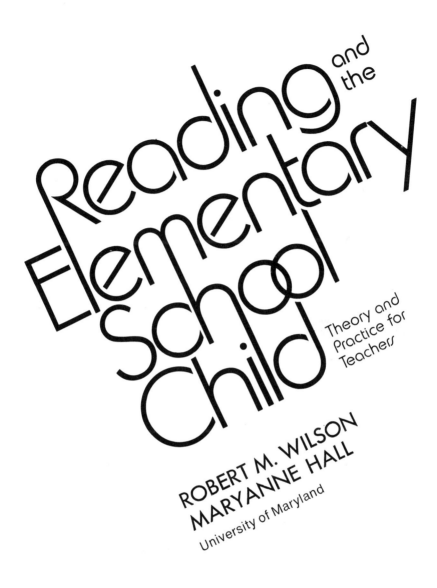

Reading and the Elementary School Child

Theory and Practice for Teachers

ROBERT M. WILSON
MARYANNE HALL
University of Maryland

D. VAN NOSTRAND COMPANY

New York Cincinnati Toronto London Melbourne

D. Van Nostrand Company Regional Offices:
New York   Cincinnati   Millbrae

D. Van Nostrand Company International Offices:
London   Toronto   Melbourne

Published by D. Van Nostrand Company
450 West 33rd Street, New York, N. Y. 10001

Published simultaneously in Canada by
Van Nostrand Reinhold Ltd.

10   9   8   7   6   5   4   3

Photographs on pages 28, 62, 100, 153, 171, 205, 271, 320, and 331 by
    Charles Bohn
Photograph on page 129 by Bruce Roberts from Rapho Guillumette Pictures

Respect the child.

—EMERSON

Contents

Foreword

This book skillfully presents a general background for effective reading instruction without neglecting the many specific teaching techniques all reading teachers seek. Recognizing that successful teachers of reading are those who formulate for themselves a basic teaching strategy within which they can recognize and promote sequences in skill development, the authors have laid down here basic principles which provide guidance in the selection of specific teaching techniques, activities, and materials.

According to the authors' view, successful teachers are those who have information on how learning occurs, who know the findings of research, who have studied reading programs devised by specialists, and who understand the theory on which each program is based. And, as Drs. Wilson and Hall emphasize so often in this text, they use their foundation of information to hit upon basic strategies practical for their own unique classrooms.

With each decade since 1920, better identification of specific objectives—the first essential for effective instruction—has contributed greatly to improved reading instruction. This book functionally identifies specific objectives in terms of attitudes, skills, and understandings. It also assists reading teachers in their attempts to anticipate skills and understandings which pupils must develop if they are to become good readers. For reading teachers must know the word analysis skills pupils need, the specific skills and attitudes which facilitate comprehension, and the key reading-study skills. They must encourage extensive reading as an integral part of a sound reading program. And their directed reading activities must be purposeful. In basal readers and in other books they must quickly recognize specific situations which may be used to develop skills appropriate for their pupils.

Successful teachers, too, use a variety of learning activities to arouse and maintain interest. They understand that a given learning activity is not equally effective for all objectives and with all pupils. They try out many activities to find those most effective with individuals in their classes. Such teachers will find in this book a wealth of specific suggestions on how to teach, for the authors have succeeded in culling from their many experiences with children those suggestions which are really practicable.

Successful teachers also understand the factors which account for differences in reading achievement, for they have command of techniques and materials which help determine the extent to which such factors are present. When essential factors appear lacking, they have ideas for remedial instruction, they study each child so that his specific needs may be met with individualized instruction, and they know what to do if conditions justify the assistance of a specialist.

Successful teachers know how to work not only with children but with parents, reading specialists, and supervisors. They are willing to work as members of a team, and they know how to do so. Since the authors are actively engaged in in-service programs, it is not surprising that their book includes apt suggestions on how all concerned may work together on reading problems.

In their writing, as in their teaching that I have witnessed, the authors reveal high respect for teachers, regarding them as professional workers seeking understanding as well as techniques. In this book teachers will find numerous ideas for immediate application while they will at the same time arrive at understandings enabling them to apply techniques intelligently.

Alvin W. Schindler

Preface

At a time when the nation as a whole and the education profession in particular are directing new efforts to the improvement of the reading experiences and skills of America's children, we hope and we believe that a new survey of the field is in order. For it has seemed to us in our work with pre-professionals, in-service teachers, colleagues from all aspects of education, and children in the schools, that an organized, relatively fundamental understanding of reading instruction has been one of the most elusive and certainly one of the most sought after goals of elementary educators. We therefore offer the present book as a broad, contemporary *gestalt* of reading theory, research, and practice. We offer it particularly to the student of elementary education who seeks an up-to-date picture of "what the field is all about"—either as an introduction or as a refresher.

In thus attempting to construct a book which would be both practical and illuminating for today's elementary reading teacher, we were mindful that he plunges very early into a complex welter of procedures, materials, theories, and intricate problems with which he cannot realistically be expected to deal effectively until he has got his general bearings. We were reminded too how ironic it is that the very innovation and reexamination which characterizes the healthy state of the reading profession today may well be least likely to provide a reassuring port in the storm from which the teacher can embark—and to which he will want to return—in his daily work with children.

So we have tried to build this book upon the principles of simplicity, unity, and a close theory-and-practice correspondence. We make minimal assumptions about background knowledge or experience the student brings to Part One, our overview of reading instruction. Yet we do move him along promptly, following four survey chapters there, into the essential skills and levels of reading in Part Two, where he encounters stages ranging from pre-reading to higher levels of study and pleasure reading. Part Three on implementation extends the theory-into-practice direction of the book through prototype lesson plans and other basic components of the reading program, and the book concludes with three appendices as further aids to implementation.

One final principle which guided us ought to be mentioned. As you read the following pages, whether for study or for self-improvement, we hope you will detect a happy tone about teaching children to read. As learning about reading becomes a *happy* experience for you, we hope you will make every effort to make reading a *happy* learning experience for the children whose lives you touch. For ultimately, of course, our major concern is that good things will happen with children in classrooms as a result of this text. That is why we have placed special emphasis on the individual child throughout the book, not just in theory but with many suggestions for practice.

Our debts to those who assisted in this exciting effort are many, not the least of which are the contributions, direct and indirect, of children and students from whom we have learned much. We wish also to acknowledge the typing assistance of Mrs. Betty Burson, Mrs. Jane Mirsetich, and Mrs. Susan Kern. To Mrs. Barbara Wainer, Assistant Professor at Prince George's County Community College, we are grateful for her diligent efforts to help us communicate our thoughts effectively and for her careful proofreading. Mrs. Rita S. Bean, Reading Supervisor of the Upper St. Clair (Pennsylvania) School District, contributed significantly to the practical nature of the applications for teachers, especially in chapters 14 and 15. And our excellent colleague Dr. Alvin W. Schindler, Professor of Education at the University of Maryland, honored us by serving as that person one finds behind every manuscript: the friend who counsels, encourages, and inspires.

RMW
MAH

Reading and the Elementary School Child

PART ONE

AN OVERVIEW OF READING INSTRUCTION

CHAPTER ONE

MAPPING THE FIELD CALLED READING

Advance Organizer

The focus of all language arts is communication, and one vital ingredient in communication is reading—a topic of major concern not only to teachers but to researchers, parents, and society in general. For the new or prospective teacher, the field of reading might be compared to an as yet unexplored region encompassing several distinct parts, all of which are necessary for a grasp of the total complex area. Such an understanding, in turn, is an imperative prior step to the planning and carrying out of instruction, since it provides the teacher with a foundation and perspective from which to proceed. Accordingly, this chapter introduces the main aspects of the reading process, all of which contribute to an overview of the field.

GETTING THE FIELD IN FOCUS

The moment the elementary school teacher, or prospective teacher, asks himself questions such as, "How much time should I spend developing sight vocabulary in first grade?" or "What are the best independent reading activities for this group of fourth-graders?", he finds himself confronted with the complexity of the reading process. The more questions he asks, the more he studies the professional literature, the more he observes and works with children, the greater will be his appreciation of not only the manifold dimensions involved in reading but also their highly subtle interrelationships.

Much is known about reading, but our knowledge is not yet so complete that we can give each new teacher a model that he can use with assurance as an accepted, organized body of data with which to correlate all his teaching and observation of reading. Each teacher must realize that his overview of the field can be only a tentative one. However, an overview is necessary so that the teacher does not work in a vacuum. Meaningful answers to his questions and meaningful programs of reading instruction for children are unlikely to be formulated unless the teacher possesses a generalized understanding of the total reading process and retains an open-minded receptivity to new developments.

Society at large has become increasingly concerned with the reading instruction of today's young people. The past decade has seen an unprecedented amount of debate—in the popular press, in academic circles, among interested laymen—about questions such as whether the average American pupil reads better than his Russian and English counterparts, or better than his father did when he was in school; and whether, in any case, he reads as well as he is capable of reading. More attention is also being paid to the question of his ability to handle the reading demands of the role he will assume after his public schooling is completed—as, for example, a freshman in college, a working member of society, a member of the armed forces, or simply as a citizen who will need to read a variety of printed materials in order to remain informed about his complex environment.

Many concerned parties are inquiring about the degree to which current reading instruction meets the needs of young people who enter school with cultural, linguistic, and economic backgrounds considerably different from those of populations traditionally served by the schools in their area. The issue is raised of modifying and supplementing existing instructional methods and materials in order to increase their applicability and relevance. Developing new instruction that meets the needs of all members of our multi-cultural population is likewise being stressed. Also significantly increasing is the public consciousness of the possibility of a full-front federal attack on reading deficiency. A concrete example is the national "Right to Read" program, which is aiming at universal literacy throughout the country and fulfillment of maximum reading capacity. In these developments in the field of reading one can identify two strong currents of thought: a general recognition that more needs to be discovered about the act of reading, how it is learned, and how it can be taught; and the awareness that action ought to be taken now to correct existing reading problems.

As happens with any topic that becomes a full-blown public issue, a certain amount of exaggeration has been vigorously asserted on every side of the reading issue. Statistics have been misinterpreted and used out of context. The air has sometimes been clouded with sensationalism and doomsday prophecies. Evidence has not always been marshalled objectively. Yet no one in education today would deny that the schools face an exceedingly difficult challenge, which they are not always able to meet, in carrying out their acknowledged mandate: Teach every child to read as well as he is able.

READING AS A COMMUNICATION TOOL

Instruction in the language arts—listening, speaking, writing, and reading—focuses on the ultimate purpose of improving the pupil's receptive and expressive skills of communication. Viewed as a tool of communication, reading is of importance in scholastic success, job success, continuing education and personal improvement, and pleasure. Let us examine in detail the role of reading in each of these general areas.

Reading for Scholastic Success

Success in school, clearly, is closely tied to success in reading. It has often been remarked that after a child learns to read, he reads to learn. The poor reader, blocked from using this major avenue of learning, experiences failure in many school situations. In the content areas of English, social studies, science, and mathematics, reading assignments are common and time-consuming. Pupils are expected to have the necessary skills to read content material accurately, but all too often the skills are missing. Even those pupils who perform well in instructional reading situations may experience difficulty with content area texts. Aside from being a handicap in specific subjects, poor reading is also a contributing factor to the total relationship of the pupil to school. Statistics on the reading achievement of dropouts and delinquents show a high incidence of reading failure.[1] Underachievement can lead to feelings of boredom or inadequacy and consequent behavioral problems.

The child with limited reading ability, therefore, is ideally placed in a modified learning situation. It is important for teachers to be alert to reading materials that present difficulty, to make program adjustments, and to provide specialized instruction which enables the pupil to adapt to the requirements of varied reading tasks. (Chapter 9 discusses problems involved in study-type reading more fully.)

Reading for Job Success

There are few occupations in today's world for which some reading skills are not necessary, and there are many occupations for which mature reading skills are virtually mandatory. Employees are expected to follow written commands in the form of messages and signs: "Danger!" . . . "No Smoking!" . . . "Wet Paint." Employers communicate through written notes, letters, and memos. Many expect employees to be up-to-date on the latest trends in their fields. Authors who write vocational materials assume that the materials will be used by persons who have the basic reading vocabulary in a particular area.

In our fast-changing world, the average wage earner finds that he must be retrained at least once during his lifetime. Government estimates suggest that 50 percent of the jobs that will be held ten years from now do not even exist today, and that future generations of Americans may pursue two or three careers during their lifetimes.[2] While employers often provide for retraining through on-the-job experiences, lectures, films, and the like, much retraining will be in the form of reading. The emphasis placed on reading instruction in Job Corps retraining efforts and the interest on the part of industry in adult literacy classes reflect the growing acceptance of reading as vital to job success.

Reading for Continuing Education

As a citizen, a conversationalist, a do-it-yourself advocate, a householder, a club member, a member of an organized religion, modern man is dependent upon the printed word. Although radio and television are effective means of communication, the listener or viewer is limited to the information and opinions conveyed. If he were reading on the same subjects, he could consult alternate sources of information, check the authority of the information, reread at will, and save certain material. He could compare one view with another in an effort to make the most intelligent decision possible. Former Commissioner of Education John Gardner, in his book *Excellence,* states the case:

> Complex society is dependent every hour of every day upon the capacity of its people to read and write, to make complex judgments, and to act in the light of fairly extensive information. Where there is not this kind of base on which to build, modern social and economic developments are simply impossible.[3]

As modern society becomes even more complex, greater reading burdens will be placed upon its members. Our consumer-based economy is a good example of a force making continuing education more and more essential. Efficient living in the home today virtually demands communication through reading. Menus, tax records, bills, and directions for operating appliances require careful reading. Intelligent buying of food, clothing, and household items is easier through reading discriminatingly than through listening to radio or television commercials.

For the teacher, continuing educational improvement through wide reading above and beyond his own specialty is vital if he is to remain conversant with the world in which his pupils are growing. It is also essential if he is to be alert to new subjects and sources of effective reading materials, without waiting for news of them to filter down through the professional literature.

Reading for Pleasure

The ability to seek pleasure through reading has long been a stated goal of school reading programs. Modern school libraries have more books for recreational reading than ever before. Many teachers set aside blocks of school time in which children can read books of their own choosing for their own purposes. They hope, as an outgrowth of this practice, that an attitude toward reading for pleasure will be developed into a habit which will carry over into the child's future life. When reading in school is considered a chore, it is not likely that a child will choose it as a leisure-time activity. However, even a child with poor reading skill can come to know the fun of reading if a teacher provides free reading opportunities with easy, interesting books that will prove rewarding, and if he makes the reading of stimulating materials to children a part of the curriculum. (More attention will be given to this topic in chapter 10.)

As automation reduces the necessity for an eight-hour workday, and as workweeks become shorter, leisure-time activities will become more central in our society, and the quality of the leisure-time activities selected will be of considerable importance in relation to the quality of modern life. Reading is sure to play a major role. Reports from public libraries and bookstores indicate ever-growing book circulation and sales. Book clubs are doing a booming business. The increase in personal reading can be attributed to the attitude among the population that reading is an enjoyable, highly satisfying recreational pursuit.

ASPECTS OF THE READING PROCESS

Certainly reading is more than sounding letters, calling words, or responding to print. It is the communication through language between an author and a reader—the sum total of the interaction which culminates in a child's relating printed word forms to ideas expressed by the author. Such a complex process comprises many identifiable aspects, each distinct, yet existing side by side, and in some sense a product of each other. It involves the cognitive, psycholinguistic, psychological, physiological, and perceptual processes of the reader. Let us examine each of these separately, realizing, of course, that the components of the reading act cannot and should not always be so separated.

Reading as a Cognitive Process

Perhaps teachers most commonly look at reading as a cognitive process. From this view, it can be subdivided into the twin skills of *decoding* and *comprehending*. Decoding, translating printed words into speech, involves visual memory for word and letter forms (configuration clues), anticipation of the ideas and words to be used by the author (context clues), ability to see large structural parts of words (structural clues), awareness of symbol-sound relationships (phonics), and dictionary skills. Good readers use a combination of these skills to decode words. In early reading many children pay great attention to the configuration of the word to be decoded. Other beginners feel comfortable relying more heavily upon phonics. Regardless of the approach stressed by the teacher, however, every reader ought to be aware that there is more than one system for decoding.

Comprehension involves the reader's recalling what he has read and relating it to real or vicarious experiences, identical or similar to those expressed in print. It cannot be assumed that a reader will automatically make associations as he decodes words. Teachers alert to the implications of the preceding statement will stimulate the reader with thought-provoking questions prior to reading and will follow the reading with discussion and with questions that extend the child's thinking. In beginning reading the teacher may need to provide questions for stimulation for nearly every line, but as the reader progresses he will need less teacher prompting, assuming more responsibility for his own learning. Although stress is placed on comprehension at all levels of the reader's development, critical and creative thinking assume greater importance as the reading material becomes more complex.

A word of caution: it is easy to become so involved in the intricacies of reading as a cognitive process that the purposes for which a child learns to read are forgotten. Many a teacher has temporarily lost sight of these purposes—information, enjoyment, insight—as he pursued skills instruction. This is, of course, a case of putting the means before the end.

Reading as a Psycholinguistic Process

Printed language must be related to the child's background of spoken language if communication is to occur. Reading is a language-based process, and a linguistic perspective helps to clarify what occurs during the act of reading. Such a perspective is provided by psycholinguistics, which draws upon both psychology and linguistics. As applied to reading, psycholinguistics focuses on several main points: the interrelationship of thought and language; how an individual learns language, especially his native tongue; how he uses the symbol system in thinking and communication; how the features of a language, which linguists have been able to identify, relate to common behavior involved in learning and thinking. Strongly stressed are the relationship between the spoken and written codes of language, and the interaction between the reader and the written language.

The psycholinguistic dimension of reading is especially significant in the initial stage of learning to read, when the child first translates unfamiliar print into familiar speech. It is then that the teacher needs to make a conscious effort to help the reader sense a relationship between written and spoken language. In this effort, the so-called language experience approach is probably the most logical, personally relevant, and theoretically justified method of introducing children to reading. This approach emphasizes the fact that children are reading not so much *symbols* as *language*— their language. It attempts to help them realize the relationship of speech and reading as they use both the spoken and written codes of the language.

The language experience approach is also recommended for other than beginning readers. It is helpful when a child's spoken language is different from the standard English found in most commercially produced reading materials. Teachers need to investigate the essential differences between the languages involved in order to understand the translation process required of the nonstandard-English-speaking learner. They also need to know the features of nonstandard language which may cue a reader incorrectly in standard English. Baratz has identified key syntactical features for black, inner-city, nonstandard speech.[4]

A great deal has already been explored by the field of linguistics which has critical implications for the teaching of reading. Yet, as Wardhaugh claims:

> It would be true to say that most reading experts have given only token recognition to linguistics in their work, with the consequence that the vast part of what is discussed under the name of linguistics in texts, methods, and courses on reading is, in reality, very far from the best linguistic knowledge that is available today.[5]

It appears likely that the growing emphasis on variant dialects of spoken English, combined with the widespread interest in teaching reading more effectively to members of subcultural groups will increase the interest in this field which bridges spoken and written language.

Reading as a Psychological Process

A positive attitude, emotional normalcy, and psychological condition are essential for successful mastery of the printed page. It is possible that a disinterested reader may read successfully without having all the emotional and psychological apparatus usually considered mandatory. This may be the case with gifted children especially. However, it is the exception rather than the rule. A positive attitude toward the content will enhance the possibilities of successful reading. It is not uncommon to hear a child say, "Do I have to read this?" or "I don't want to read this again!" When the learning situation is approached with such an attitude, learning is likely to be inefficient and retention hindered. In a general discussion of learning, Bugelski has pointed out that "an incorrect orientation—wrong attitudes . . . fear of subject matter— all can prevent acquisition of knowledge and should be eliminated before the teacher begins the learning sequence."[6]

Emotional normalcy, important in all learning, is considered especially relevant to reading. Money found that some emotionally disturbed children are reluctant to look at the printed page.[7] This problem may be helped in remedial reading sessions, where one of the prime objectives is to create feelings of success.and good self-concept so that the problem reader's attitude can change, and so that learning can be attacked with greater promise of success. The teacher who does not consider the psychological condition of his children will find in almost every group some who could have learned better if psychological factors had been considered and appropriate adjustments made.

Another psychological aspect of the reading process which the teacher needs to consider is reaction. During and after reading, the child is likely to react to those concepts that he interprets emotionally. To laugh at a funny story or to choke up over a sad tale are common reactions to reading. Good readers will be expected to react in this fashion; the authors, indeed, expect an emotional response. When children do not react to their reading or when their reaction is inappropriate, the teacher attempts to determine why.

Another major consideration is the psychological effect of reading materials on children of particular subcultural groups. There is an increasing awareness that the content of the curriculum, particularly the content of reading material, is, in part, sociologically and culturally determined. The materials a child is given to read reflect the values of his society, his school, and his teachers. To these materials the child brings the social attitudes of his subculture which have a direct influence on how he responds to adults, to books, and to learning in general. Awareness of the social implications of varying language backgrounds and recognition of dissimilarity in experiential backgrounds will help the teacher provide suitable learning situations.

To help foster this type of situation, conscious manipulation of the content material being read is usually necessary. There is little doubt that a black child reading about successful blacks in our society is more likely to feel a personal identification with the content than when he is reading about stereotyped Negroes or when the book has only white characters. Berg has pointed out that "middle class bias has tended to expect mediocrity from these [minority] groups, setting up teaching and learning situations for them primarily devoid of experiences intended to foster freedom or creativity of thought."[8]

Social attitudes are promoted through reading, as well as through direct experience. The reading teacher, therefore, ideally pursues every opportunity to present reading materials that will assist in developing children's perception of human relationships and in identifying and removing stereotyped images of various groups. The Association for the Study of Negro Life and History in Washington, D.C., is one of several groups attempting to produce relevant materials about minority groups.

Reading as a Physiological Process

Children learn to read more easily when they are physically comfortable and when their physical development is normal, than when a physically uncomfortable situation or a physical defect is present. We have all attempted to read when the room was too warm or too cold, when we were suffering from a headache, or when we were hungry or sleepy. In each case, even though we might have been able to complete the specific reading, we were aware that we could have accomplished it more efficiently had we been physically comfortable. Thus, the physical state of the reader is of concern to the teacher who is attempting to provide the best possible learning situation for all children.

Normal physical development is also an ideal condition for maximum reading achievement. Evidence suggests a relationship between certain physical impairments and reading difficulty. Malnutrition, fatigue, metabolic imbalance, speech impairment, and gross dental difficulties may cause a given child enough discomfort to keep him from reading and learning as profitably as possible. Aside from these problems directly hampering the child's ability, they may also cause him to be absent from school frequently and miss important instruction. This, in itself, limits his skill development in reading.

In a more subtle manner, the child's physical maturity, his coordination, his orientation to objects around him, the ability of his nervous system to respond, and even his chronological age are considered by many authorities to have a direct influence upon how well he responds to reading-learning situations. Naturally, it is possible to cite physically immature, poorly coordinated youngsters who read well. Such children exist, and they have the drive and motivation to learn even though they are physically impaired. Nevertheless, the more intact we find the child physically, the less likely are problems caused by physical interference.

This is not to advocate that physiological problems be corrected by the teacher. It is to point out that whenever a physiological limitation is suspected of interfering with a child's sensory experiences, a modification of those experiences may well result. The child does not stop responding, but he adjusts his response to his sensory capabilities. In so adjusting, he may have a different experience than normally expected. When facing his next sensory situation, he builds on this distorted experience. Complications of such a cycle can be compounded into serious difficulties in the development of inaccurate percepts and concepts. Furthermore, the teacher who is unaware of such adjustments and distortions is likely to misinterpret the child's reactions to events as signs of dullness or inattentiveness. Every effort ought to be made to adjust the classroom situation for children with physical difficulties.

Reading as a Perceptual Process

Perceptually, reading may be considered from two points of view. One view is simply that reading involves perceptual processes—the child is required to coordinate several sensory processes and to put them to work at will. The eyes, for example, must be controlled so that they can move from left to right across the page at the will of the reader. For children lacking the skills required for control over the sensory systems during the reading act, the initial exposure to reading must surely be frustrating and confusing.

The second view of perception as an aspect of reading stresses the relationship between the reader's present perceptions and those encountered in print. A more intricate formulation of the perceptual component in the reading process, this view has been expounded by Suchman, among others. He sees perception in reading as "the result of an interaction between whatever is 'out there' and available to our senses, and what is already internal and available to our thinking."[9] From this point of view, the more extensive and accurate the child's present perceptions, the more likely he will be to make appropriate perceptions concerning similar and related topics in the future. Conversely, if he starts with faulty perceptions, and if these go undetected by the teacher, there is a greater possibility of inaccurate perceptions developing in subsequent situations.

Strang has presented a model useful for a more detailed explanation of the role of perception in the teaching of reading:

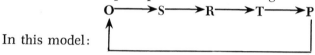

In this model:

   O = the individual and all that he brings to the learning situation

   S = the learning situation and its characteristics

   R = the response made by the child to the learning situation

   T = the trace of the response which is made on the individual's nervous system

   P = the perception which becomes a part of the individual[10]

Several examples based on this model should demonstrate how a reader may or may not form accurate perceptions. A child (O) is placed in a reading situation (S) in which the teacher tells him the word *saw*. The child looks at the word and says *was* (R). The letters *s-a-w* pronounced as *was* is the trace made on the nervous system (T). The child's perception of *s-a-w* is now *was* (P). In his next reading situation, he will probably call *s-a-w was*, forming even stronger traces. As the teacher becomes aware of this incorrect response, he adjusts the reading situation (S) so that the child can make the appropriate responses and develop accurate perceptions. Without adjustment, the reversal of *was* for *saw* might become a firm perception.

Another example might find a child (O) starting with the concept that a large body of water is the size of the pond on his farm. In a reading situation (S) in which a ship is lost at sea, this child's response may be confused or ineffective because of his previous perception (P). In this example, the child is likely to confuse the sea in the story with his previous concept of a large body of water, the pond on his farm. A teacher needs to anticipate the concepts a child brings to reading situations, so that learning can be accurate.

From Strang's model, we can see that the teacher's task in the teaching of reading is to study the individual (O), to manipulate situations for effective learning (S), and to evaluate and reinforce the child's responses (R). The teacher may often be aware of the child's response before the next reading situation. The resulting trace and the perception are quite personal and often unnoticeable. The teacher understands the trace and perception developed by the child through studying him and observing his response to the next learning situation. Since the teacher is responsible for the learning climate in the classroom, he manipulates the situation according to what he knows about individual students.

It is also necessary for the teacher to realize that the perceptions which a child brings with him to the reading situation are real for that child. The water in the pond is a large body of water and s-a-w is *was* for the children in the above-mentioned situations. An understanding of the foregoing view of perception permits the teacher to approach reading at all levels with a better chance of success. Discussions of the specific types of situation manipulation teachers can design are explained throughout the remainder of the book. The ability to control the nervous system well enough for the reading act and the awareness of how percepts develop are important aspects of the reading process to consider.

FUNDAMENTAL CONSIDERATIONS FOR THE TEACHING OF READING

Viewing these general areas of reading as a whole, the teacher of reading becomes aware of certain fundamental questions which need to be answered before an effective program of reading instruction can be undertaken. Primary among them are the following:

- What are the specific communication requirements of my pupils, and how can I best provide for them?

- How can I effect a balanced program of cognitive skill development reflecting both decoding and comprehension?

- How can I best assess my students' physical, perceptual, psychological, and psycholinguistic abilities?

From these broad considerations, the major objectives of an effective reading program can be derived.

Chapter Review

Reading is a vital means of communication and is essential for scholastic and occupational success, for continuing education, and for personal entertainment. Reading involves a number of distinct, yet related areas: cognitive processes, primarily decoding and comprehension; psycholinguistic processes by which spoken language is recognized in the printed text; psychological conditions, attitudes, and reactions, particularly those stemming from the child's subcultural background; perceptual processes; and physiological variables such as vision, hearing, sensory responses in general, and overall health.

Awareness of the various dimensions of reading permits the teacher to plan a program for children which is inclusive and to reject programs which are too narrow in scope. At this time our knowledge of how a child learns to read is incomplete. As additional information becomes known, the teacher will find it necessary to reexamine his views of the reading process and of how he teaches reading.

NOTES

[1] Ruth Penty, "Reading Ability and High School Drop-Outs," *Journal of the National Association of Women and Counselors* (October 1959): 14.

[2] David Sarnoff, "No Life Untouched," *Saturday Review,* 23 July 1966, pp. 21–22.

[3] John Gardner, *Excellence* (New York: Harper & Row, 1961), p. 37.

[4] Joan C. Baratz, "Teaching in an Urban Negro School System," in *Teaching Black Children to Read,* eds. Joan C. Baratz and Roger Shuy (Washington, D.C.: Center for Applied Linguistics, 1969), pp. 92–116.

[5] Ronald Wardhaugh, *Reading, A Linguistic Perspective* (New York: Harcourt Brace Jovanovich, 1969), p. 30.

[6] B. R. Bugelski, *The Psychology of Learning Applied to Teaching* (Indianapolis: Bobbs-Merrill, 1964), p. 184.

[7] John Money, *Reading Disability* (Baltimore: Johns Hopkins Press, 1962), p. 12.

[8] Paul C. Berg and Victor M. Rentel, "Guides to Creativity in Reading," *Journal of Reading* 10 (January 1967): 219.

[9] Richard J. Suchman, "A Model for the Language of Education," *Instructor* 76 (August-September 1966): 33.

[10] Ruth Strang, "The Reading Process and its Ramifications," in *Invitational Adresses* 1965 (Newark, Delaware: International Reading Association, 1965), pp. 70–71.

SUGGESTED ACTIVITIES

1. Compare definitions of reading from the various suggested readings.
2. Hold a discussion centering on the two views "Reading is decoding" and "Reading is thinking."
3. Write your personal definition of reading, showing how it will affect your method of teaching the subject.
4. Compare your definition of reading and your proposed teaching method with those you observe during a visit to a reading class.

SUGGESTED READINGS

Bond, Guy L. and Wagner, Eva B. *Teaching the Child To Read.* New York: Macmillan, 1966.

Chapter 1 sets the scene for reading and presents a useful development of the major objectives of a modern reading program into teacher language.

Goodman, Kenneth S., ed. *The Psycholinguistic Nature of the Reading Process.* Detroit: Wayne State University Press, 1968.

The first chapter of this scholarly book presents an elaborate definition of reading as a psycholinguistic process.

Smith, Nila B. *Reading Instruction for Today's Children.* Englewood Cliffs: Prentice-Hall, 1963.

See especially chapter 2 which emphasizes reading for today's world and the communication aspects of reading.

Strang, Ruth. "The Reading Process and Its Ramifications." In *Invitational Addresses 1965* Newark, Delaware: International Reading Association, 1965, pp. 49–73.

See especially the introduction to and explanation of the model O-S-R-T-P, used in this chapter.

Wardhaugh, Ronald. *Reading: A Linguistic Perspective.* New York: Harcourt Brace Jovanovich, 1969.

The linguistic implications of reading as presented by the author merit thoughtful consideration by educators. Also examined are phonics, comprehension, dialect, and other topics of significance for reading teachers.

CHAPTER TWO

THE EVOLUTION OF READING INSTRUCTION

Advance Organizer

The evolution of reading instruction in the United States from early times to the contemporary scene is presented in this chapter with the aim of offering a perspective of the current status of teaching reading. The objectives of reading instruction as well as the general types of methods and materials which have emerged to implement these objectives are examined. Discussion of five main objectives of modern reading instruction and analysis of the modern elementary reading program yield an awareness of an emphasis on communication processes. Also identified are theories of learning which are exerting an effect upon all instruction today.

THE CONTEMPORARY APPROACH TO READING

In general, the conception of reading today is considerably broader and more complex than at any time in the past. Our multi-part classification of reading dimensions in the preceding chapter in part illustrates this complexity, as will our examination of the component parts of reading instruction throughout the remainder of the book. No doubt this expansion of the concept of reading is in one sense simply a reflection of the growing body of research findings and of practical observation in the area; we simply know more about reading today, so that we are less satisfied with simpler definitions. In another sense, however, our entire view of the language arts has broadened considerably over the past several years, necessitating an expanded conception of reading as part and parcel of the general trend.

If we were to single out one word that seems to represent the new conception most fully, it would be *communication*. Many people, in fact, no longer speak of the "language arts" but of the "communication arts." The difference, it seems to us, is significant— reflecting as it does the new concerns of our society with the interactions of its members and with new forms of information dissemination.

Objectives of Modern Elementary Reading Programs

If reading is viewed as one medium of communication, therefore, the ultimate goal of reading instruction is enabling children to communicate effectively through reading. Accordingly, reading needs to be taught in such a way that the communication process is considered a part of all the reading activities in which children are involved every day. Developing children's facility in communicating through reading is such a broad goal, however, that we have identified several less encompassing, but still major objectives for modern elementary reading programs.

- To help children develop a permanent interest in reading and an appreciation of literature. These goals are in part achieved by exposure to fine examples of children's literature and a planned program of recreational reading included in the reading curriculum. Effective teaching of reading aims to produce children who *do* read, not merely children who *can* read.

- To equip children with the essential skills for accurate and efficient decoding of print. A modern reading program not only will teach children to attack words independently but also will demonstrate that decoding is only the first step toward interpreting an author's meaning.

- To help children to develop extensive sight vocabularies. As children progress through the elementary school, their reading vocabularies ought to be increasing steadily through direct instruction and wide reading. It is necessary for every efficient reader to have a stock of words which he can recognize instantly in print.

■ To equip children with the skills necessary for comprehension. Reading must be taught as a thought-getting process because a student employs the skills of association in order to relate the content of any reading selection to his previous knowledge and to react to an author's ideas.

■ To teach children to be versatile readers as they learn to adapt their reading skills to the demands of particular materials and situations. A versatile reader is able to adjust his rate, skills of decoding, and skills of association according to the difficulty of the material and the purpose for which the reading is done.

Implementation of these objectives rests with the effectiveness of the methods and materials utilized. Accordingly, we shall examine each in turn.

Modern Methods

A few years ago the widely respected reading authority, Nila Banton Smith commented on today's reading programs:

> Ours is a period of using new approaches, formulating new adaptations, making new applications of many of the fundamental ideas which have been previously propounded, and to which we have paid too little attention in years past.[1]

In our rapidly changing world, in the midst of an explosion of information, it is to be expected that reading instruction is changing to meet new challenges and that today's approach to teaching reading is an eclectic one that is based on a variety of historical precedents, successful classroom practices, and research findings. Modern teachers, realizing that there is no one best method that works for all children, adapt their knowledge of several approaches to the needs of a class of individuals, each learning differently. The National First Grade Studies of the United States Office of Education, which investigated a number of approaches used with 30,000 pupils in twenty-seven school systems throughout the country, indicated that no one approach demonstrated a clear superiority over the others and that a combination of approaches produced better results than did a single method of teaching.[2]

In teaching reading today, a synthesis of the best features of several methods is the teacher's best course.

Current reading methods have also been affected by recent developments in diagnostic practices, now more sophisticated and more useful for instructional purposes than ever, and by greater attention to special remedial help for pupils who experience more than average difficulty in reading. Methods in reading have also been influenced by trends in both pre-service and in-service training practices for teachers. Increasing opportunities are being made available for in-service training of teachers desirous of upgrading their reading programs, and for reading consultants who help teachers plan instructional programs. These, in turn, have precipitated innovations in classroom organization which facilitate both group and individualized instruction.

Modern Materials

Modern reading programs are characterized by a vast array of materials ranging from graded textbook series to such supplements as enrichment materials, programmed instruction, and materials designed for multi-media types of presentation. Elementary school libraries are indispensable corollaries to dynamic reading programs when children are encouraged to do wide reading and individual research. Since modern reading programs integrate reading with instruction in the other language arts—speaking, listening, and writing—pupil-composed materials are considered another important source of reading materials. Children need specific instruction in reading in the content areas, and textbooks and trade books become increasingly necessary for a well-rounded reading program.

Basal readers are still the most widely used materials for the core of instructional reading programs, although the authors of various series stress the necessity for the use of other types of materials to supplement the basals. In recent years criticism of reading books has centered around their tendency to present story content and characters pertaining to the white, middle-class child of a suburban community. It was not until 1962 that Negro characters were included in reading textbooks.[3] Multi-ethnic reading books have gained in popularity, but critics still feel that not enough attention has been directed to developing story content with which culturally different children can identify.

A COMPARATIVE HISTORICAL VIEW OF READING APPROACHES

Just as attention to the objectives of a field reveals much about its practices, so a comparison with the same field at an earlier time can be illuminating. In the field of reading instruction, where so much has been studied, reported, and discussed, a brief historical retrospective is especially informative for the light it sheds on present practices.

Earlier Objectives of Reading Instruction

The goals of reading instruction from the beginnings of America to the present, perhaps even more than the materials and methods, represent sociological concerns about the educational system. The objectives of reading can be studied from two points: 1) the ultimate use of reading in society, and 2) the particular skills thought to be important in a given historical period. In the first chapter, reading was examined not by a single or simple definition but as a multi-dimensional process which is a medium of communication. However, reading has not always been viewed as a high-level thinking process.

During colonial times the main objective of reading instruction was to equip pupils with sufficient reading facility for reciting religious content. Another goal was to develop fluency in oral reading.[4] After the Revolution, reading was considered an important means for developing loyalty to the new nation and for inculcating ideals of virtue and moral behavior, necessary for good citizenship. Since the skill stressed most was eloquent oral reading, children received instruction in correct pronunciation and elocutionary delivery.

Not until the last quarter of the nineteenth century did the goal of developing a permanent interest in literature become important.[5] Exposure to good literature was viewed as a cultural asset, and literary content began to appear in reading textbooks. As silent reading became of major importance in the present century, greater attention was directed to having pupils comprehend material rather than "word-call" in an expressive manner.

A statement of objectives can be found in the *Twenty-fourth Yearbook of the National Society for the Study of Education* published in 1925.[6] At this time the teaching of reading began to be viewed as complex and as having several broad goals rather than a single narrow one. The content of the *Twenty-fourth Yearbook* has had a significant influence on courses of study, professional books, and instructional practices. Harris states that this book may well be the most important single book about reading instruction published during this century.[7] The objectives of a modern program stated earlier in this chapter, are, in part similar to those originally identified by Gray in 1925:

- The primary purpose of reading in school is to extend the experience of boys and girls, to stimulate their thinking power, and to elevate their tastes. The ultimate end of instruction in reading is to enable the reader to participate intelligently in the thought life of the world and appreciatively in its recreational activities.

- A second objective of reading instruction is to develop strong motives for, and permanent interests in reading that will inspire the present and future life of the reader and provide for the wholesome use of leisure time.

- A third aim of reading instruction, therefore, is to develop the attitudes, habits, and skills that are essential in the various types of reading activities in which children and adults should engage.[8]

Examination of earlier methods and materials which derived from former goals for instruction shows some interesting shifts in theory.

Previous Methods and Materials

A cyclical nature can be observed through the years as one type of instruction was stressed, then discarded, then revived either in its old form or with new trappings or a new label. It seems ironic that with the wealth of knowledge and approaches available today, some critics of reading instruction have advocated return to an approach which was discontinued in the past or which utilizes a single method for teaching a process as complex as reading. An examination of practices of the past can help us to determine whether a hue and cry for changes in teaching reading is actually a demand to return to a practice of the past without due consideration of current research and the goals of a modern reading program. This is not to imply that because a practice was used in the past it is a poor one, but simply that practices should be evaluated for their relevance to an effective, up-to-date reading program.

Methods of teaching reading can be studied in conjunction with the materials through which they were implemented. One of the greatest contrasts between reading instruction in the early days of our country and the present is in the materials used to teach reading. The contrast between the materials is not only one of type of content but also one of variety and quantity. Some changes in reading materials illustrate changing goals of education as well as changing cultural values. Thus, the content of reading books popular in various periods of our history reflects the concerns and mores of the times in which they were written. The concept of variety in reading materials designed to appeal to children of diverse backgrounds, abilities, and interests is a change from past periods in which all children were expected to read the same material and in which one book represented the total reading program for a school year. In modern reading programs, teachers recognize that teaching reading as a communication process necessitates the utilization of many types of materials in addition to basic reading textbooks.

The earliest reading materials reflected the religious concerns of the colonists: the repetitive nature of the content was not designed with children's interests in mind. The first book used for teaching reading in this country, although it originated in England, was the hornbook which consisted of a sheet of paper about three by four inches fastened on a thin paddle-shaped board covered by a translucent sheet of horn.[9] Hornbooks usually contained letters of the alphabet, syllables, and religious verses. *The New England Primer*, which was the first reading book specifically designed for use in America, also contained the alphabet, syllables, and religious verses. Both the *Primer* and the hornbooks introduced reading by the alphabet-spelling method. Children studied lists of letters and then progressed to lists of syllables beginning with two-letter combinations such as *ab, ac, ad.* The lists were read aloud by spelling the various letter combinations. Reading periods during which this approach was used were characterized by repetitive drill and oral recitation.[10] Although there were some early spelling books which were also used to teach reading, the *New England Primer* was the most popular reading book from the 1690s to the time of the American Revolution.[11]

Books of the postrevolutionary period contained material of a strongly nationalistic and patriotic nature. Noah Webster's *The American Spelling Book,* often referred to as "The Blue-back Speller," was the most widely used instructional book from 1776 to about 1840.[12] It also used the alphabet-spelling method, although it emphasized lists of words more than the earlier books. Of the 158 pages of the speller, 74 contained lists of letters, syllables, and words. In addition, there were 39 pages of rules, 29 pages of moralistic advice and admonitions, and 10½ pages of fables, realistic stories, dialogs, and poetry.[13] With concentration on oral drill, memorization, and rules, it is evident that concept of meaning was not thought to be of prime importance.

As Webster's famous speller lost its foothold in American schools around 1840, some marked changes in reading methods and materials occurred. Some educators, particularly Horace Mann, expressed dissatisfaction with the rote memorization of reading content, a practice he considered devoid of meaning. He stressed the importance of the association of a word form with the meaning of a printed symbol.[14] In the word method, a picture or actual object was shown simultaneously with the printed word form. While this method was employed in some schools, the alphabet-spelling method continued to be used by many teachers because of its earlier widespread influence and acceptance. The word method, even though recognizing the role of meaning in reading, required children to study isolated lists of words before progressing to reading stories.

As an extension of the meaningful approach to reading, the word method expanded into the sentence-story method with the unit of meaning being the sentence or story. Children read a passage for meaning first. The acquisition of a reading vocabulary came after rather than before the reading of meaningful selections. To emphasize the thought of a sentence or story, the teacher often read the material aloud to pupils before they were asked to read. Like the word method, the sentence-story method was based upon the principles of Gestalt psychology which expounded the importance of the whole rather than the parts in meaningful learning.

This shift in method was not the only change in reading. The development of the graded elementary school was also of great influence, giving rise to graded series of readers. William H. McGuffey is credited with being the first author to carefully prepare such a series of readers, one for each of the elementary grades. The first of the McGuffey readers was published in 1836 and the series was very popular for the next forty years,[15] although modern opinion is not all so favorable. Smith observes that "the content is very dull and so altogether senseless that it is difficult for an adult to read."[16] The readers contained literary, patriotic, and moralistic story content and provided repetition of new vocabulary. The word method and phonic method (discussed later) were used.

After the advent of the McGuffey readers, the series concept spread, and a number of other series were also published. The bulk of the content of readers from 1840 to 1880 consisted of selections written to teach lessons in behavior and to educate pupils for intelligent citizenship. The importance of content of high literary quality began to be stressed during the 1880s as concern for the cultural development of the individual became an educational goal. Although literary content previously had been a part of school readers for the intermediate grades, such content was usually a means for providing drill exercises rather than for stimulating an interest in or an appreciation of literature. As the shift to literary content gained momentum, moralistic and informational selections declined in importance and elocutionary rules disappeared from reading textbooks.

Over a period of time, other changes in the instructional emphasis of basal readers also occurred. Increase in vocabulary control and planned repetition of words were two major changes. While standard word lists were used as a basis for word selection, there was a gradual reduction of the number of words introduced in primary readers.

The role of phonics is one of the most interesting facets of the history of reading. The earliest approach to reading, the alphabet-spelling method, did not teach letter sounds but did provide extensive practice with letter names. Gradually the teaching of letter sounds along with or in addition to letter names began to be stressed. Dissatisfaction with the word method was a factor leading to pressure for a method of reading with a heavy emphasis on phonics. While the word and sentence-story methods had many advocates, other educators were developing elaborate phonic systems in the second half of the nineteenth century. In such systems pupils were taught all the sounds an individual letter could represent and also all the rules governing each sound. Some basal series stressed a phonic approach in the beginning stages of reading instruction, while other series included study of some selected phonic elements after children learned to read sentences, stories, and words.

After the turn of the century, the progressive education movement deemphasized phonic drill in favor of reading for meaning.[17] Although phonics declined in importance, a study of the reading textbooks published during the height of the progressive education movement shows that all of them gave some attention to this subject.[18] However, some teachers did interpret the lessening in importance of phonics to mean that such instruction was of little value and should be discontinued. Therefore, in some elementary schools, children received very little instruction in phonic skills. Most reading authorities today support the teaching of phonics as part of the reading skills program, and some approaches place heavy stress on it in the initial phases of instruction. Phonics may best be looked upon as one tool of decoding which should form a well-rounded reading program.

Recognition of the difficulties in teaching phonics with the English language has led to the development of altered alphabets for use in beginning reading classes. This idea of "alphabet tinkering" dates back as far as 1570.[19] The Scientific Alphabet and the Shearer System were employed in the United States for a short time around 1900.[20] Neither of these systems was widely used although they generated some interest for a brief period. In the 1960s, school systems throughout the country were teaching first-graders to read with materials printed in the Initial Teaching Alphabet (ITA), a writing system of forty-four symbols which have a highly regular sound-symbol relationship.[21]

Besides the experimentation with alphabets and the stress on phonics in texts, basal readers continued to change in other ways over the years. The scope of the basal series was increased in 1925 with the addition of pre-primers. The appearance of the books became increasingly attractive as attention was directed to the size and arrangement of the text and to the importance of illustrations. Greater variety of reading selections was one of the most significant changes.

A practice ordinarily associated with the use of basal readers is that of grouping children according to achievement and/or ability. This practice became popular in the 1920s and 1930s as the testing and child study movements revealed evidence of the existence of a wide range of differences in achievement and ability among children on any grade level.[22] No longer could an instructional reading program consist of teaching all children in a class on the same level and from the same book.

As attention to individual differences has continued to grow in importance, there have been reactions to the inadequacies of ability grouping for meeting individual needs in reading. Plans for individualized reading, while becoming popular in the late 1950s and 1960s, also had their beginnings in an earlier period. The concept of individual children progressing at their own rate was the rationale behind the Winnetka and Dalton plans of teaching popular in the 1920s and 1930s.[23] Individualized reading programs of recent years are built upon Olson's concepts of "seeking, self-selection, and

The wide range of differences in achievement and ability among children on any grade level gave rise to the practice of grouping.

pacing"[24] as children are encouraged to select what they will read.

Supplementary reading materials which have proved to be a vital part of individualized and of general reading programs began to appear around 1910. However, basal series were still the core of the reading program or, in many cases, the entire reading program. Other supplements to basal texts were workbook materials correlated with the readers and additional materials for phonetic and vocabulary drill such as flash cards and pictures. As the activity method of teaching evolved in the 1920s and 1930s, experience chart stories and other classroom-produced materials were used as supplement to graded series of readers. Supplementary reading has continued to be an essential component of an elementary reading program, and today a wealth of material for enrichment reading is available.

A word might be mentioned here about professional materials designed to inform teachers about reading and to assist them in executing reading programs through detailed descriptions of teaching procedures. The number of professional books and courses of study about reading have increased steadily since their first appearance in the 1880s.[25] Teacher's manuals to accompany the textbooks came into general use after 1910 and have become increasingly more detailed and helpful in recent years.

THE CONTINUING INFLUENCE OF LEARNING THEORY

It is apparent from this comparative survey of reading instructional objectives, methods, and materials of present and past that many previous practices have been modified and incorporated into current procedures. These modifications have occurred in reading as the result not only of shifting views within the field but, in addition, of changing conceptions about the learning process as a whole. Parallel to research into the teaching of a given subject, throughout the course of education as we know it today, there has been active inquiry into general questions such as how children learn, how teachers can manipulate learning environments for better learning, and how to construe the interaction between the learner and the learning environment. Although the various learning theories appear to lack universal application, and although disagreement continues among theorists as to which are most appropriate in which situations, certainly the contributions of learning theorists available at this time do help provide direction for the teacher of reading.

Historically, learning theory can be said to have developed around two schools of thought. Both share a view of human behavior which recognizes a stimulus to behavior and a response to that stimulus. Expounded by the pioneer Russian physiological psychologist Pavlov, the theory of behavioral conditioning originally held that behavior could be controlled by substituting one stimulus for another.[27] Pavlov theorized that, because a teacher can control a stimulus-response chain in this way, he thereby ought to be able to evoke the desired emotional response to a new stimulus.

The American educator Thorndike, on the other hand, later introduced the element of *reinforcement* and advocated the substitution of one response reinforcement for another.[28] A stimulus leads to a response, which leads in turn to a reinforcement of that response. The reinforcement, through being either positive or negative, encourages or discourages the probability of that response's occurring again in the presence of the original stimulus. Thorndike would have the teacher praise desirable behavior and ignore undesirable behavior. Because human beings enjoy praise, he postulated, a child will repeat the desired behavior in a similar stimulus situation in order to bring about the reinforcement that success brings.

From this very brief explanation one can see several possibilities for application of learning theories to teaching situations. And today, indeed, many educators do see themselves as stimulus manipulators; that is, they assume the responsibility for providing the child with interesting reading material which is appropriate for his reading level. They also see strong possibilities in their role as reinforcers of responses. When the child reads well, follows directions accurately, and responds in a desirable manner, the teacher lets the child know that he approves. He might praise the child, let him know he'll get a positive remark on a report card, comment to his parents, or otherwise reward him. Generally, however, teachers have difficulty fulfilling the role of an effective reinforcer when the child is not responding appropriately. Criticism and punishment are not uncommon. The child who makes a genuine effort can only develop negative attitudes toward trying when such efforts are met with punishment. It is essential for a child to want to be successful and for the teacher to have the opportunity and responsibility to manipulate learning situations to provide successes so that the child can earn legitimate positive reinforcement.

Variables of an individual nature such as age, sex, intelligence, motivation, social class background, and previous experiences are important in studying each learner within a class. Variables related to the type of material to be learned also influence the teacher's structuring of a learning situation. In teaching reading, the teacher draws upon his knowledge of the individual and analyzes the nature of the learning task in order to arrange a situation which will facilitate the learning of that particular task for that individual.

We see then that a combination of the basic ideas of conditioning and behaviorism have valuable application for the teacher of today. They have led, in fact, to many other ideas about how to promote more effective learning. Listed here are some of the most prominent.

- When a child enters a learning situation, how much he can learn is directly related to his attitude at the outset. If the child has decided that learning is not worthwhile or that the topic is not interesting, little learning can take place. Therefore, the teacher has the responsibility to develop attitudes and interests before starting the instructional situation. Warm-up activities might well precede most instruction.

- A child is likely to forget material he did not learn well. While some teachers blame children for forgetting, others are aware that a child remembers when 1) he has use for the material learned, 2) he wants to remember, and 3) the initial learning is reviewed until established. Bearing this in mind, the teacher has the responsibility to provide situations for helping children to remember.

■ Meaningful material transfers better and is remembered better than material that is not meaningful. Rote learning is generally difficult for the child. Therefore, the teacher should take every effort to make learning meaningful and to point out the relationship of particular material to previous knowledge.

■ Interest and attention come from success. Conversely, disinterest and inattention come from repeated failure. Therefore, the teacher needs to structure situations for success if he desires to develop interest and attention.

■ The child should never leave the learning situation with the wrong answer. While it is often good to challenge the learner and have him probe for the answer, it is important that he obtain it and not leave the learning situation with an incorrect response. The teacher then has the responsibility for making certain that children are developing accurate ideas, particularly when future learning depends upon them.

■ While it is advisable in early learning situations to reinforce every response, it is also wise to start omitting reinforcement from time to time. This helps the child to realize that teacher praise is not always forthcoming and that there are other reasons for doing good work. In this manner, the learner becomes independent of the teacher's extrinsic reinforcement. The teacher can, therefore, start intermittent reinforcement soon after the learner is capable of making appropriate responses.

The student will find the suggested readings at the end of this chapter helpful if he is interested in pursuing the ideas of learning theorists in depth. In chapter 4, we turn to specific reading instructional approaches which embody these theoretical principles.

Chapter Review

A study of the history of reading reveals that many aspects of present-day reading instruction had their beginnings years ago. Reading was the most important subject in the first American schools and has continued to be the most stressed area of the elementary school curriculum. Instructional materials and procedures have differed during various periods of American educational history. Today's reading programs are extremely varied and are built upon a wealth of knowledge and materials. The emphasis is on an eclectic approach which is based upon historical precedents, successful classroom practices, research findings, principles of learning, and knowledge of children. Research in the field of reading is more extensive than in any other curriculum area.[26] The teaching of reading, while better than ever before in our history, is still in need of further knowledge to be learned from future research. However, greater dissemination of existing knowledge to affect classroom practice is also needed. How well teachers provide reading instruction today will be recorded for tomorrow's history.

NOTES

[1] Nila B. Smith, *American Reading Instruction* (Newark, Delaware: International Reading Association, 1965), p. vii.

[2] Guy L. Bond, "First-Grade Reading Studies: An Overview," *Elementary English* 43 (May 1966): 468–469.

[3] Gertrude Whipple, "Multicultural Primers for Today's Children," *Education Digest* 29 (February 1964): 26.

[4] Smith, *American Reading Instruction,* p. 35.

[5] Ibid., pp. 115–116.

[6] National Society for the Study of Education, *Twenty-fourth Yearbook of the National Society for the Study of Education,* pt. 1, ed. William S. Gray (Bloomington: Public School Publishing, 1925), pp. 9–19.

[7] Albert J. Harris, "Progressive Education and Reading Instruction," *The Reading Teacher* 18 (November 1964): 131.

[8] Gray, pp. 9, 11, 12.

[9] Smith, *American Reading Instruction,* p. 7.

[10] Ibid., p. 34.

[11] Ibid., p. 25.

[12] Ibid., p. 45.

[13] Ibid., p. 48.

[14] Ibid., pp. 76–78.

[15] David H. Russell and Henry Fea, "Research on Teaching Reading," in *Handbook of Research on Teaching,* ed. N. L. Gage (Chicago: Rand McNally, 1963), p. 867.

[16] Smith, *American Reading Instruction,* pp. 106–107.

[17] Harris, p. 133.

[18] Smith, *American Reading Instruction,* p. 233.

[19] John Downing, "How I.T.A. Began," *Elementary English* 44 (January 1967): 40.

[20] Smith, *American Reading Instruction,* p. 128.

[21] Downing, p. 43.

[22] Nila B. Smith, "What Have We Accomplished in Reading?—A Review of the Past Fifty Years," *Elementary English* 38 (March 1961): 143.

[23] Smith, *American Reading Instruction,* p. 195.

[24] Willard C. Olson, *Child Development* (Boston: D. C. Heath, 1959), pp. 402–404.

[25] Smith, *American Reading Instruction,* p. 122.

[26] Russell and Fea, p. 865.

[27] B. R. Bugelski, *The Psychology of Learning Applied to Teaching* (Indianapolis: Bobbs-Merrill, 1964), p. 38.

[28] Ibid., p. 51.

SUGGESTED ACTIVITIES

1. Visit an elementary classroom to observe the materials used to teach reading. Are they diversified? What would you add to improve the program?
2. Compare reading textbooks of ten to twenty years ago with today's. How are they similar? How do they differ?
3. With a group of your peers, discuss how you learned to read in the first grade. Note the methods used and why some students remember vividly, while others not at all.

SUGGESTED READINGS

Bugelski, B. R. *The Psychology of Learning Applied to Teaching.* Indianapolis: Bobbs-Merrill, 1964.

A careful development of the history of learning theory, followed by a treatment of the relation of those theories to present teaching situations.

Coleman, Morrison and Austin, Mary C. *The First R: The Harvard Report on Reading Instruction.* New York: Macmillan, 1963.

A valuable, detailed report of current instructional practices in teaching reading in schools throughout the country.

National Society for the Study of Education. *Twenty-fourth Yearbook,* pt. 1, "Report of the National Committee on Reading." Edited by William S. Gray. Bloomington: Public School Publishing, 1925.

National Society for the Study of Education. *Sixtieth Yearbook,* pt. 1, "Development In and Through Reading." Edited by Paul A. Witty. Chicago: University of Chicago Press, 1961.

National Society for the Study of Education. *Sixty-seventh Yearbook,* pt. 2, "Innovation and Change in Reading Instruction." Edited by Helen M. Robinson. Chicago: University of Chicago Press, 1968.

A comparison of the content of the above two yearbooks gives a feeling of the forward movement in reading over a period of thirty-five years. Chapter 1 of the *Sixtieth Yearbook* presents a list of trends which could currently be considered recommended practices employed in many schools. The *Sixty-seventh Yearbook* gives the historical background of the changes and innovations in reading during the 1960s, with research documentation in each chapter.

Smith, Nila Banton. *American Reading Instruction*. Newark, Delaware: International Reading Association, 1965.

The most important single source on the history of reading to date, this book is divided into nine historical periods with detailed descriptions of the goals, materials, and methods of each period.

Thorpe, Louis P. and Schmuller, Allen M. *Contemporary Theories of Learning*. New York: Ronald Press, 1954.

See chapter 13 which presents the major principles of learning important in every learning situation. The result is an eclectic view of learning theory.

Waetjen, Walter B., ed. *New Dimensions in Learning: A Multi-Disciplinary Approach*. Washington, D.C.: Association for Supervision and Curriculum Development, 1962.

This bulletin contains a collection of articles on the biological, social, and psychological forces affecting learning. All articles emphasize the multi-disciplinary aspects of learning.

CHAPTER THREE

READING
AND
LANGUAGE

Advance Organizer

Reading requires the translation of printed letters and words into speech so that the reader can associate meaning with the print. Yet, while it is concerned with meaningful reaction to ideas through written language, reading is only one dimension of language. For language is a symbol system: speaking and listening involve oral language symbols, whereas reading and writing involve printed symbols which represent speech. Indeed, reading is so intricately related with other language skills that all these interrelationships are continually in operation during all activities requiring communication. The teacher who is aware of these interrelationships will be better equipped to use reading situations to promote oral language development and to use language arts periods to contribute to skills important in reading. This chapter discusses linguistics and examines the relationship between reading and language. It stresses the view that the teaching of reading is also the teaching of language, and that reading instruction in both decoding and comprehension must be based upon a child's existing level of language development.

LINGUISTICS AND READING

What does the field of linguistics have to offer the classroom teacher of reading? In recent years, considerable attention has been directed to the writings of linguists and to the application of their findings to the teaching of reading. Although the impact of linguistics on the elementary language arts curriculum has not yet been fully realized, linguistic influences can be observed in the teaching of reading, oral language, grammar, and spelling. In examining the topic of linguistics and reading, we will consider how linguists define language, linguistic terminology, and the relationship of linguistics to the teaching of reading.

We are distinguishing between the *study* of linguistics and the linguistic *approach* to initial reading instruction. Although a specific program for teaching beginning reading based on linguistics has been developed, a broader view is presented in this chapter— that is, any approach is linguistic (See p. 68) in that language symbols must be interpreted by the reader. Therefore, linguistics as a discipline can contribute knowledge which will help teachers to help children grasp some basic concepts about their language. However, linguistics is not a method or design for teaching reading. As Betts cautions, "linguistics cannot be equated with reading instruction. Instead, linguistics is a body of knowledge that provides a systematic insight in regard to (1) word perception and recognition and (2) the ability to think in a language."[1]

Definition of Language

How does the linguist define language? When thinking of reading or even of language arts in general, we are apt to think first of written language. However, linguists emphasize that the primary form of language is spoken rather than written and that all cultures have a spoken language but not all have a written one.

One definition of language was expressed by the well-known linguist, Carl Lefevre:

In objective linguistic terms, language is a communication system of vocal symbols, patterning in objectively knowable ways within the rumbling totality of the flowing stream of speech. Speech is a complex system of intricate patterns understood in common by native speakers and native listeners.[2]

Language is a symbolic means of communication. Strickland defines language as "an arbitrary system of sounds and meanings held in common by a language community."[3] Fries, on the other hand, has said that, while all language is concerned with meaning, the meaning itself comes from man's experience and that language serves as the tool for grasping and sharing meanings.[4] Language, here, is seen not as the message designed for communication but as the system of symbols arranged in patterns for signaling the message to be transmitted through speech or print. Language functions as an indispensible tool for thinking and conceptualization, for obtaining new information, and for communicating through symbolic form the thoughts, feelings, and experiences of an individual.

Linguists have identified the language structure of children's speech and thus have provided information that can be used in the development of reading materials which are more related to children's oral language than those currently in use.

The following points summarize some of the linguistic insights into language:

- The primary form of any language is speech.

- Language is arbitrary and ever-changing.

- Language is patterned and has a definite form or structure.

- Writing is a recodification of speech. The English alphabet and punctuation conventions are representations of speech sounds and intonation patterns.

- English is based on an alphabetical principle.

- English is spoken in dialects of which standard English is only one.

- Language is a tool of communication as meaning is received and expressed.

Linguistic Terminology

One problem in studying linguistics is the number of technical terms which make many writings on this subject difficult for the student who is unfamiliar with the field. The following definitions are helpful for clarification, and the reader will probably want to refer to them while reading this section on linguistics.

Phonetics is the study and classification of sounds in language.

Phonemics is concerned with the systematic use of the speech sounds in a specific language. Fries explains the difference between phonetics and phonemics as follows:

> *Phonetics* is a set of techniques by which to identify and describe, in absolute terms, all the differences of sound features that occur in any language. *Phonemics* is a set of techniques by which to determine for a *particular language* which phonetic features form bundles of functioning contrasts to identify the word-patterns of that language.[5]

A *phoneme* is one of the set of small, single units of sound: e.g., the spoken word *box* is composed of three phonemes.

Phonology refers to the branch of linguistic study concerned with speech sounds or phonemes.

A *grapheme* is the written representation of a phoneme. The word *box* is composed of three graphemes, *b, o, x*, which are the written code for the phonemes.

A *morpheme* is the smallest meaning unit of a language. *Box* is one morpheme. *Boxes* and *boxed* contain two morphemes: *box* and the *es* or *ed* endings. Morphemes include *free morphemes* which are words that can stand alone as complete meaning units and *bound morphemes* such as prefixes, suffixes, and changes in word forms that cannot stand alone as independent units of meaning. *Box* is a free morpheme while *es* and *ed* are bound morphemes.

Morphology is the study of the meaning of language and includes the study of minimal units of meaning (morphemes) and of changes in word forms.

Syntax refers to the forms or grammatical patterns of a language. Lefevre defines syntax as "the various patternings of morphemes into larger structural units; noun groups, verb groups, noun clusters, verb clusters, prepositional groups, clauses, and sentences.[6]

Intonation is the linguistic tool for translating written language into speech. Intonation accounts for the rhythm and melody of speech and when supplied by a reader helps him to capture the meaning of a sentence. Intonation includes the features of pitch, stress, and juncture.

Pitch is the relative extent, level, or intensity of speech. Linguists have identified four relative pitch levels.

Stress is the degree of emphasis or accent with which syllables, words, and parts of sentences are spoken.

Juncture refers to pauses in speaking or reading. In written language, juncture is partially but not completely indicated by punctuation marks and spacing between words. For example, the difference between "a name" and "an aim" and between "I scream" and "ice cream" is one of juncture.

Structure words are a category of language signals which have no concrete referent. When contrasted with "full" words which have distinct referents, structure words can be called "empty" words. Words such as *when, or, and, of, that,* and *how* are examples of approximately 300 structure words which are meaningful only within the context of a sentence.

The Relationship of Linguistics to Reading

How does linguistic knowledge relate directly to the reading process? This question at once introduces others. How does knowledge of phoneme-grapheme relationships aid the reader? How does syntactical patterning of language structure facilitate reading comprehension? How can semantic study add to the interpretation of printed messages? In order to begin to answer these questions, it is helpful to identify, as Shane has done, three divisions of linguistics which are relevant for teachers interested in using linguistic knowledge to improve instruction: 1) the phonology, or sound, of the language, 2) its syntax or grammatical form, 3) its semantics, or meaning.[7] Insofar as reading is concerned, these divisions can be identified with the two major tasks of the reader: decoding and comprehension.

Linguistics and Decoding Phonology is ordinarily thought of as the branch of linguistics most related to decoding. Even in decoding, however, more than phonology is used. As children develop knowledge of sound-letter or phoneme-grapheme relationships, they acquire skill in breaking the code of written language. The English language, while based on an alphabetic code of written symbols which represent speech sounds, does not have a one-to-one relationship between sound and symbol. Some speech sounds are represented in print in a variety of ways; some letters commonly represent more than one sound. For example, the phoneme "long *a*" can be represented by *a* in *apron*, by *ea* in *great*, by *ai* in *rain*, by *ay* in *hay*, and by the silent *e* coupled with the first vowel in *hate*. *C* is an example of a letter which signifies more than one sound-letter association as illustrated by the sounds represented in *cow* and *city*.

In the study of the phonology of English, the regularity of phoneme-grapheme language patterns has been identified. Some linguists have suggested a sequential introduction of sound-letter relationships in beginning reading material; it is in this area that programs designed as "linguistic reading programs" have been focused. (See p. 68.) Linguists state emphatically that the study of phoneme-grapheme relationships is a *phonemic*, not a *phonetic*, approach to reading, since children are not studying individual speech sounds but are learning the relationship between speech and its graphic representations.

Decoding print involves language processing in addition to the sound-letter relationship level. Goodman has studied the oral reading performance of readers and has concluded that they use three basic kinds of linguistic information as they decode:

1) *Grapho-phonic.* This is the information from the graphic system, and the phonological system of oral language. Additional information comes to the reader from the interrelationships between the systems. Phonics is a name for those relationships.

2) *Syntactic information.* This is the information implicit in the grammatical structure of the language. The language user knows these and therefore is able to use this information before he learns to read his native language. Reading, like all language processes, involves a syntactic context.

3) *Semantic information.* As he strives to recreate the message, the reader utilizes his experiental conceptual background to create a meaning context. If the reader lacks relevant knowledge, he cannot supply this semantic component, and he cannot read.[8]

Even though readers use information of these three types, they do not use all the information available in the language system. Efficient readers sample and select enough cues from the existing information of the language to decode a meaningful message.

Linguistics and Comprehension The relationship of linguistics to comprehension has received much less emphasis than has that of linguistics to decoding. The field of psycholinguistics which interrelates the study of thought and language has much to offer in understanding how comprehension occurs in the reading process. Reading must give access to meaning as the reader processes the information encoded in printed symbols. Comprehension is the goal of reading and the language systems which operate in comprehension must be studied. There is a relationship between the areas of syntax and morphology and the topics of vocabulary, context, and comprehension. Therefore, the importance of a syntactical and semantic base for understanding the comprehension process cannot be overestimated. In other words, if language is a tool of thinking and if reading encompasses thinking, the importance of language in reading comprehension cannot be denied. If attention is given to reading language structures, comprehension in reading can be enhanced.

By applying knowledge of language structure to reading comprehension, Lefevre has done significant work with language signals in sentence patterns. He identifies "poor sentence sense" as the basic fault in poor reading and suggests that, if the sentence is the minimal meaning-bearing structural unit of most communication, children need to read whole language patterns at the sentence level.[9] He defines a sentence as "not a sequence of words, but a unitary meaning-bearing pattern of grammatical and syntactical functions; the individual words are relatively minor elements in such unitary patterns."[10] In understanding meaning in sentence context, the language signals of intonation, structure words, word-form changes, and functional order in sentence patterns are major language signals of meaning. Indeed, flexibility of language expression and comprehension within basic patterns is essential for effective communication in oral and written language. Loban reports that the degree of flexibility within patterns of meaningful spoken language—not always sentences in the strict sense—is one factor which distinguishes high and low reading achievers.[11]

The study of semantics, or meaning, is an important consideration in developing listening, speaking, and reading vocabularies. To read effectively, a child must have speaking and listening vocabularies with which to connect written word forms for association of meaning. The semantic content of a sentence must be understood, for words take on meaning as they are combined into sentence patterns. For example, structure words and word-form changes acquire meaning only within the context of a sentence.

Likewise, the reader has to combine the words into patterns and understand the individual morphemes in relation to their use in a sentence. As he studies word-form changes (plurals, verb endings, possessives, prefixes, and suffixes) within sentence patterns, a child is increasing his semantic understanding of language. Words are a minor language unit and when they are studied out of context, they lose the characteristic pitch and stress they receive in speech. Goodman states that "children learning to read should see words always as units of larger, meaningful units. In that way, they can use the correspondences between oral and written English within semantic and syntactic contexts."[12] As stressed in chapters 6 and 7 on vocabulary and word attack, word study is most effective in contextual settings. Knowing sentence patterns and word-form changes can aid in the use of context clues to determine an unfamiliar word. In other words, a reader must read the sentence patterns of the language, not separate words.

Linguistics and Oral Reading

The relationship of linguistics to expressive oral reading should be examined also. If readers are taught to understand the intonation signals of pitch, stress, and juncture in understanding sentences, they will realize that oral reading is not reciting words but that it is speaking written language with the emphasis used in their own speaking. Hildreth refers to this process as using the "melodies of speech."[13] Perceiving these melodies should be reflected in fluent oral reading; this in turn is a reflection of the understanding of the syntactical patterns in reading material. Children's ability to supply melody for the written language code is dependent upon their previous experience in understanding and using the spoken code. Intonation accounts for the rhythm and melody of a language and must be supplied by a reader in order to truly translate print into speech. Since the alphabet and punctuation marks are imperfect representations of speech, the reader must supply the missing language signals through intonation and syntactical groupings of words.

Summary of Contributions of Linguistics to Reading

The explorations into language undertaken by linguists can be applied to reading in many ways. Linguistic information can be used to:

■ Identify the alphabetical nature of the English language and provide a basis for developing an understanding of the phoneme-grapheme relationships.

■ Furnish information about the meaning-bearing patterns of the language, thus supplying an intonational and structural basis for understanding the relationship between spoken and written language.

■ Provide knowledge of intonation patterns which in turn can lead to better oral reading.

■ Supply information about the major spelling patterns of the language, with the result that children become more adept at recognizing and using these patterns in reading and writing.

■ Heighten the learning of letter names in the pre-reading stage. (For other factors also responsible for the emphasis on letter names, see p. 109.)

■ Provide a syntactical base for teaching comprehension of units, especially the sentence.

■ Furnish information for structuring the language in reading materials, especially at the beginning levels, to correspond more closely to spoken language.

■ Provide information about how children initially learn to speak the involved symbol system of their native language.

■ Help bilingual children to read by supplying information about similarities and differences between the spoken and written codes of the native language and English.

■ Help reading specialists to develop instructional reading materials that are related to the speech patterns of different subcultures in the country. For example, if we know the dialects of the urban, culturally different child, of the child in Appalachia, of the Mexican-American in the Southwest, and other groups with dialects different from standard English, materials which use the language patterns of specific groups can be developed.

■ Support the language experience approach as children learn to read through their existing language patterns and to see the relationship between speech and print.

Linguists are not reading specialists, and their function is not to develop complete reading programs apart from consideration of individual differences or principles of learning. Joint efforts of linguists, reading specialists, and teachers can lead to improved teaching of reading as a communication and a thinking process. As Shane states, "Linguistics is a source of information; reading theory and methods should be concerned with the strategy and tactics for employing this information."[14]

It is hoped that greater understanding of our language and of the relationship between other aspects of language study and reading will result in improved programs for teaching the skills of communication.

RELATIONSHIP OF ORAL LANGUAGE TO BEGINNING READING

The relationship between spoken language and reading is of immense significance in the initial stages of reading. Competency in understanding the spoken language facilitates learning the written language code. A child's background in oral language affects his readiness for dealing with print which must be translated into speech. Hildreth writes, "The more extensive the child's experience in the language of speech, therefore, the better equipped he is likely to be in getting an author's meaning."[15]

When they enter school, most children have mastered the basic sentence patterns of their native language and have extensive speaking and listening vocabularies. They have internalized and employed all the language signals of effective communication. Their oral language development provides the base for developing skill in decoding and comprehension in reading. The ability to hear and to distinguish likenesses and differences in speech sounds is a part of auditory readiness for learning the phoneme-grapheme relationships to decode print efficiently. As a child learns to read, he learns that writing is a representation of oral language and that meaning is connected with decoded symbols. He also has to associate printed words with words which are already a part of his speaking and listening vocabularies. Not only words, but also his understanding of sentence patterns is essential to comprehending the ideas of a passage.

Many authorities agree that reading programs should take these ideas into account and that much still needs to be done in this area. Ruddell writes, "The research and opinion would suggest that an instructional program designed to develop an understanding of the relationship between the child's familiar spoken system of communication and the written language would facilitate his ability to comprehend reading material."[16] Loban concludes from his extensive study of children's oral language that "it would be difficult not to conclude that instruction can yet do more than it has *with oral language*. Many pupils who lack skill in using speech will have difficulty in mastering written tradition."[17] Until very recently, minimal attention was given to relating the sentence structure in children's reading books to the sentence structure of their speech. In a study of children's oral language and of the language of elementary textbooks, Strickland reports that the children's oral language was more advanced than the sentence patterns employed in the textbooks.[18]

TEACHING READING WITH THE OTHER LANGUAGE ARTS

Since reading is so intricately related to all language activities, it must be related to instruction in listening, speaking, and writing. Understanding vocabulary, using contextual clues to meaning, comprehending sentence patterns, and thinking abstractly and creatively are functions of both oral and written language. Without facility in all communication skills, indeed, the value of reading as a communication process is not fully realized. Reading instruction, therefore, occurs not only in the reading period but is fostered through all language instruction and experience.

Reading and Listening

A child first learns language by listening to the speech of others. In the primary grades, listening is the main avenue for receiving information and continues to be an important means of learning throughout the elementary years. However, instruction in the skill of listening is often taken for granted. In a study of the content of elementary language arts textbooks, Brown found that direct instruction in listening rarely was stressed although the authors of the texts stated that this is the most used language art.[19]

Some obvious parallels exist between reading and listening. Both are receptive facets of language, and both require attention to language signals. Punctuation signals serve as clues for the reader;

intonation patterns of pitch, stress, and juncture are clues to meaning for the listener. The ability to interpret information in both reading and listening depends upon past experiences and knowledge. Both listening and reading involve the same levels of thinking in the comprehension process; and comprehension, in turn, depends upon the quantity of material presented and on the purpose for listening or reading.

There are also differences between receiving information in listening and reading. When reading, a child may vary his rate, pause, or reread. If he does not know a word, he can consult a dictionary or ask for clarification. But in listening, the speaker controls the rate of speech and the presentation of ideas. The listener has the advantage of hearing intonation patterns and interpreting gestures or facial expressions as aids to meaning.

Starting with the earliest school experiences, children ought to be instructed in the skills of careful listening. In the pre-reading and beginning stages of reading, a teacher needs to provide opportunities for children to develop listening skills. Opportunities to hear the language model of the teacher, to enjoy hearing interesting children's literature, and to hear the speech of their peers can add to children's vocabularies and concepts. The term *auding* is sometimes used to denote listening with comprehension as distinguished from hearing without comprehension of meaning. Listening to follow a sequence of events, to find main ideas, to remember specific details, and to follow the thread of a story relate to reading comprehension. In fact, whenever children are having difficulty comprehending reading material, it is recommended that the comprehension skills which are causing difficulty be presented in a listening situation. (See p. 176)

Reading and Speaking

Speaking is an expressive facet of language in which thoughts are formulated and expressed verbally. As a child speaks, he uses the intonation patterns of his language. As he reads orally, he is transposing print into speech and seeing the relationship between the spoken and written language symbols. The reader relates words in reading to words already in his listening and speaking vocabularies. To the extent that "sentence sense" is a basis for comprehension in reading, sentence patterns need first to be employed by the pupil in his speech.

All the statements made in the section on oral language and

beginning reading are applicable here. Much has been written about the relationship of oral language to beginning reading instruction, but oral language facility is also significant to reading achievement at higher levels. A good elementary reading program must extend listening and speaking vocabularies because the greater the degree of linguistic facility, the greater the ability to translate print into meaningful ideas.

Providing frequent opportunities for speaking is one of the most significant factors in the development of effective oral communication. As children have frequent opportunities for dramatization, story-telling, conversation, reporting, choral speaking, taping their speech, and discussions, oral language development can be fostered.

Reading and Writing

Writing, like speaking, is a means of expressing meaning rather than of receiving meaning. Tiedt and Tiedt define writing as "thought transferred to paper."[20] This definition points out the importance of writing as a communication medium rather than as a mechanical skill of reproducing the letter forms of the language. Writing is best taught as a function of thought expression. Handwriting and typing are merely the mechanics for facilitating self-expression and encoding meaning through writing.

Attention to writing during the beginning reading phase has been supported by recent research reports. Chall's review of beginning reading programs,[21] as well as that of the National First Grade studies,[22] found that attention to writing in the initial stages is helpful. Children can be encouraged to dictate personal experience stories and through these stories be guided to see that writing is a record of their spoken thoughts. Further, writing can provide practice in associating spoken and printed words and in using words in meaningful sentence patterns.

Viewing writing as communication can reinforce aspects of communication skills also important in reading. Correlating writing and reading experiences can encourage the productive and critical thinking essential in the higher level comprehension skills. Organization of ideas through titles, headings, topic sentences, and outlining can be taught through functional writing. Exposure to a wide variety of literature and writing styles helps develop a language awareness important in stimulating children to write creatively. Independent reading presents a valuable source of stimuli and ideas for independent writing. Learning language signals such as punctuation and capitalization is reinforced through writing experiences. Individual writing is a means, too, of helping children realize that the writing system of English is alphabetic and is an imperfect representation of speech.

READING AND LANGUAGE FOR THE LINGUISTICALLY DIFFERENT CHILD— A SPECIAL SITUATION

Reading instruction for the child who is "linguistically different" necessitates special consideration. Most linguistically different children come from homes where the native language is not English or where a nonstandard dialect of English is spoken. The terms "culturally disadvantaged," "culturally deprived," and "culturally different" have been used to describe some children who fit into the linguistically different category. For those linguistically different children who have also been called "disadvantaged," the problems of learning to read are greater than just those problems related to the differences between the language of the school and the language of the child. Our intent is not to examine the environmental and learning problems of these children; rather, the concern here is with the reading and language difficulties encountered by children whose speech differs from standard English. Whatever the reasons, a high failure rate exists among speakers of nonstandard English.[23] While it cannot be stated that language difference is the reason for reading failure, the difference needs to be examined and adjustments made to facilitate learning.

Theories concerning language deficiency and language difference have been postulated to explain the language of the nonstandard-speaking child. Prior to the 1960s nonstandard English was considered deficient. However, linguists now support the idea that the nonstandard form is a complete language system satisfactory for communication in the home and cultural group. The nonstandard-speaking child internalizes the features of his language system by the time he enters school, just as the standard-speaking child evidences control of the patterning of his language by age five or six.

Three positions related to the dialect problem are described by Fasold and Shuy:

1) The goal of the first position is *eradication* through correction of children's speech and writing to rid their language of nonstandard features. The eradication philosophy is now

rejected by the sociolinguists who feel that this approach does not improve children's linguistic ability and that it results in damage to the self-concept.

2) The second position of *biloquialism* stresses the addition of standard English to the individual's spoken and written language skills. Eradication of the dialect is not the goal; the addition of another form of the language is. A child's speech is not rejected as sloppy or inferior. Instead, the emphasis in this position is on development of the understanding of the appropriateness of different language forms according to the situation. It is vital that children who speak a nonstandard dialect not be discouraged from expressing themselves for fear of correction. A feeling of rejection of themselves or their language must not be developed.

3) A third position, *appreciation* of dialect differences, is that of accepting a nonstandard dialect without attempting to change it or without encouraging the addition of standard English to the child's linguistic background. At present, little research has been conducted on this position. While the viewpoint may seem desirable, children still must be equipped to deal with materials written in standard English.[24]

Dialect is a variation of a language, not a language deficiency. It is not considered wrong or unacceptable but is acknowledged as one factor which may account for part of the difficulty certain children experience in reading because of the mismatch between their spoken language and the standard English language forms in reading material.

The language difference problem is of special concern in the initial stage of reading as children translate printed symbols into speech. If their speech differs from the language represented in print, the reading task is compounded in difficulty. Goodman supports the importance of recognizing the effect of dialect interference, stating that "the more divergence there is between the dialect of the learner and the dialect of learning, the more difficult will be the task of learning to read."[25] Baratz affirms this idea in extensive writings concerning one group speaking a variant of standard English—black inner-city children. She writes that "the dialect of Negro nonstandard [English-speaking] children is sufficiently divergent from standard English so as to cause difficulty for children who are attempting to learn to read in a dialect which is not similar to the dialect that they speak."[26] However, it must be re-membered that not all black children speak nonstandard English and that many children speaking variants of English have learned to read well.

Several alternatives for working with beginning readers in these special cases have been suggested in the literature on this topic. One is to delay formal teaching of reading until oral standard English has been learned. A drawback to this approach is the time required with the resultant delay before reading is introduced. Shuy comments, "It is more important to learn to read than to speak Standard English."[27] A second alternative is to use commercial reading materials written in dialect. At present the development of such materials is largely experimental, but the use of reading materials written in dialect is a development to observe closely in the coming years.

Perhaps efforts should be directed to the development of beginning reading materials which are dialect-free, using standard forms but excluding any language patterns or vocabulary items not known by the linguistically different speaker.

A third alternative is to use existing standard materials, but to permit children to read them in their dialect. Teachers will need to be knowledgeable about the features of nonstandard speech so that they realize when a child's reading reflects changing print into *his speech*. Teachers will then not correct children for an oral reading response which seems incorrect in standard English, but which is really a reflection of their speech.

Still another option is to use language experience materials written in dialect. This idea has its drawbacks if teachers are not familiar with the syntactical patterns of the divergent speech. We would encourage teachers to use standard spellings when writing experience stories but to record the words and sentences the child speaks. For example, if a child says "dat" for *that* or "des" for *desk,* the correct spelling should be used, but the grammatical forms should be those of the speaker.

A problem occurs if some children use nonstandard forms while others in the group speak standard English. The teacher may accept the child's language but indicate that it can be said another way, thus helping children realize that some of them say it one way, some another. In any case, the teacher uses standard English in his language model and offers many situations for fostering oral language development.

The child whose native language is not English also faces difficulties in reading if sufficient attention is not given to the relationship of reading and language. One approach in this area is to teach the bilingual child to read first in his native language, then to teach him oral English either along with or after the initial reading in the native language, and then to teach reading in English. Venezky comments:

> By teaching reading in the native language, reading instruction can begin at an earlier age than if the standard language had to be taught first; the child's cultural heritage is honored; and a most difficult task—learning to read—is undertaken in the language that the child will always be most comfortable—his own.[28]

However, he cautions that the native literacy approach has not yet been proven superior.

An alternative to the preceding approach is teaching oral English intensively in kindergarten and first grade and then teaching reading in English—bypassing the first teaching of reading in the native language. Just as with teaching oral standard English to the nonstandard speaker, this approach delays the process of learning to read.

In working with the oral language of linguistically different children, a teacher needs to provide active learning situations requiring communication in listening and speaking. Many pictorial aids, actual experiences, language development kits, tape recorders, literature materials, and listening stations can be utilized in a program to foster communication skills.

Chapter Review

All reading is linguistic; therefore, the teaching of reading must be based on knowledge of the interrelationships of reading and language. Linguistic science can offer insight into these interrelationships and also provide the teacher of reading with an understanding of the structure of our language and of the relationship of the spoken and written codes of English. Reading specialists and linguists can use this information to collaborate in the development of improved materials and practices.

The thinking processes in reading are facilitated by stressing the close link between reading and listening, speaking, and writing. Reading must be taught as communication through language.

NOTES

[1] Emmett A. Betts, "Reading: Linguistics," *Education* 83 (May 1963): 524.

[2] Carl A. Lefevre, "Language and Self: Fullfillment or Trauma?, pt. 1," *Elementary English* 43 (February 1966): 126.

[3] Ruth G. Strickland, "Innovation in the Language Arts," in *Readings on Contemporary English in the Elementary Schools*, eds. Iris M. Tiedt and Sidney W. Tiedt (Englewood Cliffs: Prentice-Hall, 1967), p. 5.

[4] Charles C. Fries, *Linguistics and Reading* (New York: Holt, Rinehart and Winston, 1962), p. 99.

[5] Ibid., p. 150.

[6] Carl A. Lefevre, *Linguistics and the Teaching of Reading* (New York: McGraw-Hill, 1964), p. xv.

[7] Harold G. Shane, *Linguistics and the Classroom Teacher* (Washington, D.C.: Association for Supervision and Curriculum Development, 1967), p. 13.

[8] Kenneth S. Goodman, "Analysis of Oral Reading Miscues: Applied Psycholinguistics," *Reading Research Quarterly* 5 (Fall 1969): 17–18.

[9] Lefevre, *Linguistics*, p. 5.

[10] Ibid., pp. xix–xx.

[11] Walter D. Loban, *The Language of Elementary School Children* (Champaign, Illinois: National Council of Teachers of English, 1963), pp. 68–84.

[12] Kenneth S. Goodman, "Words and Morphemes in Reading," in *Psycholinguistics and the Teaching of Reading*, eds. Kenneth S. Goodman and James T. Fleming (Newark, Delaware: International Reading Association, 1969), p. 32

[13] Gertrude Hildreth, "Linguistic Factors in Early Reading Instruction," *The Reading Teacher* 18 (December 1964): 177.

[14] Shane, p. 41.

[15] Hildreth, p. 172.

[16] Robert B. Ruddell, "Reading Instruction in First Grade With Varying Emphasis on the Regularity of Grapheme-Phoneme Correspondence and the Relation of Language Structure to Meaning—Extended into Second Grade," *The Reading Teacher* 20 (May 1967): 731.

[17] Loban, p. 88.

[18] Strickland, p. 10.

[19] Kenneth L. Brown, "Speech and Listening in Language Arts Textbooks," *Elementary English* 44 (April 1967): 341.

[20] Iris M. Tiedt and Sidney W. Tiedt, *Contemporary English in the Elementary School* (Englewood Cliffs: Prentice-Hall, 1967), p. 145.

[21] Jeanne Chall, *Learning to Read: The Great Debate* (New York: McGraw-Hill, 1967), pp. 66–67, 124–125, 234.

[22] Richard L. Venezky, "Nonstandard Language and Reading," *Elementary English* 47 (March 1970): 339–340.

[23] "National First Grade Studies," *The Reading Newsreport* 2 (January 1968): 41.

[24] Ralph W. Fasold and Roger W. Shuy, eds., *Teaching Standard English in the Inner City* (Washington, D.C.: Center for Applied Linguistics, 1970), pp. ix–xiv.

[25] Kenneth S. Goodman, "Dialect Barriers to Reading Comprehension," *Elementary English* 42 (December 1965): 853.

[26] Joan C. Baratz, "Beginning Readers for Speakers of Divergent Dialects," in *Reading Goals for the Disadvantaged*, ed. J. Allen Figurel (Newark, Delaware: International Reading Association, 1970), pp. 79–80.

[27] Roger W. Shuy, "Some Conditions for Developing Beginning Reading Materials for Ghetto Children," in *Language and Reading*, ed. Doris V. Gunderson (Washington, D.C.: Center for Applied Linguistics, 1970), p. 88.

[28] Venezky, p. 336.

SUGGESTED ACTIVITIES

1. Discuss the reasons for accepting the language of the linguistically different child and for using it in preparing reading materials.
2. Tape children talking at nursery school, kindergarten, and first grade. Listen for the sentence patterns employed by them at these levels. Are they standard patterns? Do the children communicate? Summarize your impressions.

SUGGESTED READINGS

Baratz, Joan C. and Shuy, Roger W. *Teaching Black Children To Read.* Washington, D.C.: Center for Applied Linguistics, 1969.

> Excellent, scholarly collection of papers on the topics of dialect and nonstandard English and their significance in the teaching of reading.

Fasold, Ralph W. and Shuy, Roger W., eds. *Teaching Standard English in the Inner City.* Washington, D.C.: Center for Applied Linguistics, 1970.

> Emphasizes the educational implications of teaching reading and language to nonstandard speakers. Features of black dialect are examined and programs for teaching suggested.

Figurel, J. Allen, ed. *Reading Goals for the Disadvantaged.* Newark, Delaware: International Reading Association, 1970.

> A comprehensive collection of papers on reading for the culturally and linguistically different child, with one major section about the urban child and another about the bilingual child and his problems.

Fries, Charles C. *Linguistics and Reading.* New York: Holt, Rinehart and Winston, 1963.

> See chapter 2 for a treatment of the development and description

of types of linguistic study. Chapter 5 presents definitions of phonics, phonetics, phonemics, and other terms.

Greene, Harry A. and Petty, Walter T. *Developing Language Skills in the Elementary Schools.* Boston: Allyn and Bacon, 1967.

Chapters 2 and 3 emphasize the general characteristics of language and the interrelationships of all the language skills. Throughout, the importance of both structured and informal experiences in developing communication skills is stressed.

Horn, Thomas D., ed. *Reading for the Disadvantaged, Problems of Linguistically Different Learners.* Newark, Delaware: International Reading Association, 1970.

A collection of articles exploring the social, economic, psychological, and linguistic settings for understanding the reading problems of culturally different children. Especially helpful are the discussions of specific groups, such as whites, blacks, American Indians, and Spanish-speaking persons.

Lefevre, Carl A. *Linguistics and the Teaching of Reading.* New York: McGraw-Hill, 1964.

One of the most frequently cited works on linguistics and reading. It stresses the meaning-bearing patterns of language and is particularly detailed on intonation, functional order in sentence patterns, structure words, and word-form changes.

Shane, Harold G. *Linguistics and the Classroom Teacher.* Washington, D.C.: Association for Supervision and Curriculum Development, 1967.

Synthesizes for the classroom teacher the major aspects of linguistics and points out the major applications of linguistics to reading and to other language study.

CHAPTER FOUR

BASIC APPROACHES TO READING INSTRUCTION

Advance Organizer

This chapter introduces the major tenets of methods-and-materials combinations or approaches in use today in elementary reading instruction. The following approaches to teaching reading are discussed: basal reader, language experience, individualized, linguistic, Initial Teaching Alphabet, phonic, and programmed. Each is described in terms of its characteristic emphases, the level or levels in the elementary school where it is generally used, the materials commonly employed in conjunction with it, the activities it fosters, and the advantages and disadvantages frequently associated with it.

Following the treatment of these approaches is a discussion of ways for combining aspects of several of them and occasions when this is advisable.

Emphasis in the chapter is on the variety of highly developed approaches available for teaching reading. Each approach should be evaluated for its strengths and weaknesses and for its contributions to an effective instructional program.

INTRODUCING THE BASIC APPROACHES TO READING INSTRUCTION

The varying types of reading instruction are referred to in this chapter as reading *approaches,* to signify that they are more than a set of objectives, more than a method, more than a series of materials. They are *roads into* reading—some more highly structured or more tied to specific materials and procedures than others, but all providing some means by which it is possible to guide the young child from pre-reading into reading. At the close of the chapter, combinations of features from several of the basic approaches are suggested.

THE BASAL READER APPROACH

The basal reader approach is centered around the use of one or more series of graded reading textbooks as the core of the reading program. It is the most commonly used approach for teaching reading. In a survey of school systems in the United States in 1963, Austin and Morrison reported that over 95 percent of the primary teachers and over 90 percent of the intermediate grade teachers in the survey employed basal readers as the main approach to reading.[1]

The books for grade one in the basal reader approach usually include reading readiness workbooks, three or four pre-primers, a primer and a first reader. The additional materials for the beginning reading stage usually include a "Big Book" which is a large reproduction (generally twenty-four-by-thirty-six inches) of the first five or six stories in the first pre-primer, picture cards, word and phrase cards, letter cards, and a word card holder. Above the first grade level, most series include two books for grade two, two books for grade three, and one book each for grades four, five, and six. Some series also have junior high school materials. For independent work with each reader there are accompanying activity books which correlate with the stories and skills taught in readers. Some series provide parallel readers which are designed to provide supplementary materials and extra practice before children progress to the next book or level. Filmstrips, tapes, and records are also available with several series.

Basal readers are characterized by careful control of the rate of vocabulary introduction with a planned amount of repetition. Table 1 lists the number of cumulative words in basal readers at the different levels.[2]

TABLE 1   Cumulative Vocabulary in Basal Readers

Basal Reader	*Cumulative Vocabulary*
First grade	
Pre-primers	40 to 110
Primer	120 to 310
First Reader	230 to 475
Second grade	950 to 1700
Third grade	1900 to 3300
Fourth grade	2800 to 3500
Fifth grade	4500 to 6000
Sixth grade	6000 to 8500

When basal readers are used, children are usually grouped according to reading ability. This type of grouping permits the teacher to instruct the various groups within a class at different levels of difficulty. (For more detail on grouping and classroom organization for reading see chapter 12.)

The pattern of teaching with basal readers is usually referred to as Directed Reading Activity (DRA). This is the vehicle for teaching skills in vocabulary, word attack, and comprehension. DRA consists of several steps: preparation or readiness, guided reading, skill development, and enrichment. While the terminology may differ from one series to another, the overall pattern is similar and can be adapted to teaching reading with other materials in other curriculum areas.

In the preparation stage, the teacher develops the necessary background for understanding the ideas of the story and introduces the new vocabulary. Vocabulary introduction receives different emphases from series to series and from one level to another. The preparation stage also identifies the general purposes for reading. In his intensive work in developing thinking abilities with basal readers, Stauffer puts particular emphasis on having children identify *their* purposes for reading.[3]

The guided reading step consists of both silent and oral reading, as well as discussion. As they read silently first, children seek answers to questions posed during the purpose-setting phase of the preparation stage. Discussion of story content is included as a follow-up to silent reading. There may be oral reading of a particular passage which answers a question or proves a point. The amount of oral reading decreases when children move beyond the initial stages of instruction and comprehension is stressed more than decoding.

In the skill development step of the reading lesson, intensive attention is given to teaching vocabulary, word attack, and comprehension skills. (See chapters 6, 7, and 8.) Selected workbook pages or teacher-designed activities can be employed as a means of reinforcing the direct skill instruction.

The enrichment step gives the teacher an opportunity to relate reading to the other language arts and to other curricular areas. Supplementary reading of trade books on the same topic as the particular story treated in the directed reading period may be recommended to pupils. Dramatization of a story, creative writing, and other types of enrichment activities can broaden children's reading experiences.

Basal readers have many advantages:

- They provide a carefully graded set of materials with a systematic progression of difficulty in vocabulary and reading skills.

- The vocabulary is carefully controlled in beginning readers to promote success in the initial stages, although this control is not necessarily considered an advantage by all authorities.

- The skills of both decoding and comprehension are stressed.

- They are colorful and attractive and contain numerous illustrations.

- Teachers can simultaneously use materials of various levels of difficulty for the pupils who are working at different levels in the same class.

- The detailed teacher's guides contain clear explanations of the total reading procedure and step-by-step outlines for each lesson.

- The accompanying manuals provide numerous suggestions for enriching the total reading program used in a class.

- Basal readers save teacher time and effort with the readily available books, workbooks, and other supplementary materials.

There are also limitations to the instructional approach using basal readers:

- They have been criticized for stilted language patterns, rigid vocabulary control, lack of interest appeal, lack of literary content, and middle-class suburban settings and values.

- The teacher's manuals have been criticized for presenting too structured a program and for not allowing flexibility in teaching procedures.

- Children may too easily be placed in groups which are using readers of an inappropriate level.

Stauffer cautions against the use of basal readers in a stereotyped fashion which may not encourage thinking on the part of the teacher in reading instruction. He also warns that "at no time should a basic reader program, even in jest, be referred to as 'the reading program.' "[4]

The preceding limitations are in part related to the materials themselves. For example, stilted language patterns occurring in the early levels result from limited vocabulary, but as the material quickly becomes more difficult, the sentence patterns become more natural. However, the limitations of basal readers may also be a result of poor use. Teacher's manuals are not meant to be followed slavishly, but rather to guide the teacher in his planning and teaching techniques. Likewise, the readers were not designed to provide a literature program and in any class the teacher needs to encourage recreational reading by providing many experiences with children's literature. Recently, attention has been devoted to publishing multi-ethnic texts with urban settings. For numerous children they present more realistic content than the former stereotyped situations.

Graded basal textbooks are also used in the linguistic approach, with the Initial Teaching Alphabet, and with some phonic approaches. However, in most classrooms the basal reader approach refers to the use of a series of books with which the teacher presents reading through the DRA procedure as he works with vocabulary, stresses reading for meaning, provides careful development of reading skills, and correlates reading with other classroom activities.

THE LANGUAGE EXPERIENCE APPROACH

The language experience method is used as an approach to initial reading, to remedial reading, and as a supplement to other approaches and materials beyond the beginning stages. Allen has written widely of this approach and has expressed the rationale for it in a child's terminology:

> What I can think about, I can talk about.
> What I can say, I can write—or someone can write for me.
> What I can write, I can read.
> I can read what I can write and what other people can write for me to read.[5]

In this approach, the *language patterns* of the reading materials are determined by a child's oral language, and the *content* of reading materials is determined by his experiences. There are three major characteristics of this approach:

1) The majority of reading materials is pupil-produced.

2) The teaching of reading is integrated with instruction in the other language arts.

3) Vocabulary is not controlled since any words a child uses in his speech can be used in the reading materials.

Communication of meaning is built into the three steps of creating personal reading materials:

1) The child relates an experience through speaking.

2) The child or teacher records the child's thoughts.

3) The child reads the written record of his story. This step includes subsequent work on vocabulary and skill development.

Meaning is stressed for the reader as he communicates his thoughts through speech, as he writes or watches the teacher record his thoughts, and as he reads his story by decoding the print and associating the meaning with his previously spoken thoughts. Figure 1 illustrates the communication sequence by stating the child's actions as he communicates in the language experience framework. As the reader observes his thoughts being encoded into graphic symbols, the communication of the meaning of his speech in written form is evident to him. As he decodes the printed symbols and associates them with his previously spoken thoughts, he is communicating through reading.

The reader must also learn that reading materials other than his own involve the communication of meaning. He begins to realize

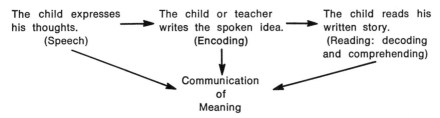

Figure 1 The Communication Sequence in the Language Experience
Approach[6]

that other authors have expressed their thoughts and ideas in
printed language in order to communicate meaning.

The major reading materials used in the language experience
approach are group and individual experience stories and word
banks. Other supplementary materials such as children's literature
materials are also used in conjunction with a child's personal writing. (In chapter 11, a sample lesson is given for developing a group
experience story following the steps of oral discussion, recording
the spoken language, and reading the written record.)

An individual word bank is built as a child identifies words in a
group experience chart or in his individual story. These words are
written on cards which then comprise his personal word bank. A
word bank indicates to the teacher the words in the reader's sight
vocabulary and furnishes examples for skill instruction. As different
categories of words are studied, group word banks are built within
a class. For example, a group word bank may include such categories as descriptive words, color words, or action words. Both the
individual and group word banks are valuable reference resources
when children are doing creative writing. The group word banks
are available in the classroom writing center.

In organizing reading instruction using the language experience
approach, a large block of time is devoted to reading and to other
language activities. The teacher conducts individual pupil-teacher
conferences during which children create, read, and review their
stories. Some small group and some total group instruction is
included as individual stories are read to other children, as group
experience stories are composed, and as instruction in skills is conducted with a small group needing the same skill. Skills are taught
not in the sequence outlined by basal textbooks, but as needed by
children in the reading of their personal reading materials.

The advantages of the language experience approach are its em-

The teacher records the child's words as he relates his experience watching
a locust in the jar.

phasis on meaning, its stress on the relationship between spoken
and written language, the high degree of personal involvement and
interest, language patterns which are comprehensible for the
learner, and the exposure to a wide variety of words rather than
to a controlled vocabulary. Reading is introduced gradually with a
natural transition from pre-reading to beginning reading. Success
is stressed, and a child is not forced into reading books too early.
The language experience approach has some particular advantages
for culturally different children. Basal readers contain stories and
language patterns which may be unrelated to their experiences and
language, while the experience materials are meaningful in both
language patterns and content.

The language experience approach is not without limitations since it is based upon the child's own experience and language. While from one viewpoint the uncontrolled vocabulary is considered to be an advantage, this feature may also be a limitation. Confusion rather than acquisition of a basic sight vocabulary may result. It is possible for a child to memorize story content instead of developing reading skills. Skills may be neglected since the teacher is not following the structured sequence of a basal reader. Pupil-developed materials may not provide enough variety in reading content to develop sufficient skill in comprehension. Group interaction in discussing stories may be omitted, and a child may not receive enough direct instruction in getting meaning from reading. The absence of a detailed teacher's manual and the lack of a sequential plan for reading may result in an inadequate reading program especially with weak and inexperienced teachers. A teacher may have difficulty evaluating his students' level of achievement or progress in reading.

The preceding limitations do not mean that the language experience approach cannot be an effective way of teaching reading if the following suggestions are put into practice.

- It is necessary to develop a system of record-keeping with regard to each child's mastery of specific skills. (The types of record-keeping suggested for individualized reading can be used with the language experience approach. See p. 66)

- The teacher needs to be well-informed about the skills needed by individual children and should plan periods for direct instruction in skills.

- Supplementary reading materials and experiences with children's literature must be included in order to have an enriched reading program.

- Time must be provided for small groups to hear each other's stories and for group interaction through language discussions.

Stauffer reported a study in which teachers received in-service training in using the language experience approach in grade one. He concluded that the language arts (language experience) approach was an effective method of beginning reading instruction, that this method can be used effectively with all children, and that results in reading performance, word attack skills, spelling, vocabulary development, and facility with written language were excellent.[7]

THE INDIVIDUALIZED APPROACH

Adapting instruction to individual differences should be of primary concern to teachers of reading. Since 1950 professional literature has given great attention to the individualized approach which stresses principles of child development in the implementation of an instructional reading program. The terms *individualized instruction* and *individualized reading* are not synonymous. While individualizing instruction is a basic tenet of any effective approach to teaching reading, this discussion treats the specific approach known as *individualized reading.*

The major characteristics of individualized reading are:

- Pupils select their reading material from a wide variety of books available in their classroom and/or school library.

- Each pupil reads different material and moves at his own pace through the material he has selected.

- Direct instruction occurs in a pupil-teacher conference rather than in a reading group.

- The reading materials are trade (library) books rather than basal readers.

In organizing an instructional reading program employing the individualized approach, the teacher needs to give attention to the selection and availability of reading materials; to procedures for conducting the individual pupil-teacher conference; to provisions for skill instruction; to types of records to be kept; and to organization of the reading period to provide a balance between conferences, independent silent reading, and enrichment activities involving reading.

A successful individualized reading program requires a wide selection of reading material. Barbe suggests an minimum of three books per pupil and of not less than one hundred books in the classroom library.[8] At best they cover a wide variety of subjects and include a wide range of levels in order to provide appropriate materials for the range of interests and achievement within a class. Adequate school library facilities are also a must for this approach. While the growth of elementary school libraries has been encouraging in recent years, large numbers of elementary schools do not have adequate libraries. Although teachers may bring in their personal book collections and use public library facilities and packaged collections of literature materials now available from many publishers, a wide school library collection is considered essential if an individualized reading program is to provide sufficient material.

The individual pupil-teacher conference is crucial to the instruction in the individualized approach. During the conference, the teacher talks with the pupil to check his choice of material, asks questions to guide his reading, questions the pupil's understanding of his reading, reviews vocabulary and other skills, and notes his progress. The length of the conference usually varies from five to ten minutes with one or two conferences with each child per week. Some teachers have children sign up voluntarily when the children feel they need a conference. Other teachers prefer to have these conferences scheduled on a regular rotating basis so that all children are reached regularly.

Darrow and Howes identify the following concerns of the teacher in the conference.

Diagnosis of Reading Problems
—discovering how the pupil attacks new words—use of context clues, phonetic clues . . .
—asking general and specific questions about the story, main idea, details of an episode . . .
—observing the child read orally and silently
—evaluating progress in locating materials through use of indices, table of contents . . .
—checking word meaning, interpretations of ideas . . .
—discussing reading difficulties, asking the pupil what he needs help with . . .

Selection of Material
—seeking the child's opinion on the quality of his reading material
—pointing out other stories by the same author
—discussing possible choices for next reading
—developing ways to evaluate reading material, criteria for selection . . .

Plans for Next Steps
—selecting appropriate worksheets or practice materials
—discussing possible independent activities, creative art work, dramatizations, preparation of material to share with others . . .

—sharing testing results
—looking at the child's reading plans

Records of Progress
—going over the child's reading records
—planning for kinds of records for the child to keep
—sharing the teacher's records of pupil progress
—bringing the records up to date

Plans for Parent-Teacher Conference
—developing an "agenda" for parent-teacher conferences
—sharing results of conference
—preparing a folder of child's material for conference[9]

Direct instruction in reading skills grows out of the observations made during the conferences. Occasionally the teacher forms small groups for work on skills needed by a number of children. Some skill instruction occurs incidentally in the pupil-teacher conferences, but additional instruction needs to be included for most children. The teacher may wish to use the teacher's manuals of basal readers as a source for the content and procedures to be used in the direct teaching of skills.

Carefully kept records are an essential of individualized reading since pupils are not following a carefully ordered sequential program in reading. Some teachers employ a card file system of record-keeping, while others prefer a class notebook. Notes taken during the conference are one source of records for each child. It is recommended that teachers prepare checklists of the skills in word attack and comprehension and that they check off a child's name when he has mastered a particular skill. The records are a valuable reference during conferences with parents and for continuous evaluation of a child's progress.

Records kept by children are also important in encouraging self-evaluation in reading. The types of records kept by children usually include a list of new vocabulary words and a list of books read. Children may be directed to summarize their reactions to books as part of their personal records.

The advantages of this approach are expressed through the philosophy of having each child read what interests him at his own pace. Veatch states that "this new reading program is based on the idea that children can and do read better, more widely, and with increased interest when allowed to choose their own reading materials."[10]

An individualized reading program does not force a slow reader to work at a level which is too difficult and the advanced reader is not penalized by being confined to the pace of a group which is not up to his level. The labels of "fast," "average," and "slow" reading groups are removed, and the tension and pressures of group competition are eliminated. The stigma of being in the slowest group is minimized, and a child's self-confidence may improve when he does not have to read in a group with his classmates. As a result of the one-to-one relationship, there may be improved pupil-teacher rapport in the conference plan of instruction.

The disadvantages most frequently cited for individualized reading relate to the organizational problems and the lack of a sequential plan for teaching. Record keeping is time-consuming, and the teacher may not have an accurate indication of a child's progress in reading. The amount of direct instructional time each child receives in the conference is minimal when compared to the time he would receive in direct group instruction. Class size may also be a limiting factor. Individualized reading is easier to organize if the class size does not exceed twenty-five pupils. However, this is true of any approach, and class size is not necessarily the major factor determining the choice of approach for teaching reading.

A frequently stated criticism of individualized reading is the neglect of instruction in skills. However, this need not be the case if the teacher incorporates skill instruction into the regular organization of the reading program. When children are permitted to choose their own materials, there may be some pupils who are not sufficiently motivated to read and others who may choose materials which are inappropriate in level of difficulty. Some children may not be able to work independently or to read carefully with a minimum of teacher guidance. The advantage of group interaction in providing for depth of comprehension will be lost unless the teacher includes occasional group activities related to reading.

The wide variety of books used in individualized reading presents still another problem for the teacher. It is unrealistic for a teacher to be familiar with all the library books which children will be reading. If he is to check children's comprehension, can he do it adequately without knowing the material? It is possible for teachers to keep a file of summaries or reviews of books with some suggested questions to check comprehension. As the teacher continues to use the individualized approach, his familiarity with the available books will increase. Another frequently cited limitation of individualized reading is that it requires a teacher to be especially capable in organizing a thorough instructional program. However, capable teachers are necessary for any approach to be effective. The merits of any approach must be evaluated in relation to the total reading program offered to pupils.

The research evaluating the superiority or inferiority of individualized reading to other approaches is inconclusive.[11] Most of the research reports achievement in reading skills and does not measure reading attitudes or interest. Thus, one of the greatest assets of individualized reading, the encouragement of wide independent reading, is not measured. Individualized reading, like other approaches, can be an effective way of teaching reading. In the preceding discussion, this approach has been described separately from other approaches, but in actual practice many of its features can be combined with other approaches.

THE LINGUISTIC APPROACH

Another approach to the teaching of reading is the linguistic approach which developed as the findings of linguistics were applied to the teaching of reading. Linguistics is the scientific study of language and encompasses different types of language study. Since reading is a facet of language, all approaches are linguistic. However, some materials are labeled specifically as linguistic.

One group of linguists, the structural linguists, are concerned with the structural elements of language that influence the meanings conveyed by language. Lefevre has elaborated upon the implications of language structure for reading instruction.[12] Another group of linguists, the phonologists, are concerned with studying the speech sounds of language. They have shaped the linguistic reading programs now in use. However, while there are some differences between them, there are a number of common features. In some series the program extends through the second and third grades, although linguistic readers are designed primarily for initial instruction in reading. After the completion of linguistic materials, children are expected to transfer to regular reading materials. Linguistic readers stress the controlled introduction of vocabulary guided by regular spelling patterns. In the linguistic approach there is heavy emphasis on decoding the print because, as Fries claims, the child already knows the meaning of the words which he is decoding. Since several linguists feel that pictures encourage children to guess rather than to recognize printed word forms, pictures are omitted in their linguistic series. In one series of linguistic readers, pictures are used to make the books more attractive, but do not correlate with the story content.

Beginning reading programs with a linguistic emphasis introduce monosyllabic words which follow regular spelling patterns. Words are introduced with a "read-spell-read" procedure. For example, if the teacher is introducing the word *can*, he would write the word, spell it for the children, and then say it again. The children would be directed to repeat the word, name the letters, and read it again. Since linguists view beginning reading as basically a process of recoding print into sounds, learning the phoneme-grapheme (sound-letter) relationships of the language is the child's first task in learning to read.

Words are presented in an orderly development of regular spelling patterns with minimal differences between the words in a patterned set. For example, the first group of words in the *Merrill Linguistic Readers*[14] includes *cat, nat, fat, hat.* There is only one letter which is different in each word, and all the words follow the spelling pattern of consonant, short vowel, consonant. Through the read-spell-read procedure and the minimum-contrast feature, children learn to deduce the sounds associated with particular letters although they are not instructed in phonics. Bloomfield developed linguistic materials following the above principles in 1942, and they are now available both in a single book and as a set of readers.[15] The reading material in his book, *Let's Read,* consists of isolated lists of words presented in a carefully developed sequence. Other more recent series of linguistic readers are similar to Bloomfield's but also include sentences and stories. The *Merrill Linguistic Readers* introduce some "sight words," that is, words which are irregular or which follow patterns not yet introduced but which permit greater flexibility in the sentences and stories.

The major advantages of the linguistic approach are inherent in its definite structure and its systematic, sequential instruction. Presenting words which are regular in spelling patterns to establish solid learning of the phoneme-grapheme relationships eliminates the confusion present when there is random selection of vocabulary for beginning reading materials. The linguistic materials provide frequent repetition to insure over-learning of the major spelling patterns and of the phoneme-grapheme relationships. The feature of "minimum contrast" presents learning in small steps which are closely related to previous learning, thus simplifying the child's task. From the beginning stages of instruction it requires the child to observe small rather than gross differences in words. For example, he learns to notice the difference between *sat* and *rat* instead of making the gross discrimination required to distinguish between words such as *jump* and *look*. The elimination of pictures facilitates concentration on the printed word forms rather than on a picture clue for guessing story content.

The major disadvantage of the linguistic approach is the lack of attention to the thought-getting nature of reading. At present, the linguistic approach to reading gives little consideration to communication in reading while placing great stress on the decoding nature of the process—and on only one decoding technique at that. There is danger that the beginning reader may view reading as naming words rather than as a process of responding to the meaning of print. We stated earlier that a good reading program utilizes a variety of methods and that no one approach is effective with all children. If a linguistic approach is used with all pupils in beginning reading, some children are unnecessarily penalized.

Other criticisms of the linguistic approach are concerned with the content of the readers. In the easiest of the reading books of one linguistic series, the language is stilted and artificial, and the stories are unrelated to the experience backgrounds of the children. (The same criticism was stated for the first grade basal readers because of the controlled vocabulary.) The omission of pictures in some of the linguistic readers diminishes their attractiveness and appeal to primary children.

However, linguistics can be of help in reading programs. As more is learned about the relationship between spoken and written language, such knowledge can be considered in planning instruction and in developing reading materials which employ the language patterns used by children in their speech.

THE INITIAL TEACHING ALPHABET (ITA) APPROACH

Since its introduction in England in 1960, the Initial Teaching Alphabet has been the subject of much interest in both the United States and England. Developed by Sir James Pitman, ITA is an "altered" alphabet of forty-four symbols designed for use in the beginning stages of reading instruction to provide greater regularity between speech sounds and their representation in print. The forty-four symbols include twenty-four of the letters of the regular alphabet (*q* and *x* are omitted). Only lower case letters are used.

Downing emphasizes that the ITA is a "medium" through which

TABLE 2 The Initial Teaching Alphabet

æ face	b bed	c cat·	d dog	ɛɛ key
f feet	g leg	h hat	ie fly	j jug	k key
l letter	m man	n nest	œ over	p pen	ɼ girl
r red	s spoon	t tree	ue use	v voice	w window
y yes	z zebra	ʒ daisy	wh when	ch chair
th three	th the	ſh shop	ʒ television	ŋ ring
ɑ father	au ball	a cap	e egg	i milk	o box
u up	ω book	ω spoon	ou out	oi oil

reading is taught, not a "method" of teaching.[16] Ordinarily children learn to read through the "medium" of the twenty-six letter English alphabet, or as it is called, traditional orthography (TO). Using ITA, most children who make satisfactory progress in reading in grade one transfer to reading in TO. Some transfer earlier, and some later. ITA is not designed for use beyond the initial stages of reading instruction.

When ITA is the medium of reading instruction, the use of basal readers and experience charts, the study of phonics, and the individualized reading of trade books may be included as methods and materials in the overall program. Thus, in practice, ITA is often a combined approach. In some instructional programs using ITA, independent creative stories have been encouraged. With the added advantage of increased phonics instruction and independent writing activities, some children using ITA have had an enriched reading program. Therefore, the question of whether the children's achievement in reading can be attributed to the medium of ITA or to other components of the reading program must be raised.

Downing lists the following advantages of ITA for the beginning reader:

1) Easing the initial task of learning to read.
2) Reducing the ambiguity of conventional spelling.
3) Making the coding of English phonemes less complex.[17]

Because of the high degree of regularity (although not perfect) between sounds and their graphic representations, it is possible to include more phonics instruction in beginning reading with ITA than is usually done with other approaches. In ITA a child learns only one form for each letter, while in traditional orthography he must learn both upper and lower case forms, as well as deviations in printing styles. Spelling with ITA is consistent, and the beginning reader can use his knowledge of phonics to spell. Thus ITA enables him to write independently as he is learning to read.

A basic question is, "Is ITA necessary?" If most pupils can be instructed effectively in TO and eventually must use TO as the medium of print, is it desirable to teach another alphabet which must then be unlearned? In the report of the National First Grade Studies continued through the second grade, Dykstra reported no significant difference in reading comprehension between pupils taught with ITA and those taught with the basal reader approach, but that the ITA taught students were superior on measures of word recognition and spelling.[18]

Other questions about ITA are related to spelling instruction, availability of materials, and the transition to TO. Children who have learned phonetic spellings in ITA must relearn these words with TO spelling and they may have developed the habit of phonetic spelling which perhaps will not equip them to spell correctly with the TO alphabet. The lack of sufficient supplementary reading material has also been considered a drawback in some instances. The transition to TO is not considered by the advocates of ITA to be a major problem if children have progressed satisfactorily in ITA during the first year of instruction.

ITA is not a panacea or automatic answer to the complexities of teaching beginning reading. Further research, some of which is now being carried out by Downing and others, is needed to ascertain the value of this approach. Research studies of ITA are complicated by other factors affecting reading achievement, such as amount of phonics instruction or related language activities, which must be controlled in the research.

VARIOUS PHONIC APPROACHES

Phonic approaches to intial reading instruction put more weight on learning sounds than on the recognition of whole word forms. These approaches stress letter-sound relationships and the decoding facet of the reading process. The term *phonic approaches* may be misleading; these are not broad approaches which view reading as a developmental process extending over a relatively long time span and which include instruction in all reading skills essential for a balanced reading program. However, since we wish to describe a number of ways of approaching reading and since the question of the role of phonics usually occurs when approaches to reading are discussed, we will use the above-mentioned term in this chapter.

It should be pointed out that although the basal reader, language experience, and individualized approaches are not labeled "phonic," this does not mean that the study of phonics is omitted. Phonics instruction begins in the pre-reading program as part of any approach when children receive auditory training in hearing likenesses and differences in beginning and ending sounds of spoken words. The study of phonics is continued as children progress in reading, since knowledge of letter-sound relationships is one important skill needed for independence in reading.

Approaches to phonic instruction can be classified as synthetic or analytic. These two approaches differ chiefly in the attention given to meaning in beginning reading, the amount of phonics in initial instruction, the method of teaching sounds of letters, and the importance of developing a sight vocabulary in the beginning phase.

Synthetic phonic approaches start with the study of individual letter sounds and build words by combining the separate sounds into a pronounceable unit. The old alphabet-spelling method based on the naming of letters in order to learn words was a synthetic approach. Analytic phonic approaches start with a whole unit (a word, sentence, or story). After the whole unit is understood, it is broken down for a more detailed analysis of the smaller parts.

Analytic approaches stress the meaning component of the reading process and the importance of building a sight vocabulary. The reader studies phonics by analyzing a group of known sight words which illustrate the particular phonics content to be learned. For example, if the child has learned the words *red, ride,* and *run* in reading, he may then study the sound of the initial consonant *r* with those words as examples.

Several synthetic approaches are described below. Generally, approaches specifically designated as *phonic* are synthetic since they begin with individual letters and sounds rather than with analysis of known words.

The Phonovisual Method

One supplementary phonics program is the *Phonovisual Method*[19] which can be used with other reading materials. Phonovisual materials stress game-type drills to provide practice in letter-sound associations with letter sounds presented in isolation rather than in words. The materials are intended for kindergarten and primary grades and for remedial instruction with pupils who are deficient in phonics. Included are two large charts (one for consonants and one for vowels), a teacher's guide, pupil workbooks, and game materials.

One drawback of this method is a rigidly outlined sequence which may not be correlated with the skills needed by the children in the materials they are using for regular reading instruction. The phonovisual drills may thus be isolated from reading activities and may not help children transfer phonic knowledge to attacking unfamiliar words. However, these materials do provide systematic instruction in phonics through the use of colorful charts and they do teach the use of auditory and visual clues in combination as keys to analysis of words.

Phonetic Keys to Reading

The *Phonetic Keys to Reading*[20] is a supplementary phonics program consisting of teacher's guides and pupil workbooks for grades one through three. In the period of initial instruction, forty separate phonetic understandings are taught. As children progress through the three first grade workbooks, they learn various rules or "keys" for sounding letters. This program has a heavy emphasis on rules.

Vowels are taught before consonants and are taught in the middle position in words. A great amount of practice in sounding out words is provided even though the words being sounded have been presented frequently enough to be in the reader's sight vocabulary.

Emphasis on sounding individual letters and on learning a number of complicated and often unreliable rules is open to question. There is a very real danger that exposure to this type of instruction may result in word-calling rather than comprehension.

The Carden Method

The *Carden Method*[21] is another set of materials and procedures for teaching phonics synthetically. The three books in this method are written for first grade children to use before they use basal readers. The Carden materials teach vowels first with emphasis on vowel rules. Consonant sounds are isolated and may result in distortions such as *b—buh, g—guh*. Spelling and writing are stressed in this initial instruction in reading. These materials present phonics content in a mechanistic and unnatural way with undue emphasis on isolated letter sounds. Heilman comments that

> . . . it should not be concluded that children exposed to this type of instruction in grade one will not "learn what is commonly measured at the end of grade one as reading achievement." This is a tribute to children, but perhaps an unfortunate educational phenomena since the fact that "learning takes place" is often cited as a justification for the use of such procedures.[22]

Words in Color

The *Words in Color*[23] scheme of teaching letter sounds uses a series of twenty-nine large wall charts to present thirty-nine different sounds, using thirty-nine different colors. Every time a particular sound appears on the chart, it has the same color regardless of the letter representation of the sound. Drill is provided through the use of chalkboard presentations and the demonstration of the charts. Children are exposed to the visual representation of a letter with the particular color while hearing the letter sound. Initial consonant sounds are taught in connection with a following vowel sound. For example, *b* is taught in the combinations *ba, be, bu,* and so on. Reading books are included in the *Words in Color* materials, but these books are printed without color.

When children transfer from the *Words in Color* drills to regular reading materials, they will not have color crutches to help them determine sounds of letters. It is possible, too, that some children will have as much difficulty distinguishing between different shades of colors as they do between forms of letters.

The major advantage of the synthetic approaches described above is the systematic instruction provided for one important skill in reading. The teaching of phonics in these systems is definitely not left to chance or to incidental learning. The careful identification of the content may be a guide for the inexperienced teacher. Teaching materials such as charts and suggested game activities are usually considered to be helpful aids. When used as a supplement to other approaches, some phonics systems may be valuable.

Harris summarizes the shortcomings of synthetic alphabetic and phonic approaches:

1) The English language has so many irregularities and exceptions that an adequate phonic system has to be quite complicated and difficult to learn.
2) The synthetic methods tend to produce slow, labored reading.
3) They encourage attention to the words and do not place enough stress on the thought-getting side of reading.[24]

Approaches to reading which stress word-calling rather than comprehension of ideas are a matter of concern. The child does not benefit from a flood of phonics content without training in learning to read for meaning. If the reader develops inefficient habits of word analysis, they may be detrimental to the later development of his reading skill. The role of phonics is one important method of word attack but not the major emphasis of a reading program. Children need to learn a variety of techniques for word attack. It is imperative that the correct emphasis be placed on phonics in reading.

THE PROGRAMMED READING APPROACH

As acceptance of the concept of programming learning has grown in recent years, it has been applied to the teaching of reading.

We are using the term *programmed reading* to refer to one particular set of materials entitled *Programmed Reading*,[25] and to the procedures for using materials of this type. *Programmed Reading* includes a pre-reading series and Series I, II, and III for use in the primary grades and in conjunction with remedial readers. Storybooks for independent reading are also available. The pre-reading series begins with detailed oral instruction for learning letter names and sound-symbol relationships. The oral pre-reading activities are followed by the introduction of the first pupil book, the programmed primer. With the primer the teacher gives oral directions to the entire group, and pupils respond by marking in their books. Upon completion of the primer, the children are ready for the first book in Series I. After the children have progressed to page 18 of Book I in Series I, they work independently at their own pace. Series I, II, and III each include seven books.

The pupil books are of a workbook nature with the content presented frame by frame, and children must make a written response in each frame. The responses required are usually to choose *yes* or *no*, select the appropriate word from two or three choices, or write the missing letter or letters of a word. The teacher's role is to supervise and observe the pupils' independent work. Tests are included for each book, and the teacher can use the results of these tests as a record of each child's progress and for diagnostic information regarding a child's particular reading needs. The teacher gives individual help as needed. As he circulates around the class while pupils are working independently, he may ask some children to read a frame to him or to answer a question about their reading.

Several features of programmed reading merit special attention. Pupil responses are immediately reinforced or corrected so that in all of his reading a child is informed of the correct response. The learner advances steadily from frame to frame by very small steps in which new learnings are related to previous ones in a logical, sequential development. The feature of permitting each child to progress individually at his own rate is another advantage of the programmed approach. Frequent testing is included so that there is continuous evaluation of each child's progress.

Programmed Reading has been used with remedial readers in both clinic and classroom situations. For children who are reading at primary levels in the intermediate grades, programmed materials offer one means of providing reading instruction on the appropriate instructional level. Since these materials can be used independently, they can be utilized without placing excessive demands on the teacher's time. The cartoon-type format of the programmed books may be of greater interest to remedial readers than are basal textbooks on their level.

Other materials with features of programmed learning for independent progress are multi-level reading kits. A well-known example is the SRA Reading Laboratories which contain booklets of reading material graded in difficulty and covering a wide range of reading levels. A number of the laboratories or kits are available for different grade levels, and within each kit the range of levels is wide. In addition to the reading booklets, the laboratories also contain materials for skill instruction, rate improvement, and listening training.

The multi-level materials are regarded as supplements to other approaches to reading. If, however, they are used by all children in a class as the main approach, they are intended for only part of the school year. Such materials can add variety to a program, offer a collection of material on a variety of levels, and encourage self-learning and evaluation as pupils become aware of their progress.

The greatest disadvantage of the programmed materials is the omission of critical reading. When responses are of a limited nature, when learning is dissected into minute units, and when there is no provision for group and/or pupil-teacher interaction and discussion, little instruction in comprehension is provided. There is a danger too that reading can be a simple stimulus-response type learning with great attention given to mechanics but little attention directed to the role of communication in reading. The supplementary reading books which accompany the workbooks do not provide sufficient material for independent recreational reading; however, the teacher can make other library books available. Another disadvantage is that instruction in oral reading may be neglected when programmed materials are used.

COMBINED APPROACHES

Research does not show conclusively the clear superiority of one approach over others. We believe that combined approaches have considerable merit for the improved teaching of reading. The direction for modern elementary teachers is toward an eclectic program, drawing the most pertinent features of several approaches into a total program that is sufficiently flexible and enriched to provide for individual differences in a given class. In fact, Bond has reported that one major finding of the National First Grade Studies was that the effectiveness of any approach was increased when enriched by some features of another approach.[26]

The basal reader, language experience, and individualized approaches offer a number of possibilities for combined approaches. Because many teachers feel the structure provided through basal readers is essential, they may prefer to rely upon the readers as the main approach. For those children who seem unable to profit from basal reading instruction, an individualized approach may be employed. For example, the teacher may be using basal readers with the majority of his students but using an individualized approach with those students at the top and bottom of the range of reading achievement.

Some teachers may combine the basal approach and individualized reading by alternating the time devoted to reading instruction between basal readers and individualized reading on different days of the week. Some teachers may employ individualized reading for the top group only, or rely on the basal approach for most of the school year and then, for an enriched program of wide reading, move into an individualized program later in the school year. The pupil-teacher conference found in individualized reading can be incorporated into a program using basal readers. Through the conference technique, a teacher can have children share their recreational reading.

The language experience approach can be combined with both the basal reader and the individualized approaches. If the language experience approach is used as the major approach to beginning reading, the individual reading of trade books can be gradually introduced after pupils have developed an initial sight vocabulary. The language activities in the language experience approach provide a valuable means of correlating reading with instruction in the other language arts of speaking, listening, and writing. The use of pupil-created stories and individual word banks can be encouraged as independent activities in all approaches to teaching reading. Beyond the first grade, a teacher may wish to use the language experience approach for those pupils who are reading on a first grade level.

For pupils who show deficiencies in phonics, a teacher may wish to use one of the supplementary phonics approaches to provide the needed instruction. A phonics supplement may be used in combination with other approaches, although caution must be exercised so that comprehension receives sufficient attention.

As mentioned before, programmed reading materials may be used for pupils below the reading levels of most of the class. It is possible too for the first or second grade teacher to use these materials as a means of permitting faster learners to progress at their own rate. In a combination approach, a teacher may employ some of the kits of multi-level reading materials to provide additional reading materials.

Many combinations of approaches are possible and desirable in a reading program which provides a balance in the various reading skills. In planning reading instruction for those pupils who seem unable to work satisfactorily with the main approach, a teacher should consider the advisability of using a different approach.

When using a combined approach it is assumed that systematic instruction in phonics is included as a necessary part of reading instruction and that reading instruction is correlated with other language activities. It is also assumed that, regardless of the approach or combined approaches used, the total reading program includes as essential features recreational reading and individualization of instruction.

Chapter Review

We have seen that several basic approaches to reading instruction have evolved. They are not mutually exclusive, and a combination of them offers an enriched instructional program. Each has special features and together they provide a sound basis for an effective total instructional program. Each approach should be evaluated for its strengths and limitations and for its contributions to the teaching of reading. For poor readers and for exceptional readers, various approaches that stress certain dimensions can be used to complement and enrich the main emphasis of the reading program. There is no one answer to the question of how to teach reading, and educators are constantly seeking many avenues for improving instruction.

NOTES

[1] Mary C. Austin and Coleman Morrison, *The First R* (New York: Macmillan, 1963), p. 54.

[2] George D. Spache and Evelyn B. Spache, *Reading in the Elementary School* (Boston: Allyn and Bacon, 1969), pp. 77, 83, 89.

[3] Russell G. Stauffer, *Teaching Reading as a Thinking Process* (New York: Harper & Row, 1969), pp. 11–150.

[4] Russell G. Stauffer, "Time for Amendment," *The Reading Teacher* 20 (May 1967): 685.

[5] R. V. Allen, "The Language Experience Approach," in *Teaching Young Children to Read,* ed. Warren G. Cutts (Washington, D.C.: U.S. Office of Education, 1964), p. 59.

[6] Adapted from MaryAnne Hall, *Teaching Reading as a Language Experience* (Columbus: Charles E. Merrill, 1970), p. 5.

[7] Russell G. Stauffer, "The Effectiveness of Language Arts and Basic Reader Approaches to First Grade Reading Instruction," *The Reading Teacher* 20 (October 1966): 24.

[8] Walter B. Barbe, *Educators Guide to Personalized Reading Instruction* (Englewood Cliffs: Prentice-Hall, 1961), p. 33.

[9] Helen Fisher Darrow and Virgil M. Howes, *Approaches to Individualized Reading* (New York: Appleton-Century-Crofts, 1960), pp. 47–48.

[10] Jeanette Veatch, "Children's Interests and Individualized Reading," *The Reading Teacher* 10 (February 1957): 160–161.

[11] Mary K. Huser, "Reading and More Reading," *Elementary English* 44 (April 1967): 378–382.

[12] Carl A. Lefevre, *Linguistics and the Teaching of Reading* (New York: McGraw-Hill, 1964).

[13] Charles E. Fries, Rosemary Wilson, and Mildred Rudolph, *Merrill Linguistic Readers, Teacher's Guide for Reader 1* (Columbus: Charles E. Merrill, 1966), p. 7.

[14] *Merrill Linguistic Readers*

[15] Leonard Bloomfield, *Let's Read—A Linguistic Approach* (Detroit: Wayne State University Press, 1961).

[16] John A. Downing, "What's Wrong with I.T.A.?" *Phi Delta Kappan* 48 (February 1967): 262.

[17] John A. Downing, "Beginning Reading with the Augmented Roman," in *Teaching Young Children to Read.*

[18] Robert Dykstra, "First-Grade Reading Studies Follow-up," *Reading Research Quarterly* 4 (Fall 1968): 62, 64.

[19] Lucille D. Schoolfield and Josephine B. Timberlake, *Phonovisual Method* (Washington, D.C.: Phonovisual Products, 1960).

[20] Theodore Harris, Mildred Creekmore, and Margaret Greenman, *Phonetic Keys to Reading* (Oklahoma City: The Economy Company, 1964).

[21] Mae Carden, *The Carden Method* (Glen Rock, New Jersey: 1953).

[22] Arthur W. Heilman, *First Grade Reading Programs,* ed. James A. Kerfoot (Newark, Delaware: International Reading Association, 1965), pp. 59–60.

[23] Caleb Gattegno, *Words in Color* (Chicago: Learning Materials, 1962).

[24] Albert J. Harris, *How to Increase Reading Ability* (New York: David McKay, 1961), p. 69.

[25] Cynthia D. Buchanan, et al., *Programmed Reading* (St. Louis: McGraw-Hill, Webster Division, 1963).

[26] Guy L. Bond, "First-Grade Reading Studies: An Overview," *Elementary English* 43 (May 1966): 468–469.

SUGGESTED ACTIVITIES

1. Examine a set of basal readers, especially a beginning volume and an advanced one. Would you like to use such materials?
2. Prepare and teach a directed reading lesson from a basal reader. You will find helpful hints in the manual.
3. Compare a basal reader for first grade to the linguistic reading texts for the same grade. How are they alike and how do they differ? Which would you like to use?
4. Examine and read a book printed in the ITA. Why is it so easy for you to read the ITA?
5. Visit a classroom where the language experience approach is used and observe how the children respond.
6. Observe an individual pupil-teacher conference in individualized reading. What happens? Who does the talking? Will you try this?

SUGGESTED READINGS

Chall, Jeanne. *Learning To Read, The Great Debate.* New York: Mc-Graw-Hill, 1967.

Chapter 1 presents a clear and concise description of different approaches and materials. In chapter 2, advocates of the various approaches state answers to philosophical questions about reading.

Cutts, Warren G., ed. *Teaching Young Children To Read.* Washington, D.C.: U.S. Office of Education, 1964.

Concise and clear descriptions of the ITA and the language experience approaches are provided. The beginning reading period is also discussed in great detail.

Darrow, Helen Fisher and Howes, Virgil M. *Approaches to Individualized Reading.* New York: Appleton-Century-Crofts, 1960.

A practical explanation of how to initiate, conduct, and evaluate individualized reading programs.

Goodman, Kenneth S. and Fleming, James T., eds. *Psycholinguistics and the Teaching of Reading.* Newark, Delaware: International Reading Association, 1969.

Discusses in detail the relationships of thought and language with emphasis on the linguistic contributions related to comprehension.

Heilman, Arthur W. *Principles and Practices of Teaching Reading.* Columbus: Charles E. Merrill, 1967.

See chapter 4 for a discussion of the basal reader, language experience, ITA, and phonics approaches. Chapter 8 treats linguistics and reading, while individualized reading is the topic of chapter 11.

Kerfoot, James A., ed. *First Grade Reading Programs.* Perspectives in Reading, no. 5. Newark, Delaware: International Reading Association, 1965.

Presents detailed descriptions of a number of approaches to beginning reading.

Spache, George D. and Spache, Evelyn. *Reading in the Elementary School.* Boston: Allyn and Bacon, 1969.

The advantages and limitations of each approach and the practical implementation of a combined approach are clearly outlined.

Stauffer, Russell G. *Teaching Reading as a Thinking Process.* New York: Harper & Row, 1969.

See chapters 2, 3, and 4 for an extensive coverage of the Directed Reading Thinking Activity procedure. Chapters 5 and 6 are devoted to individualized reading.

PART TWO
THE SKILLS AND LEVELS OF READING

CHAPTER FIVE

PRE-READING

Advance Organizer

The modern view of reading maintains that a child's experiences and skills prior to beginning reading are just as important as those he develops once formal reading instruction has begun. Such early preparations for reading take place during the stage known as *pre-reading,* and they contribute to what is called a child's *readiness* for reading. Although evaluation of individual pupils and consequent adjustment of instruction according to the information learned from evaluation are vital at all levels, they are especially critical in pre-reading, when successful preparation for later work is so important.

This chapter examines the period of pre-reading and the composite skills and experiences of reading readiness: physical, perceptual, cognitive, linguistic, psychological, and environmental-experiential— each of which develops differently in each child and influences the teacher's endeavor to provide for children's individual differences.

THE DEVELOPMENTAL NATURE OF READING

One day a child may be unaware that there is meaning to be found in the symbols next to pictures on a cereal box, or the markings on the billboards along a highway, or the brief parts of television programing that flash by without people or places in them. He may, in fact, barely be aware of them at all.

Another day, the same child studies these symbols more closely, sensing that other people derive messages from them. And at some point—probably with the encouragement of an older person—he experiences his first dawning recognition of the identity between certain of these strange symbols and the familiar sounds of the language he hears and speaks every day. At this moment he begins to unlock the code which until then has isolated him from a world open to all literate members of his society and from its written traditions. At this indefinable point in the experience of the child who cannot read, there occurs the beginning of a staggering intellectual accomplishment.

Authorities differ on the nature and timing of the various stages of development that young readers must master before mature reading is possible. There is general agreement, however, that everyone begins at a level that can be called *pre-reading,* moves to a *beginning reading* stage, and passes to succeeding levels at which earlier skills are refined and extended.

The notion of each child engaging in multiple phases of development, at his own rate and in his own style, challenges certain educational practices. The student of elementary reading instruction will no doubt observe, for example, that a developmental view of reading seems at odds with the lock-step grade levels still present in some elementary schools, and he is correct in this observation.

It is impractical, of course, to expect schools to reorganize grouping practices for reading instruction overnight. It has proved possible, however, for individual classroom teachers to place children in instructional settings which are appropriate, first and foremost, to each child's level of development—whether or not they correspond to the elementary school grade to which the child happens to be assigned. A basic premise of the present text is that viewing children by developmental levels is desirable in elementary reading instruction. Throughout the text, accordingly, the following four levels are used as organizing concepts:

LEVELS		*GENERAL RANGE*
A	Pre-reading leads to →	Home—Pre-school − 1
B	Beginning Reading expands to →	K − 1
C	Basic Skill Development results in →	1 − 3+
D	Wide Independent Reading	3 − adulthood

Figure 2   A Child's Reading Development

Level A: Pre-reading

The child is living, maturing, experiencing, learning his language. Skills at this level precede formal reading. They may be learned at home before the child comes to school, or in nursery schools, or in a program such as Head-Start. Within the school, pre-reading is usually associated with kindergarten and first grade children. Whenever a child lacks pre-reading skills, however, instruction needs to focus on them regardless of the child's grade level. Skills at this level are therefore also appropriate as topics for review at later stages.

Level B: Beginning Reading

Entering into play at this stage are all those skills necessary for the child's first interpretation of print: the skills necessary to decode language and to comprehend it. The bridge is made between spoken and written language and a reading vocabulary begins. Although this level lasts only a short time in comparison with levels which precede and follow it, beginning reading is generally treated as a distinct level because of the importance attached to initial reading instruction.

Level C: Basic Skill Development

Once a child has made his first steps in formal reading and has gained beginning skill in word recognition and in communicating with an author, he moves gradually to a level at which a concentrated effort can be made to teach him advanced skills in word recognition and comprehension. The reading vocabulary expands and word attack skills are acquired and applied. Higher level comprehension skills are developed.

Level D: Wide Independent Reading

At Level D the child continues to refine even further all the skills he has previously learned. He learns to communicate with the author without the intervention of the teacher, as part of a general movement away from teacher-directed reading to independent reading. The reading diet is varied and the child learns to read both factual and fictional material. He learns how to study and choose widely from reading materials for information and pleasure.

THE CONCEPT OF READINESS

Until the emergence of the modern testing and child study movements in the first quarter of this century, there was virtually no formal instruction at the pre-reading level. In contrast, modern elementary school instruction takes into account a stage in reading development which precedes formal reading behavior. This stage, pre-reading, is considered prerequisite to beginning reading in that it entails certain experiences and skills generally thought to be necessary before the complex reading act can occur. The presence of these building blocks for reading has come to be called *reading readiness*.

Acceptance of the concept of readiness in learning assumes acceptance of the significance of individual differences, for it acknowledges that readiness for a particular learning is not attained by all pupils in a class at the same time. Indeed, it has as much to do with the teacher's willingness to adjust instruction as with the child's level of development. As it pertains to reading, readiness has three major meanings—all of which are of major significance in the total elementary reading program.

1) Reading readiness refers to the level of development necessary in order for a child to be successful with beginning reading instruction, particularly with the types of materials and approaches used in a specific classroom situation. Before reading, the child needs a combination of background experiences, knowledge, skills, and maturation in order to decode and to comprehend printed symbols.

2) The term reading readiness is also used to denote the preschool, kindergarten, and first grade instructional program which provides specific training in skills needed before formal instruction in beginning reading is undertaken.

3) The term is also used in a broader context: readiness for every step in learning. Thus, readiness for each lesson and skill must be considered in the teaching of reading at all levels.

This chapter is concerned with the first two meanings of readiness—those relating specifically to the first level of reading development.

What constitutes readiness for learning to read? The answer is not a simple list of essential factors and skills, for readiness is a part of the total personality and background of an individual. Indeed, the presence or absence of any one generally accepted component of readiness does not in and of itself imply that a child is or is not ready for reading. Rather, it is the composite pattern of interrelated factors which determine a child's readiness. How a child listens, expresses his thoughts, looks at a line of print, works in a group, relates to others, how eager he is to know what a book says, his exposure to books and exploration of the world around him, his mental alertness, and his physical maturation all influence readiness for reading. And, as stressed above, the teacher's acceptance of and adjustment for a child's strengths and limitations can be as significant as the factors themselves.

Figure 3 presents the generally acknowledged components of readiness, focusing on the multi-dimensional nature of a child's reading readiness and on the obligations of the teacher for evaluation and adjustment of instruction to an individual's pattern of readiness. There is some overlapping within the broad categories. For example, the home background influences development in the other areas, while linguistic and intellectual readiness cannot truly be separated. An additional point to bear in mind when studying the figure is that, as he analyzes a child's readiness, the teacher must distinguish between those factors which indicate referral for remedial purposes and those which indicate his own instructional obligations.

Physical Readiness

The relationship of physical factors to the reading process was discussed in chapter 1. It is in Level A of the child's reading development that these factors are considered so that any physical barriers to learning can be identified, corrected, or compensated for in the instructional program. The teacher has the responsibility to be aware of symptoms which may indicate a physical problem and to make necessary referrals to the appropriate specialists. Vision and hearing merit consideration, since reading involves adequate functioning of these senses. General health, age, and sex also affect reading readiness.

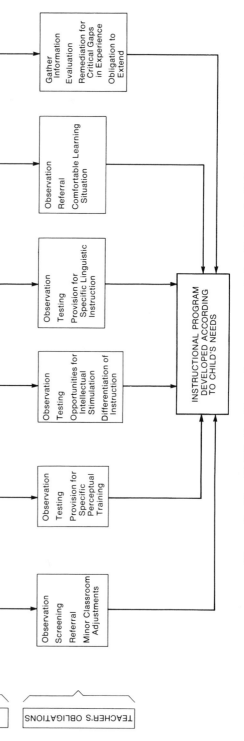

Figure 3   The Child's Readiness Components and the Teacher's Obligations

Vision In pre-reading, attention to vision is deserved since certain visual defects can cause difficulty in learning to read. The teacher is expected to be knowledgeable about symptoms which may indicate a visual deficiency. If any are present he always refers a child to a vision specialist. This is especially important because the visual screening commonly conducted in schools may not identify a number of visual problems.

Monroe and Rogers list the following symptoms of eye difficulties which may be observed by the teacher:

1) Unusual positions of holding book or head.
2) Narrowing the shape of the eye while looking at the chalkboard. (Near-sighted children try to shorten their eyeballs by pressing the lids against the ball of the eye, or pushing the outside corners of their eyes up.)
3) Frequent looking up from close work or glancing out of the window to rest eyes. (This is characteristic of the far-sighted child.)
4) Rubbing the eyes to brush away the blur.
5) Holding hand over one eye while looking.
6) Watering, red-rimmed eyes.
7) Comments that words or pictures "jump" on the page, that objects are doubled or blurred.
8) Inability to keep the place in the book.[1]

Although a child may be able to function adequately enough visually to learn to read, the visual adjustment required in reading may trigger discomfort for him. If he is uncomfortable, his attitude toward reading may not be favorable, and he will probably avoid reading as a leisure-time activity. Some children with serious visual defects can and do learn to read, but their progress and attitudes probably would be better if the visual problem had received earlier attention.

In the regular classroom setting, the teacher's responsibility is to provide an advantageous visual situation by appropriate seating and lighting and by alternating tasks requiring close visual attention with other types of activities.

Hearing Teachers should also be alert to symptoms which would indicate hearing problems. Wilson identifies the following symptoms:

1) Speech difficulties (particularly with consonant sounds).
2) Inability to profit from phonic instruction.

3) Tilting of the head when being spoken to.
4) Cupping of the ear with the hand in order to follow instructions.
5) Inability to follow directions.
6) General inattentiveness.
7) Strained posture.
8) Persistent earaches.
9) Inflamation or drainage of the ear.
10) Reports of persistent buzzing or ringing in the head.
11) Excessive volume needed for comfortable radio and phonograph listening.[2]

In schools auditory screening through the use of the audiometer is generally adequate for identifying children who have hearing difficulties serious enough to warrant referral. Special efforts are made to ensure that the child with a hearing loss is seated advantageously, that distractions to listening are lessened, and that directions are clarified or repeated if necessary.

General Health   Other physical factors which may influence learning are the general state of health and level of energy, eye-hand coordination, nutritional status, level of physical development, speech problems, and any physical handicaps. Children with physical impairments may find reading more difficult than those without, but the presence of a physical problem does not necessarily present a great obstacle to reading. However, it is important for the teacher to be aware of any possible interference in the learning situation and of the effect of a physical problem on a child's adjustment. For example, if the child has a speech defect, his barrier to learning may be the discomfort in group situations because of his awareness of the impediment rather than the impediment itself.

Chronological Age   Admission to school is generally based on chronological age, but meeting that standard does not ensure readiness for reading. Any group of children of a given age will differ greatly in both maturation and experience. Therefore, mental age in conjunction with other aspects of development is considered as more important than chronological age in readiness for reading.

In an extensive study of school readiness, Ilg and Ames recommend that school entrance be based on developmental level rather than on chronological age.[3] They conclude that vast numbers of children are overplaced in school and are experiencing continuing frustration by being asked to perform at a level too advanced for their level of development. Adaptation to individual differences is more important than the chronological age which can be accorded too much weight in evaluating readiness.

Sex   Research has shown that boys experience more difficulties in learning to read than girls.[4] The alert teacher can spot the possible difficulties and provide for special needs of boys in pre-reading and beginning reading. Attention is directed to motivating them to read and to consideration of their interests in planning pre-reading activities. (A number of explanations for sex differences in readiness and in reading achievement are discussed in chapter 12.)

Perceptual Readiness

Since reading requires perception of printed word forms, readiness for reading includes a perceptual dimension involving the ability to perceive printed stimuli. Although children may have satisfactory vision and hearing, they still need specialized training to recognize printed words and letter sounds in spoken words. The initial steps in learning to read can be described as the matching of new stimuli (printed words) to old responses (spoken words). The two major means of perception employed in reading by children with adequate sensory functioning are visual and auditory. In addition to these, the ability to use left-to-right direction in observing printed words is necessary.

Visual Perception   Learning to read requires visual perception that permits accurate association of a printed word form to the spoken language the child has already mastered. Visual perception in reading may be defined as the reception and identification of the stimulus of the printed word. A number of reading authorities have stated that visual perception abilities are needed for success in reading and some, notably De Hirsch have suggested "that children with reading disorders have trouble with visual perception."[5] Spache, stressing the significance of visual perception as an important factor in reading readiness, cautions that it cannot be assumed that all children in the first grade have a sufficient degree of development in this area for beginning reading.[6] The period of maximum development in visual perceptual development for most children occurs between the ages of 3½ and 7½, although some writers, notably Frostig and Horne, have suggested that some children have a lag in this respect.[7] For children with a severe lack of perceptual development, certainly, special instruction is necessary.

Auditory Perception   Another skill used in reading is auditory discrimination. A child who is able to distinguish likenesses and differences in individual sounds within spoken words may have an advantage in learning to read. As was true for visual perception, it cannot be assumed that a child comes to school with sufficient auditory perception to proceed to the perceptual demands of an auditory nature required in reading.

Dykstra reports that performance on measures of auditory discrimination does not show high correlations with reading achievement at the end of grade one and that no direct cause and effect relationship exists. He comments that the research "indicates that the ability to make auditory discriminations *may* contribute to success in learning to read."[8] Durrell feels that auditory perception is the most important yet most seriously neglected subskill in reading and that chances for success in beginning reading can be enhanced through training in auditory discrimination.[9] Although the research differs on the relationship of auditory discrimination to subsequent reading achievement, building awareness of the sounds of spoken words should begin in Level A because it is the foundation for more detailed phonics instruction at higher levels. However, this skill alone will not ensure reading success.

Directional Perception   Reading requires left-to-right progression across a line of print, and provisions for instruction can prevent later difficulty. In Level A a teacher emphasizes left-to-right eye movement through both direct instruction and informal situations until it becomes automatic for a child to approach print with the correct directional orientation.

Cognitive Readiness

Because children respond to and interpret the meaning of printed symbols, reading is a cognitive activity requiring the use of thinking skills. In the pre-reading stage, the teacher considers the mental maturity of pupils as he evaluates their readiness for reading. A child's level of mental development and intellectual ability does affect reading, although attainment of a specified level of mental development does not, in itself, guarantee success in learning to read.

The mental age necessary for learning to read has been the subject of considerable discussion and research. Monroe and Rogers state that for most children, a mental age of 5½ to 6½ is appropriate.[10] A widely quoted study by Morphett and Washburne reported in 1930 that 6½ was the optimum mental age for the introduction of reading.[11] However, other studies have shown that mental age is not as significant in determining reading success as is the type of instruction offered.[12] When the program is geared to an individual's learning abilities, a child with a mental age lower than 6½ can be successful in reading in the first grade. It is well to remember Spache's comment that it is only

> stereotyped, inflexible, and mass-oriented reading programs which demand a higher mental age and make intelligence such an important factor in reading success, in our primary class-rooms. The demands of the average or poor classroom in effect create a condition in which only the fittest (the brightest) can survive and meet these demands. This is why intelligence seems to be an important factor in early reading success.[13]

Misinterpretation of the importance of attaining a certain mental age has often resulted in delaying the time of reading introduction rather than in adapting the program for individual children.

It can be seen that there is no single criterion for readiness. Considerable evidence is now available which confirms that children of younger mental ages than six can learn to read successfully. (The issue of presenting formal reading instruction at home and in kindergarten is discussed later in this chapter.)

Linguistic Readiness

As we have noted, reading is a linguistic process in which the child associates printed words with meanings he already knows. His oral language background provides the base for attaching meaning to printed symbols. Thus the teacher can "build" readiness by teaching the child certain words and concepts used in instruction: words like *word, first, under, over, read*, etc. A child's language facility develops rapidly in the pre-school years, and most children enter the first grade with sufficient language development to deal with the language patterns and vocabulary in the beginning reading books. These materials should not contain any difficulties in meaning so that the beginning reader can concentrate on learning the printed symbols for words already in his speaking vocabulary.

The children in any kindergarten or first grade group will demonstrate great variance in their verbal communication and listening skills. The child who has a limited vocabulary and uses incomplete sentence patterns is likely to encounter difficulty in learning to read. On the other hand, the highly verbal child evidences many skills needed for beginning reading. Strang states that skill in listening comprehension is "one of the best single predictors of reading ability."[14] Since listening is the major tool of learning until children become independent readers, a child's ability in this area is of particular importance in the first years in school. The teacher will need to evaluate a child's ability to comprehend the oral language of others, listen to stories, follow oral directions, and restate ideas, stories, or events in logical sequence.

It is important for the teacher to be aware of environmental factors which contribute to or detract from the development or mastery of oral language. Growth in oral language facility is related to many factors, among which are intelligence, opportunities for talking, and exposure to varied experiences. Culturally and linguistically different children have specific language problems with these last two factors which must be recognized in the pre-reading period. Also, many children with limited backgrounds have not been exposed to experiences which contribute to their language development.

Since the other components of readiness must also be developed, verbal facility alone does not insure a successful experience in beginning reading. However, the teacher needs to evaluate his pupils' language development and provide needed experiences and instruction to remedy deficiencies and promote further development.

Psychological Readiness

Just as teachers recognize the physical, perceptual, intellectual, and linguistic aspects of readiness, they also examine personal adjustment factors which affect learning. A child's attitudes toward himself, toward others, and toward school have a significant influence. Adjusting to a school situation is not easy for some children, and regardless of their physical, linguistic, and intellectual development, poor adjustment or emotional problems may interfere with learning. Anxiety, hostility, aggressiveness, withdrawal, excessive shyness, extreme dependence upon adults, feelings of inadequacy, and negative attitudes toward authority or toward other children are examples of problems which may detract from learning. Children with severe emotional problems should be referred for further study.

Some children enter school feeling that they must learn to read to please their parents and teachers. The effects of such pressure, if excessive, can be detrimental and produce long-range adverse effects. This does not mean that negative personality factors necessarily mean problems in learning to read, but factors relating to adjustment have to be considered and their possible interference with learning acknowledged. A teacher has to adjust the learning situation for some children and provide a classroom climate conducive to effective learning. Young children need to become acclimated to classroom routines and expectations, to develop rapport with the teacher, and to feel comfortable in the classroom. For children with feelings of inadequacy, it is especially important that experiences in the pre-reading and beginning reading stages be successful.

Environmental—Experiential Readiness

Each of the previously discussed aspects of readiness is greatly influenced by home background, opportunities, and experiences provided by parents prior to school experience. The child's adjustment, language development, intellectual development, attitude toward learning, and exposure to the world around him are products of home environment. Fortunately, many parents do provide a home environment which fosters favorable attitudes and they do give their children stimulation and background important for learning to read. When evaluating readiness and planning appropriate pre-reading experiences, the teacher considers information about a child's pre-school background.

EVALUATING A CHILD'S READINESS

"Is this child ready for a successful experience in beginning reading?" This is a question a teacher must answer for each pupil before introducing reading instruction. To comprehensively evaluate the child's readiness, he employs several tools: observation, reading readiness tests, intelligence tests, and information from school records and from parents.

Careful evaluation is basic to our philosophy of teaching reading. Good instruction is based on diagnosis and some deficiencies or possible problems in learning to read can be prevented through adjustment of the total program. Careful evaluation of readiness for reading accomplishes the following:

- Utilizes information from a number of sources rather than from only one criterion or test score.

- Results in a pre-reading and beginning reading program which is differentiated according to identified needs.

- Helps make initial experiences in reading successful ones.

Teacher observation is a major means of evaluating pupil readiness.

■ Prevents the introduction of reading before children have the necessary level of maturity and prerequisite skills to be successful.

■ Emphasizes in Level A the importance of early identification of children likely to encounter problems in learning to read.

Teacher Observation

Careful teacher observation is a major means of evaluating pupil readiness. Kindergarten and first grade teachers are sensitive to pupil differences, and their awareness of these differences can be vital in assessing readiness. As he observes children's responses in group situations, the teacher evaluates the physical, perceptual, intellectual, linguistic, and personal adjustment dimensions of readiness. He may notice reluctance to participate in discussions, aggressiveness, or fascination with reading. Of particular interest to the observant teacher are a child's reactions to activities with words, such as reading names, plans, experience charts, signs, and other printed materials in the classroom. As the teacher conducts the instructional program, he observes alertness in learning as well as knowledge of specific skills, such as matching or naming letters. A checklist of readiness factors is usually a helpful tool in guiding evaluation.

Because teacher estimates of readiness do present some limitations, their value varies with the individual teacher, generally increasing with his level of experience and his capability. De Hirsch points out that a teacher's assessment is a subjective judgment and that "not all teachers possess the training, intuition, or experience that would enable them to make a reliable evaluation of a child's readiness."[15]

Another limitation of the teacher's observation in evaluating readiness is that it may not be specific enough to identify a particular weakness or deficiency. Therefore, it is preferable that teacher observation be combined with information provided by readiness tests and other sources.

Also, while teacher observation may be sufficient for those children who *are* ready and for those who *are not* ready, there are always some children who do not attract attention. A teacher may not be able to estimate their readiness by their reactions in a group or by their classroom performance.

Readiness Tests

Standardized readiness tests provide another means of evaluating children's readiness for reading. These tests are used to predict success in beginning reading, to group children according to their scores, to determine how an individual child ranks in readiness in relation to his classmates and in relation to the test norms, and to evaluate performance in particular skills in order to plan appropriate instruction. The crucial questions for a teacher to answer are: "What does the particular readiness test I am using actually test?" "What readiness factors does it *not* measure?" "How can information from the test best be used?" "How does information from the test influence the content I teach in Level A?"

It is important to again emphasize both the multi-dimensional qualities of readiness for reading and the failure of any one test to completely evaluate all physical, perceptual, intellectual, linguistic, and psychological facets of readiness. Readiness tests vary in the skills tested and the teacher therefore needs to examine the test used with his class to determine which readiness skills are measured. In 1965 Barrett commented:

> One might expect that thirty-five years of research into predictive validity of readiness factors would have produced a high degree of agreement in the content of commonly used standardized readiness tests.[16]

However, in an analysis of five widely used tests, he found that there was not a high degree of agreement in the content of the tests. While tests of visual discrimination, auditory discrimination, following directions, vocabulary, sentence comprehension, and knowledge of letter names are included in many readiness tests, not every test covers all these areas. If, for example, a particular test did not include auditory discrimination, a teacher would perhaps want to give an additional test to gain diagnostic information on this facet of readiness. (Appendix C contains a description of various reading readiness tests.)

Research has shown that the correlation between readiness test scores and reading achievement at the end of grade one is not sufficiently high to warrant using the scores as predictors of reading success or failure.[17] One explanation of the poor predictive value of readiness tests may be that deficiencies were corrected through good instruction, thus lowering the correlation between the test score and later achievement in reading. The fact that these tests are not accurate predictors of success is sometimes stated as an argument against their use. However, they can be valuable in identifying children with specific problems and a need for special instruction.

When readiness tests are used as the sole criterion for grouping children or for labeling a child ready or not ready for reading without consideration for the type of instruction needed, the test is being misused and the principles of evaluation are not being followed. Readiness tests should be used diagnostically with the performance on various subtests identifying individual strengths and weaknesses. Instruction can then be adapted accordingly. The tests are ideally used in combination with information gathered from observation and from pupil records.

Intelligence Tests

Since reading is an intellectual activity, the level of mental functioning is considered in the evaluation of readiness. While teachers may feel it is desirable to have an estimate of a pupil's mental age and of his IQ, such information ought to be interpreted with caution. In most school systems, group intelligence tests are used. Performance on a single standardized group test of intelligence is not regarded as a comprehensive evaluation of a pupil's intellectual capacity. For those children with low scores, a teacher can request that an individual test be administered.

Intelligence test scores are misused if they are accorded too much weight or if their limitations are not recognized. Some children perform poorly on standardized tests due to personal discomfort and lack of motivation; some are unduly penalized by the speed factor on timed tests. Because most intelligence tests are oriented toward the middle-class child, children from other backgrounds are penalized by items related to experiences totally foreign to them. For those children who are not adept at comprehending verbal symbols, what is tested may be previous exposure to learning rather than capacity for learning. Intelligence tests, combined with teacher observation and with standardized readiness tests, may help identify children who have difficulty learning and need adjustments in instruction. Our discussion of mental age as a factor affecting readiness stressed that adaptation of instruction in pre-reading and beginning reading is of more importance to reading success in grade one than is a specific mental age.

Other Sources of Information

While the major sources for evaluation of pupil readiness for reading will come from teacher observation, readiness tests, and intelligence tests, other sources such as pupil records and information supplied by parents will also be valuable. Cumulative pupil records, begun upon entrance to school, may contain pertinent information for estimating readiness. If a child attended kindergarten, records of that experience may indicate any particular problems or special needs. Notations or records of any physical problems should be available to the teacher.

Parents may supply information through questionnaires or through parent-teacher conferences. A teacher can obtain information about a child's adjustment at home, the parents' attitude toward the child, the extent of experience background and opportunity for pre-school learning, and the parents' educational background. The influence of the home on the child in the preschool years must not be underestimated; therefore, information from parents is of great value to the teacher.

PRE-READING INSTRUCTION

A major responsibility of the teacher at Level A is to conduct an instructional program by providing learning situations which promote skill development in several areas. An adequate pre-reading program can prevent many difficulties in the beginning reading period, if the following three objectives are used as guidelines:

- Provide perceptual training in the skills of visual discrimination, auditory discrimination, left-to-right progression, and letter recognition.

- Promote interest in reading.

- Develop language facility in conjunction with enriched experience and conceptual backgrounds.

The preceding objectives of pre-reading are also important in beginning instruction, and the similarity of the objectives illustrates that there is no sharp dividing line between the two levels. Likewise, there is ideally a natural transition from one to the other with attention directed toward acquiring a reading vocabulary, interpreting the meanings of printed words, and more intensive work with word attack as children move from pre-reading to beginning reading.

In developing the skills of pre-reading, two major approaches to instruction are commonly employed. Some teachers base instruction on the use of published pre-reading programs such as reading readiness workbooks, language development kits, sets of pictures, and other commercially produced materials. Other teachers employ a language experience approach and children create many of their own materials, such as experience charts and personal stories, while they discuss their interests and experiences. With the latter approach, Level A is naturally integrated with Level B.

Published materials usually are attractively illustrated, contain helpful suggestions for teachers, and provide specific skill training. However, various materials differ in content, and not all pre-reading skills are taught in all workbooks. The materials generally provide a structured program, while the language experience approach relates more directly to the pupils' interests. This method integrates skill training with informal experiences in speaking and listening, but may need to be supplemented by some activities for specific skill training included in workbooks or other published materials.

The two approaches are not mutually exclusive, and a teacher can use procedures from both to accomplish the objectives of Level A. The activities, materials, and techniques suggested in this section for developing the skills of the pre-reading level can be adapted for use with both approaches.

Developing Visual Discrimination

In the pre-reading period provision for visual discrimination training is a major responsibility of the teacher. Such training is related to perceptual tasks involved in reading and deals with letter and word forms rather than with discrimination of objects, geometric forms, or pictures of objects. A child may be able to make gross discriminations between objects pictured in a workbook but may not be able to discriminate between word forms such as *can* and *car* or between letters such as *b, d,* and *p.* Research on the predictive value of certain readiness factors shows that visual discrimination of letters and words has a higher predictive relationship with first grade reading achievement than does visual discrimination of geometric designs and pictures.[18] The ability to remember word forms by their distinctive configuration is important in word recognition; and an important prerequisite for skill in configuration is the ability to visually discriminate between letters and between words.

Several examples of visual discrimination activities follow:

- The teacher displays a chart similar to the following using the names of children in the group. Each row contains some names beginning with the same letter.

Tim	John	Tim	Tommy	Tim
Bill	Bobby	Bill	Bill	Tim
Ann	David	Sandra	Susan	Ann
Diane	Diane	David	Diane	Bill

The children look at the first name in the row and identify or mark all other words which are the same as the first one.

- The children match their name cards with the names on a chart such as the one illustrated above or with a list of all the children's names.

- For visual discrimination of letter forms, a chart or worksheet of the following type can be used. Starting with gross differences, then moving to more difficult discriminations is recommended.

s	t	s	g	s	t
b	b	d	b	b	d
p	q	b	p	d	p
r	n	n	s	r	r
w	w	m	w	t	f
t	t	b	f	t	l

Children look at the first letter in a line and find all others which are the same.

- The teacher displays four or five letter cards on the chalkboard ledge or on a flannelboard. The children name the letter which is different from the others.

This same activity can be done with word cards containing the children's names.

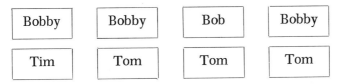

- Sequential exercises in symbol tracking, visual tracking, and word tracking are provided by the Michigan Tracking Program.[19] Emphasis in this program is placed upon the ability of the child to move visually from left to right making accurate discriminations and working as rapidly as possible.

- The matching of word, phase, and sentence cards with the identical word, phrase, or sentence on experience charts is one of the most meaningful types of visual discrimination practices. The matching of word cards to the content of daily plans and other printed words used in daily activities can also be utilized for incidental practice.

Developing Auditory Discrimination

The training in auditory discrimination provided in Level A is the foundation upon which later instruction in phonics is built at higher levels of reading development. As was true with visual discrmination, training in auditory discrimination is related to the task demanded in a reading situation and therefore is concerned with hearing likenesses and differences in sounds of spoken words, with attention given to beginning and ending consonant sounds and rhyming words.

Some suggested activities follow:

- Children listen as the teacher pronounces groups of three or four words. In each group, all the words but one will begin with the same consonant sound. The children then say the words which begin alike or name the word which is different from the others.

- The preceding type of activity can be done with groups of rhyming words.

■ Many rhymes and jingles are read to children. After these listening experiences with rhymes, children are asked to name the rhyming words and also to supply a rhyming word to complete a jingle.

■ Children name objects in the classroom which begin with the same sound as a word named by the teacher.

■ Children listen to a sentence and say all the words that begin or end like the key word named by the teacher.

■ In listening activities, the children respond by using "every-pupil response cards," developed by Durrell.[20] For example, the teacher may give each child one card with *yes* on it and another with *no*. As the teacher says a list of words, the children hold up the appropriate card to indicate whether or not each word named begins like the key word. With this technique every child can answer every item. (More will be said about every-pupil response in later chapters.)

■ Training in combining auditory discrimination of beginning sounds with contextual closure is a part of Level A experiences with auditory discrimination. For example, children can listen to the beginning sounds in the words *little, leaf,* and *like* and, by using both sound and context clues, then can complete a sentence, such as: "A baby sheep is called a _____."

Developing Left-to-Right Orientation

The activities listed below for developing left-to-right sequence can, to a large extent, be incorporated into other lessons. However, a teacher should use many "incidental" situations for teaching this important skill.

■ In writing experience charts, a teacher points out the left-to-right direction of print. When reading the charts aloud, he moves his hand from left to right as the words are said.

■ The teacher points out the left-to-right progression of a line of print while reading any material from the chalkboard or bulletin boards.

■ He stresses left-to-right direction when children are matching word, phrase, and sentence cards to experience charts.

Children are taught to begin at the left of each word when matching cards.

■ In both reading and writing activities, the teacher indicates that the left is the beginning and the right the end of the word or sentence.

■ As children arrange a series of pictures in sequence, the teacher stresses that the pictures be arranged from left-to-right.

■ The meaning of left and right can be taught through games such as "Looby Loo" or through informal game-type activities with directions, such as "Touch your left eye" or "Lift your left foot."

Developing Letter Recognition

Letter name knowledge refers to the ability to identify a letter by name when shown its printed form. A child may be able to recite the alphabet by rote and still not be able to identify printed letter forms. Although the research literature is not unanimous on the directness of the influence that letter name knowledge has on early reading, there is some evidence that such knowledge has a higher correlation with success in beginning reading than other factors tested by readiness tests.[21] Therefore, attention to letter names is warranted in Level A.

Some pre-reading programs (*Programmed Reading* and some linguistic series) are emphasizing letter name knowledge as the major content of pre-reading instruction, perhaps to the neglect of some other experiences which belong in an enriched pre-reading program. Too much attention to letter names may cause children to examine the first words met in reading letter-by-letter rather than with the quick recognition desirable in developing a reading vocabulary.

The following activities can be used to teach letter names:

■ Individual children are given two sets of letter cards, one lower-case and the other upper-case letters. In teacher-directed activities all children in a group who are working with letter names respond by holding up the appropriate letter card. If the teacher is using a chart or has written letters on the chalkboard, he asks the children to hold up the card for a capital letter as he points to it.

- As the teacher uses the class's name chart, he asks children to hold up the letter at the beginning of various names. He may also ask a child to bring up a letter card to compare to a letter on the chart.

- The teacher uses children's literature ABC books to call attention to particular letters.

- Children make ABC books modeled after the literature examples.

- As children learn to write letters, their attention is called to the names of the letters.

Promoting Interest in Reading

In the pre-reading period, one of the teacher's primary objectives is to stimulate interest in reading. Children's literature materials, which are used primarily for enjoyment, may do more to develop favorable attitudes toward and interest in reading than do instructional materials designed for developing specific skills. Realization that reading is pleasurable and that meaning comes from the printed page is best developed through hearing fictional stories. Fortunately, many children come to school from home situations where interest in reading has been encouraged through pleasurable experiences with books. However, for those children who have not had experience with books in the pre-school years, it is even more essential that literature experiences be included in Level A.

Experiences with books can promote vocabulary development, provide excellent opportunities for developing listening skills, lead to oral discussions, and stimulate a desire to read. Many skills which are important to story comprehension in reading at higher levels have their foundation in Level A as children listen to stories read by the teacher. Comprehending the main idea, following a sequence of events, predicting story outcomes, and responding to the mood and tone of a story begin in Level A.

While most experiences with literature involve fictional books, other types, such as Mother Goose collections, counting books, ABC books, and concept books, also have particular value. ABC books can provide additional experiences with hearing letter names and seeing printed letter forms. Exposure to the rhyming qualities of Mother Goose can sharpen auditory awareness. Concept books, which do not tell a story but instead explain, clarify, define, or elaborate a particular concept or main idea, are particularly valuable in extending conceptual background. For example, in the concept book, *Fast is Not a Ladybug*,[22] the concept of speed is explained in relative terms at a young child's level of understanding. Books about colors, weather, seasons, and other common topics provide an excellent source of materials for enriching informational background. (See Appendix A for book selection sources.)

The following considerations are essential for developing interest in reading in Level A:

- Part of every school day should be devoted to enjoying children's literature through story reading or telling. The primary purpose of this activity is enjoyment.

- In every classroom, a library corner or table should be made available so children can examine and enjoy books in a free-choice activity. The books should be attractively displayed and frequently changed.

- Visits to the school library should be included as a part of the weekly schedule. During these visits, each child is encouraged to select a book which he can take home for his parents to read to him.

Developing Language Facility, Concepts, and Experience Backgrounds

Oral language is the base upon which reading is built, and a child's concepts and experiences determine the meaning he brings to a reading situation. Language and concepts develop through experiences and opportunities to discuss those experiences. From the list of suggestions given below, a teacher should not conclude that only a few activities can provide adequate experience in this component of pre-reading. Language development must be viewed as a part of a child's total experiences in school and must be fostered through the total school program. It cuts across every curriculum area and activity. Shane comments, "Like any other living thing, language cannot be pulled to pieces and doled out in small bits but must be seen as a whole."[23] In fact, in all pre-reading activities, a teacher's alertness can provide opportunities to develop concepts, experiences, and language. In working with oral language, a teacher is constantly concerned with expanding a child's speaking and listening vocabularies, with improving his ability to express ideas orally, and with increasing his listening comprehension. It is obvious, then, that numerous opportunities for speaking and listening in functional settings need to be provided in Level A. The language experience approach, which stresses oral language, has particular value in this dimension of pre-reading instruction. The teacher in Level A can benefit from the following list of specific suggestions, bearing in mind that these types of experiences should be integrated with the total classroom program.

- Reading stories to children increases vocabulary and provides interesting listening experiences. Occasionally, a teacher may select particular words for discussion before or after reading a story.

- Children can be asked to talk about pictures. In this type of activity, the teacher asks questions which require children to do more than name the objects in the picture; he asks the children to state the sequence of events, suggest what might happen, or tell what they might do in a similar situation.

- Discussions of class experiences are of great value in providing functional opportunities for speaking and listening.

- Composing group experience charts and personal experience stories encourages children to express ideas in oral language. In the development of experience stories, the teacher stimulates children to formulate ideas in sentence and in story units.

- Children can classify pictures and objects according to categories, such as food, clothing, sounds, and people. In the classification activity there are many opportunities for stressing word meanings and for asking children to define words. This activity provides a base for association with sight vocabulary in Level B.

- Language development kits available from several publishing companies contain many materials and ideas for developing language and concepts.

- Dramatic play situations contribute to effective communication with oral language. Simple stick or hand puppets can be used to encourage conversation.

- Listening stations permit a group of children to listen independently to tapes of stories while the teacher is working with other children.

ISSUES IN PRE-READING

Although the concept of readiness has gained wide acceptance, different viewpoints and some disagreement exist on several topics relevant to Level A. In surveying the literature and the research, the following questions seem to trigger the most controversy and are pertinent for the teacher of reading: What is the role of maturation as contrasted with specific skill training in pre-reading? When should a child learn to read? Should parents be involved in teaching their children to read? Are reading readiness workbooks valuable instructional materials at the pre-reading level?

Maturation Versus Training

What is the relative importance of maturation as contrasted with skill instruction in pre-reading? If readiness is viewed as a state of maturation, can it be "taught?" One view which became popular as the concept of readiness was evolving is that readiness is a developmental process that unfolds over a period of time. An opposing position is that the maturation factor can be over-emphasized and that children can learn to read by formal training in the skills of pre-reading and beginning reading.

The issue of maturation versus specific training in readiness is a false one, since both maturation and skill training contribute to a child's ability to profit from reading instruction at any given time. Hillerich describes readiness as representing progress in two areas of living: "The one area is time—time for growth and development; the second is experience or training."[24] If an immature child is placed in a learning situation where the demands are too difficult, the result will be frustration, not positive learning. However, while recognizing the significance of maturation, the teacher cannot rely on time alone to provide the essential background for a successful beginning reading experience.

If we know that certain skill training can facilitate learning to read and if we are sure the children have the necessary maturity to understand and profit from that instruction, we then can and should provide it. Although certain readiness skills can best be developed through a planned instructional program, the role of maturation must be recognized. Systematic instruction without regard to the maturation levels of individual children is a violation of what is known about learning and child development.

When Should Children Learn to Read?

One of the most controversial subjects in reading today is early reading instruction. Proponents of teaching reading before the first grade are vocal and persuasive. Opponents express strong feelings against lowering the age for beginning formal reading instruction. Because some of the widely accepted thinking about readiness is being reexamined, this issue rightfully merits discussion. If readiness is commonly viewed as the "best time" for instruction dependent upon the necessary background, maturation, and skills, does this "best time" occur earlier than the first grade for some children?

Studies have shown that children younger than six can and do learn to read. Some researchers reported that reading skills learned by young children tend to lack permanence and that the initial advantage is not maintained beyond the first grade.[25] Recent research shows that children who learn to read before the first grade do maintain the advantages of early instruction.[26] The study of reading instruction in the kindergartens in the Denver schools has received considerable attention. Researchers in this study concluded that beginning reading skills can be taught to kindergarten children and that these children were superior in reading achievement throughout the elementary grades to children who did not learn to read until the first grade.[27] In two other studies of children who learned to read before the first grade, Durkin reported that the early advantage in reading achievement persisted through the elementary grades.[28] She also reported that early reading did not result in problems for the children she studied.

Even though the question, "Can children learn to read in kindergarten?" can be answered affirmatively, the question, "Should reading instruction be offered in the kindergarten?" cannot be answered so easily. Of course, some children do develop sufficiently to be ready for reading in kindergarten. Many come to school today exposed through television, print on commercial products, books, magazines, and newspapers to a world filled with words. However, a large number of kindergarten children will not be ready for reading. If the emphasis moves toward lowering the grade level at which reading instruction is initiated, there is a danger of frustration for the unready children with severe detrimental effects caused by the pressure for learning to read. If reading instruction becomes the primary focus of kindergarten, many other values of this level may be overlooked, such as: providing an environment conducive to building background experience, creating interest in reading, promoting language development, fostering social and emotional adjustment, and identifying children with possible learning problems.

If kindergarten reading instruction is to be offered, the instruction has to be appropriate for those children who give evidence of being ready. Some kindergartens are presenting a first grade program a year earlier. Durkin talks about narrow kindergarten programs "cluttered with phonics and noisy with workbooks"[29] which are not offering challenging instruction for ready five-year-olds.

The question of reading in the kindergarten has to be answered in light of the backgrounds and needs of children in a given kindergarten class. Individualization of instruction at this level is particularly important. Also, special adaptations must be made for children who enter kindergarten or first grade already knowing how to read. Part of the reluctance to encourage early reading results from the school's failure to offer differentiated instruction for those who read before entering school.

What Is the Role of Parents in Pre-reading?

The role of parents in both pre-reading and beginning reading stages is related to the issue of when a child learns to read. It has long been recognized that the child from a home setting which values reading and which provides exposure to books, as well as to a wide variety of experiences, has an advantage in reading. Parents are encouraged to provide opportunities and stimulation for talking, to read to their children, and to promote a healthy attitude toward learning. In this respect, most parents do an amazing job of preparing their children for school.

Currently articles and books are urging parents to give direct instruction to their children, and many parents are doing so. In the Denver study of reading in the kindergarten, television programs were designed to show parents how to instruct their four and five-year-old children in reading skills. Parents' concern in giving their child a good start in reading can be attributed to two motivating factors: publicity about children who read poorly and the challenge of early reading to the unusually capable. Unfortunately, it is also true that a child's accomplishments may become a status symbol for some parents. The parent who boasts, "My child learned to read at three," may unconsciously be saying, "Notice what a fine parent I am." Pressure in the learning situation must again be considered. Durkin comments on early learning in upper-socio-economic levels by saying, "the drive to achieve is so dominant as to be psychologically suffocating."[30]

Nevertheless, many parents are not clear about the role they ought to assume in the pre-school years. Durkin interviewed parents of children who learned to read early and of children who did not learn to read until first grade. She found that many parents expressed confusion and concern about what to do and what not to do concerning pre-school help. While some publications such as *Teach Your Baby to Read*[31] may appeal because of the novelty rather than the educational soundness of the points expressed, there is a need for educators to assume a position on helping parents understand how they can assist their children in the pre-school period.

Durkin's findings about children who learned to read at home would be of interest to parents. Children who read early came from homes where they were read to regularly, where the parents valued reading, and where the mother or another individual spent a great deal of time answering the child's questions. Parents need to be informed about the importance of providing a reading environment in the home, taking their children to the local library to attend story hours and to borrow books, encouraging them to talk, and exposing them to varied experiences. Generally, formal instruction in reading is best left to the school. However, if a child starts to read independently, fine!

Do Readiness Workbooks Contribute to the Development of Readiness?

For many years, the materials most commonly used for pre-reading instruction have been readiness workbooks which are a part of basal reading series. In some classes the workbooks have been the total instructional program in pre-reading. Are they effective? Exactly what are the merits of materials widely used throughout the country?

Research has shown that other types of materials and activities are as good as or superior to readiness workbooks. Ploghoft found that the use of readiness workbooks in a kindergarten situation did not result in greater readiness than a program not using workbooks.[32] Blakely and Shadle reported that workbooks did not result in greater readiness than an experience-type program among girls at the kindergarten level and that the experience-type program did result in significant differences when contrasted with workbook instruction for boys.[33]

Other research indicates that workbooks do contribute to the development of readiness skills. Hillerich reported that a kindergarten program using readiness workbooks was more effective than a program without workbooks.[34] In interpreting these results, it should be mentioned that many readiness workbooks include material related to the skills tested on the readiness tests; thus, it might be expected that workbook instruction would lead to improved performance on a readiness test.

Workbooks need to be evaluated in the light of the objectives of the pre-reading program. Do the workbooks provide the type of perceptual skills needed in beginning reading? Are the visual and auditory discrimination exercises related to skills needed in beginning reading? Do the workbooks require children to listen for likenesses and differences in beginning sounds and to rhyming words? Do the workbooks allow expression of ideas in oral language, development of vocabulary, speaking and listening, stimulation of interest in reading, development of left-to-right progression across a line of print, and extension of experience and conceptual backgrounds? The preceding questions are posed not to be overly critical of workbooks but to stress that they cannot by themselves provide an adequate pre-reading program. The answer to some of the questions are, of course, positive, but various workbooks differ to the extent to which a particular skill is included.

It is advisable that workbooks of several series be available for reference and that the teacher adapt those exercises which relate to the needs of particular children. For example, if the teacher feels that exercises with picture interpretation in one workbook are worthwhile, he may utilize that workbook as a helpful resource for that type of instruction. By examining manuals for several workbooks, a teacher will find additional sources of ideas for pre-reading instruction. However, using workbooks as the complete readiness program was never intended by their authors and cannot be condoned.

Chapter Review

What happens *before* initial reading instruction is important. If the goal of a successful reading experience for all children is to be achieved, Level A must be regarded as of great significance. The assessment of readiness and the provision for overcoming deficiencies provide the foundation for a successful beginning of the reading act. Better tools for evaluation of readiness and enriched programs of instruction in pre-reading skills are goals for the future. The question of *when* reading should begin is dependent upon the quality of the reading instruction offered and it must be answered in terms of individuals instead of grade level standards.

NOTES

[1] Marion Monroe and Bernice Rogers, *Foundations for Reading* (Chicago: Scott, Foresman, 1964), p. 161.

[2] Robert M. Wilson, *Diagnostic and Remedial Reading* (Columbus: Charles E. Merrill, 1967), p. 52.

[3] Frances L. Ilg and Louise B. Ames, *School Readiness* (New York: Harper & Row, 1964), pp. 15–16.

[4] Arthur W. Heilman, *Principles and Practices of Teaching Reading* (Columbus: Charles E. Merrill, 1967), p. 408.

[5] Katrina de Hirsch, Jeanette J. Jansky, and William S. Langford, *Predicting Reading Failure* (New York: Harper & Row, 1966), p. 89.

[6] George D. Spache and Evelyn D. Spache, *Reading in the Elementary School* (Boston: Allyn and Bacon, 1969), pp. 40–41.

[7] Marianne Frostig and David Horne, *The Frostig Program for the Development of Visual Perception, Teacher's Guide* (Chicago: Follett, 1964), p. 8.

[8] Robert Dykstra, "Auditory Discrimination Abilities and Beginning Reading Achievement," *Reading Research Quarterly* 1 (Spring 1966): 32.

[9] Donald D. Durrell, "Learning Factors in Beginning Reading," in *Teaching Young Children To Read*, ed. Warren G. Cutts (Washington, D.C.: U.S. Office of Education, 1964), p. 72.

[10] Monroe and Rogers, p. 188.

[11] Mabel V. Morphett and Carleton Washburne, "When Should Children Learn To Read?" *Elementary School Journal* 29 (March 1931): 496–503.

[12] *See* Arthur I. Gates, "The Necessary Mental Age for Beginning Reading," *Elementary School Journal* 37 (March 1937): 497–508; *and also* R. W. Edmiston and Bessie Peyton, "Improving First Grade Reading Achievement by Readiness Instruction," *School and Society* 61 (April 1950): 473–476.

[13] Spache and Spache, p. 56.

[14] Ruth Strang, *Diagnostic Teaching of Reading* (New York: McGraw-Hill, 1964), p. 13.

[15] De Hirsch, Jansky, and Langford, p. 79.

[16] Thomas C. Barrett, "Predicting Reading Achievement Through Readiness Tests," in *Reading and Inquiry* (Newark, Delaware: International Reading Association, 1965), p. 27.

[17] E.E. Panther, "Prediction of First-Grade Reading Achievement," *Elementary School Journal* 68 (October 1967): 44–48.

[18] Thomas C. Barrett, "The Relationship Between Measures of Pre-reading Visual Discrimination and First Grade Reading Achievement: A Review of the Literature," *Reading Research Quarterly* 1 (Fall 1965): 51.

[19] R. Robert Geake and Donald E.P. Smith, *Michigan Tracking Program* (Ann Arbor: Ann Arbor Publishers, 1967–1968).

[20] Durrell, p. 75.

[21] Barrett, "Relationship Between Visual Discrimination and Achievement," p. 71.

[22] Miriam Schlein, *Fast Is Not a Ladybug* (New York: Wm. R. Scott, 1953).

[23] Harold G. Shane, Mary E. Reddin, and Margaret C. Gillespie, *Beginning Language Arts Instruction with Children* (Columbus: Charles E. Merrill, 1961), p. 14.

[24] Robert L. Hillerich, "An Interpretation of Research in Reading Readiness," *Elementary English* 43 (April 1966): 359.

[25] Sarah L. Leeper, "Early Reading in the Kindergarten," in *Speaking to the Issues, Position Papers in Reading* (University of Maryland: Reading Center, 1967), pp. 110–116.

[26] Dolores Durkin, *Children Who Read Early* (New York: Teachers College Press, 1966), pp. 41, 84, 133.

[27] Joseph Brzeinski, "Beginning Reading in Denver," *The Reading Teacher* 18 (October 1964): 16–21.

[28] Durkin, p. 139.

[29] Ibid.

[30] Ibid.

[31] Glenn Doman, *How To Teach Your Baby To Read* (New York: Random House, 1964).

[32] Milton H. Ploghoft, "Do Reading Readiness Workbooks Promote Readiness?" *Elementary English* 36 (October 1959): 423–426.

[33] W. Paul Blakely and Emma L. Shadle, "A Study of Two Readiness for Reading Programs in Kindergarten," *Elementary English* 38 (November 1961): 502–505.

[34] Robert L. Hillerich, "Pre-reading Skills in Kindergarten: A Second Report," *Elementary School Journal* 65 (March 1965): 312–317.

SUGGESTED ACTIVITIES

1. Examine several reading readiness tests. What skills are tested? What important readiness factors are not evaluated? Which one of these would you like to use?
2. Observe a group of five-year-olds at play. What signs of readiness do you observe? Watch one child and jot down specifics, then do the same for another.

3. Develop an experience chart which could be used with children at Level A. See Lesson Plan 1 in chapter 11.
4. Prepare for one side of a discussion based on the topic: Children can be taught to be ready for reading. Hold the discussion and have the rest of the class draw conclusions.

SUGGESTED READINGS

De Hirsch, Katrina; Jansky, J. Jeanette; and Langford, William S. *Preventing Reading Failure*. New York: Harper & Row, 1967.

Recommended for the reader interested in the detailed evaluation of perceptual, motor, and language factors related to learning to read. The significance of early identification of possible problems is stressed.

Durkin, Dolores. *Children Who Read Early*. New York: Teachers College Press, 1967.

Two longitudinal studies of children who learned to read prior to first grade are reported. Of particular interest are her conclusions and implications regarding the curriculums of kindergarten and grade one.

Hymes, James L. *Before A Child Reads*. New York: Harper & Row, 1958.

Emphasizes the role of experience and development in the years before formal training in readiness or in reading is begun. The author states that a good program for young children is geared to their present needs rather than to "preparation" for later experiences.

Ilg, Frances L, and Ames, Louise B. *School Readiness*. New York: Harper & Row, 1964.

Describes a program of extensive evaluation of children which determines their classroom placement according to their "developmental level." The reader may wish to examine the tools of pupil evaluation.

Monroe, Marion and Rogers, Bernice. *Foundations for Reading*. Chicago: Scott, Foresman, 1964.

Presents a comprehensive discussion of factors involved in readiness and many practical suggestions for teaching.

CHAPTER SIX

DEVELOPING A READING VOCABULARY

Advance Organizer

Instant recognition of printed words, ability to pronounce these words correctly, and association of meanings with the words are the objectives of vocabulary development in reading. Reading vocabulary, in this sense, includes all words that the child can recognize and comprehend on a consistent basis. Frequently known as *sight vocabulary,* reading vocabulary is distinct from the listening and speaking vocabularies which children bring to school, and from the writing vocabulary which they develop in school. The teacher who sees the interrelationship of these vocabularies is better equipped to find numerous opportunities for extending vocabulary knowledge.

This chapter examines the processes involved in moving children from the pre-reading stage to the acquisition of sight vocabulary. Discussion centers on materials and methods which have been found effective at Level B, where a basic sight vocabulary is introduced, through Levels C and D, at which point thousands of words are recognized at sight and integrated skillfully with surrounding words and word groups. As a child develops a large stockpile of words that he can pronounce and comprehend in varied contexts, he moves toward independence in reading.

THE FOUR FACETS OF VOCABULARY

A child may listen with one vocabulary, speak with another, write with yet another, and read with still a fourth. When discussing the vocabularies of children, therefore, it is important to distinguish accurately between these four basic vocabularies.

There is no doubt that a child listens long before he speaks, reads, or writes in words. His listening vocabulary, thus, quickly becomes quite large. In fact, many an individual's listening vocabulary remains his largest vocabulary throughout his lifetime. Shortly after his listening vocabulary begins to develop, however, a child starts to speak. This vocabulary too develops rapidly, so that, by the time the average child comes to school, he has a fairly sizable speaking vocabulary. In this connection, Lorge and Chall have cited studies indicating vocabulary ranges of from 2,000 to 20,000 words for first grade children.[1]

Writing vocabulary, on the other hand, tends to be considerably smaller than any of the other three. Even the most fluent writers report that their reading brings them into contact with words which, while fully or partially understandable to them in the context of someone else's writing, lie outside their own writing vocabularies. The child's writing vocabulary usually develops slowly, especially when complicated by spelling difficulties.

For mature readers, the reading vocabulary may become their largest vocabulary. During reading, unlike listening, they can reread, look for meaningful word parts, or stop to think about how words are being used in a given contextual situation. For some children, exposure to new vocabulary through wide reading exceeds exposure through listening situations. Reading vocabularies tend to exceed speaking and writing vocabularies when children, making good use of word study techniques, are able to derive meaning from words which they cannot pronounce with certainty. In turn, the speaking and writing vocabularies come to reflect the children's new understanding of words they have learned through listening and reading.

READING VOCABULARY

This chapter examines the development of reading vocabulary, commonly referred to as *sight vocabulary*. As the child moves from pre-reading into beginning reading, the focus shifts from listening and speaking to sight vocabulary. In general, the teaching of sight vocabulary development proceeds according to three objectives:

1) Instant recognition of studied words
   The term *sight vocabulary* refers to words which a child "knows" instantly as he glances at them. If a child can pronounce a word instantly, he has met the first criterion of sight vocabulary.

2) Consistent recognition of studied words
   The reader has to be able to recognize and consistently pronounce a word correctly—today, tomorrow, next week, and in subsequent reading situations. Consistent recognition is the second criterion for a word becoming part of a reader's sight vocabulary.

3) Effective association of known words
   The reader needs to be able to make associations with printed words and phrases from his previous experiences. In beginning reading, these associations may be relatively simple in their connotation. Eventually, however, for a word to be considered a sight word in any context, a child ought to be able to discuss its various meanings. The richness and depth of a child's vocabulary is as important as its range.

The reader's sight vocabulary, then, consists of words which are pronounced instantly and consistently with effective association of meaning.

Children acquire sight vocabularies in several ways. Teachers, peers, or parents may tell a child the pronunciation of words or he may use word attack skills to decode words which he does not know. Several such encounters with a particular word may make the word easier for the child. When he "knows" the word—that is, when he can recognize it instantly and consistently in varied contexts, it has become a sight word. It is hoped that practically all words a child first analyzes through methods introduced by his teachers will become part of his sight vocabulary. Certain words, however, are encountered so infrequently that they may never become sight vocabulary words.

The Skills of Sight Vocabulary

Several related skills are involved in developing sight vocabularies effectively. Oral language skills, auditory and visual discrimination, skill in looking at word configurations and remembering them, and skill in associating word meaning in varied contexts are especially important.

Oral Language Development At all levels, oral language background affects comprehension in reading and the facility with which children associate meaning with printed words. If a child has heard a word prior to encountering it in print, and if he uses the word in his speech, learning to read the word is simplified. If he does not use the word and has not heard it before, then oral language must enter into the reading lesson in which the word occurs. Clearly, children with well-developed speaking and listening vocabularies are best equipped to deal with print.

Visual Discrimination The ability to note likenesses and differences in word forms is, as we have seen, of major importance in the pre-reading period. In this period, attention is first given to matching word, phrase, and sentence cards with the contexts of language experience stories or with other printed materials. Children are then provided experiences in which they are to identify words which are different only in the initial, medial, or final letters, such as: *can—man, went—want, back—bath.* As sight vocabulary for reading is developed and the child moves from Level A to Level B, visual discrimination sharpens.

Memory of Word Configuration Closely related to visual discrimination skills are the skills required in remembering word configurations. Getting to know words which are encountered daily involves not only discrimination but memory as well. Children who seem to have learned a word on Monday but cannot recognize it on Tuesday can be trying to teachers at all levels. It is necessary then to use strategies to reintroduce such words using highly motivating techniques. When difficulty persists, teachers have noted that it often tends to occur with words which are similar in formation (such as *big, bag,* and *beg*) or with words which are abstract enough to cause the child difficulty in association (such as *was, the, this,* and *it*). The fact that the "average" child learns rather easily any word which is introduced and reviewed appropriately tends to call even more attention to those having difficulty remembering word forms.

Associating Meaning with the Word Because of the large reservoir of words in children's oral language vocabularies, association of word meaning with experience is not usually difficult, provided the instructional materials are consistent with the children's experience. Many children, however, especially in initial reading activities, work so hard merely to decode the print that they do not even think about word meanings. It is vital to help such children to visualize what they have read, to relate it to experiences they have had, and to place themselves in the stories. It is not enough for a child to know a single meaning for a word. He must be able to understand the use of that word as it appears in many different contexts. It is important to remember too that deriving meaning from sentences involves more than associating meaning with separate words. Words must be considered as parts of larger meaning-bearing language patterns.

TECHNIQUES FOR TEACHING VOCABULARY

Attention is given to sight vocabulary development at all levels of reading. At Level A, pre-reading activities in oral language concentrate on enriching the word meanings children can bring to the learning situation. Visual discrimination of likenesses and differences in words and phrases lays the foundation for the memory of printed word forms essential to the acquisition of a sight vocabulary.

Attempts to develop oral language ability, auditory discrimination, and visual discrimination also have direct relationship to the techniques to be used in Levels B, C, and D. Level B emphasizes the mastery of a basic sight vocabulary, containing those several hundred words which are used over and over in all printed material (*the, and, in, house, boy,* etc.). Word meaning and usage are also stressed, through continuous exposure to words in varied contextual situations. Level C is a continuation of sight word development, stressing both pronunciation and meaning. Thousands of words are mastered at this level, opening the door to many books which are now accessible to children. Level D finds the child with a large sight vocabulary and well-developed listening and speaking vocabularies. Varied meanings of words and phrases are stressed in material of widely differing subject areas. Words which a child does not know at Level D will be learned through independent word attack activities. Meanwhile, writing vocabulary develops along with the reading vocabulary at all levels at a slower rate.

Level B

A core of sight words which are used frequently in the speech and the writing of others is the target of Level B. Their mastery is essential to all future reading. Let us examine the two basic approaches used to develop this core of sight words: the basal series and language experience approaches.

In basal readers, words are selected for the child by the authors. They are introduced and repeated in a carefully planned manner. Although the basal manuals vary in the instructions offered the teacher, the following techniques are usually employed at the beginning reading levels. Several words are selected for introduction. The teacher places these words on the board, on a chart, or in a word card holder. Preferably, they appear in a contextual situation.

I am a *boy*.	boy
See me *run*.	run

The teacher asks the children if they know the word. If some do, they pronounce it. Then all the children pronounce it and a common meaning for the word is discussed. They then read a story in which the words learned are used repeatedly. Word cards are usually available (and easily prepared if not) for reinforcing the word. Using the card, children are asked to match the word card with a word in the story, with words which start the same or end the same, and with another identical card. Word cards may also be used for brief drill periods in which pairs of children work together showing the card and pronouncing the word.

After the reading, the same words are usually discussed, using their context in the story. At the next reading session, the words may be used again on cards and are repeated in the reading selection along with the new words for that day. In such a manner, most children learn between 300 and 500 basic sight words during their first year of school.

When using the language experience approach, the technique changes. The stories are dictated by the children after stimulation of oral language on a topic of interest. The children select the words from the story which they can read and which are most interesting to them. These words are placed on word cards, each child having his own set. On occasion the teacher may also pick several words from a given story and add them to the word cards of the children. The word appears on one side of the card and the word in a phrase or sentence appears on the other side.

school

I like our school.

Word cards are used for games and drills to develop sight vocabulary. Children can work in pairs reading their word cards to a partner. They can select words starting with the same letter and start to alphabetize. They can even place words into categories such as people, places, or action words.

The words placed on cards are words which the children *can* read and which they will encounter again in other language experience stories. Words are learned in two ways—through repetition in reading and through activities with word cards. In general, many of the same words are learned through the basal and language experience techniques to initial reading; however, in the language experience approach, the vocabulary is not controlled or predetermined, and a wider variety of words will probably be used.

With either approach the teacher directs the child's attention to peculiar configurations of words. Such configuration clues are particularly valuable in early reading instruction. For example, the teacher points out the common elements in *ran* and *pan* or the *j* and *p* extending below the line in *jump*. It is important that children see how words are alike and how they differ. It is also essential that children learn how to use them in sentences. Although most children develop their own personal systems for recognizing words by configuration, it is helpful to have other configuration clues called to their attention. Several of the following activities recommended in most teachers guides ask the child to:

- Match a word on a card with the same word as it appears in a sentence.

- Underline words that begin or end alike or have certain configuration characteristics.

- Underline a certain word every time it appears in a sentence.

- Point to the word which means . . . or to the phrase or sentence that tells . . .

- Identify a word in a story which means the opposite of . . .

The last two activities are examples of the use of meaning clues for word pronunciation.

In Level B, word meaning is stressed along with word pronunciation. Words common to the child's oral language are used with a connotation which is appropriate for his oral language background. Exposure to the word in other contexts stressing other connotations helps the child to see how varied word meaning is. For example, in the first pre-primer of one basal series, the following sentences are seen early in the book:

> Pet a hen?
> Let me! Let me![2]

On the following page, one reads:

> And then she let me.
> She is a pet.
> She is a pet hen.[3]

Notice the manner in which the word *pet* is used in different contexts to help the reader become aware of a variance in meaning. The instruction of word meanings in basal readers is made easy for the teacher. When using the language experience approach, the teacher can assume that the child already knows the meaning of the word since he first used it orally; however, alternate word meanings will need to be developed. Children can share with one another the sentences or phrases which they used on the back of their word cards. It is likely that the varying contexts will result in different uses of the word. The teacher is also alert to the possibilities of pointing out changes in meaning when he notes them in subsequent stories. Children need to be made aware of the effect of context on word meaning.

A teacher will often feel that children bring adequate oral vocabularies to school and that word meanings do not need to be stressed; however, a real danger exists that children will develop the idea that word meaning is not an important part of reading. The teacher can encourage them to see word changes in meaning by shifting the context, thinking of different contexts, and using synonyms and antonyms. These are activities which children enjoy and from which they readily learn.

While most children find vocabulary instruction to be easy and pleasant, some find it difficult and distasteful. There are several things a teacher can do to promote the learning of vocabulary while making it a more pleasant activity in Level B.

Tracing techniques have long been suggested as a means to

help children learn words. The child is instructed to trace the letters of the word with his fingers, pronouncing it at the same time. After several tracings, the child should copy the word, pronouncing it as he writes it. After trying this a few times, the child is usually able to write the word from memory. Although tracing is time-consuming, the sensory reinforcement of touch and movement seems to be what some children need. Other teachers have found it useful to have children trace the words at their seats, then form them in the air. In this manner, the teacher can observe the children, identify those experiencing difficulty, and then provide personalized instruction.

The language experience approach can be extended for children having difficulty learning vocabulary. In such cases, the reading

Using word cards and stories which they have written, children work in small groups or in pairs to master their words.

from other materials such as the basal are withheld until the child has had considerable success with the language experience ap-proach. Working with word cards and stories which they have written, these children work in small groups or in pairs to master their words. They build new sentences with their word cards, quiz one another, read their language experience stories to other children, and practice the words with the tracing techniques men-tioned above. Use of the language experience approach places emphasis upon activities which permit a child to demonstrate his strengths—a highly desirable emphasis for troubled learners.

Some children seem to learn better when the initial introduction of sight words is done with words which have minimal differences in configuration (*ran, fan, can, man*). Materials prepared with a so-called linguistic emphasis generally contain controlled vocabu-laries presented with stress on minimal differences. Use of these materials helps children to pay careful attention to the small differences in words from the beginning of their learning of sight vocabulary.

Programmed materials are yet another way to supplement the program for children having difficulty with initial learning of sight vocabulary. These materials add the advantage of being self-pacing and self-correcting. The child moves as fast as he is able, but does not need to "keep up" with the rest of the group. Each answer is reinforced with an immediate exposure of the appropri-ate answer. In this manner, only accurate responses are practiced.

Teachers have found it useful to assist children's learning by making games out of their work. In general, the idea is for two or more children to use their sight vocabulary to play such games as lotto, matching, or checkers using a board upon which review sight words are written. Games add the dimensions of fun and success to what is otherwise an often not too pleasant task.

Some children who are experiencing difficulty in remembering words may be attempting to learn them at too fast a pace. The teacher may lower the number of words introduced in any given lesson to assure mastery of those words.

Most children will be able to learn sight vocabulary easily. For those who do not, the above suggestions usually are of help. The teacher can take pressure off these children by not pressing them to keep up with the group and by not placing them with a reader before they are ready for it. In our efforts to help first grade teach-ers, we have found that children can learn basic words easily and that it is the pressure of time that starts to bother both the child and the teacher. However, time is a man-made pressure and can be relaxed. The important factor to remember is that these early experiences should be successful and pleasant.

Level C

When a child has developed a sight vocabulary of about 1000 words, he finds he can actually read many books which he finds in the library. Having had pleasant and successful experiences in reading, his curiosity leads him to many books on different topics. The child is now moving from Level B to Level C, where he will refine the skills of sight vocabulary and develop a large stockpile of known words.

Perhaps the best, single way to enlarge the sight vocabulary is to read. A child ought to be encouraged to read everything he can, since it is by reading that he becomes adept at quickly and accurately identifying common words. Reading and finding words in print where communication is stressed is preferable to drill-type exercises for developing word knowledge. The teacher must assist a child, structuring meaningful reading situations and reinforcing the child's efforts. It is necessary to make a wide variety of easy-to-read books available and encourage free reading by allowing school time for it on a daily basis. Frequent trips to the library are a useful stimulus. Parents can also help by supplying books, library cards, and distraction-free areas for reading at home.

While reading itself is the most profitable way to reinforce the vocabulary already learned, there are many other activities which a teacher can promote to help the child enlarge his vocabulary. Short paragraphs can be used to have children experiment with synonyms and antonyms. The children change certain words to others with the same or opposite meaning. For example, antonyms such as *happy* and *sad* can be used in sentences: *John was happy. John was sad.* The children think of as many words as they can that mean the same as *happy* and substitute them in the first sentence. Then they proceed in the same way with an opposite of the word. In such a manner, the study of synonyms and antonyms is useful and interesting. This activity is best done in contextual situations, thereby illustrating how changes in vocabulary change the context.

Games with words which contain varied meanings are also interesting and useful. The teacher starts with the word *run* and asks teams of children to work together to think of as many meanings as they can for the word. They can place the new meaning in a sentence. For example: *I can run fast. I was fishing in a run behind my house.* Many other words such as *store* and *bank* can be used in a similar manner. Not only do children enjoy these games, but they extend word meanings when they share their answers.

Level C is the time in a child's schooling when word attack techniques are being refined. Words studied in word attack exercises ultimately appear in a child's sight vocabulary. Such transfer can be accelerated by the teacher if he points out words in reading which have already been used in other activities. Helping the children remember that they have worked with a word previously often assists them to recall the word. Continued use makes the word part of the sight vocabulary.

In still another activity, the children engage in definition writing. The skill with which a child can write definitions in his own words has much to do with his understanding of the word and its uses. Definition writing can be taught when dictionary usage for word meaning is taught. Normally, it is advisable for a child to start with words which are well known to him and, as his skill increases, to move to words which are less familiar, using a dictionary and context clues as his major sources. Definition writing has four steps: 1) Write one common meaning for the word; 2) Write less common meanings for the word, if known; 3) Follow each definition with the word in an appropriate sentence; and 4) List several synonyms following each definition. It is often valuable to begin such exercises with group participation before asking children to work independently.

Another activity is categorizing known words. Beginning as picture sorting or listening activities in Level A and continued into Level B as a reading activity, children group printed words according to categories, such as the work people do, the buildings in which they work, animals, transportation, and vehicles. As a child develops skill in this activity in Level C, he is expected to move to more subtle categorizing. For example, he may group words which show mood, concern, or irritation. The use of such words in child-made sentences shows whether he understands the meanings. Word banks are particularly useful in this activity. As a child shares his words or as he works in teams, he becomes conscious of personal vocabulary development.

Word banks developed during Levels A and B can be used in Level C to continue the development of sight vocabulary. Teachers may encourage children to use group word banks and to submit words for these banks based upon their knowledge of the words.

Words can be selected because they represent action, names of things, descriptions, or many other classifications. One advantage of the word bank over notebook type lists is that the card format for each entry permits great flexibility in reclassifying for different purposes. Children can be encouraged in their reading to be alert to words which could be discussed with the group and then added to the group word files.

Vocabulary work at Level C contains several hazards. Children frequently develop the idea that words are more important than the thoughts which they convey in context. Continuous efforts by the teacher to place word activities in contextual situations tend to minimize this hazard. Another problem is that word drills can be frustrating to some children and boring to others. Constant attention must be employed to guarantee that children are not participating in activities which hold little meaning for them. Still another problem is that vocabulary seems to grow very slowly for some children. These children become dismayed at the limited achievement obtained for their great efforts. Teachers can help children note their progress through the use of charts, graphs, and word banks, each of which can illustrate to the child what he has accomplished. Such extrinsic motivation has proven to be of considerable value in reading clinic cases.

For Level C, however, it is the prospect of being able to read using words which one has already learned that holds the most promise. Children who can read and who are given time for it in school find their reading to be the best motivation available.

Level D

Complete independence in sight vocabulary does not exist since a reader never knows all of the words he comes upon in reading. However, in Level D in sight vocabulary, the child is equipped to deal with all unfamiliar situations that may arise. He either knows the word at sight or knows a way of obtaining its pronunciation and meaning without further help from the teacher.

At Level D a great deal of time simply spent reading is the best way of developing word power and a wider and stronger vocabulary. The child who gains a degree of independence in sight vocabulary is the one who reads. All efforts must be made to think of ways to develop the desire to read. For example, book fairs, exciting displays of books to read, designing book covers, and sharing books which generate excitement are useful ideas. Teachers who have used these techniques and who have allocated large amounts of school time for reading supply an ample and stimulating selection of books to read.

Exercises in writing may also be used to strengthen and reinforce vocabulary knowledge. Creative writing stimulates the child to express his thoughts in imaginative language as he stretches his mind. Children will find their writing vocabulary containing some of the same words as their reading vocabulary. To help locate certain appropriate words, books such as a thesaurus are introduced and used. Scott, Foresman has developed two thesauri, both called *In Other Words,* which are helpful references for word study and for independent writing.

It is inappropriate at Level D to place fairly independent readers in a basal reading group listening to the teacher explain how to pronounce new words in a story and discussing the meaning of these words. Unfortunately, such activities are not uncommon in many classrooms. It is preferable that the child be permitted to read independently. He will obtain the meaning of the author and work out word pronunciations and meanings in his own manner. Following the reading, questions may be asked to determine the caliber of the child's efforts and to correct misconceptions. However, unless the child is free to attempt his own attack on new words, he is not encouraged to be independent.

Summary of Levels A through D

The following list summarizes the important concepts developed in the discussion of Levels A through D in sight vocabulary:

- A teacher introduces a few words at a time with commercial reading materials. Children, especially in beginning reading, often become confused when too many new words are presented at once.

- A teacher asks a child to choose those words which the child *can* read from language experience stories, not those which he cannot.

- Since children learn at different rates, a teacher is prepared to reintroduce words which have been forgotten. In such cases, it does no good to chastise a child for not remembering. Instead, patient reteaching is the solution.

- A teacher calls attention to words which have been introduced in previous reading lessons. A reminder such as, "Look at this word; we had it yesterday in reading class," helps a child realize the utility of what he has been studying.

■ Tracing is a useful technique to reinforce the learning of vocabulary for children who are having difficulty.

■ Words which have direct meaning for a child are easier to learn than those which are unrelated to his experiences. Teachers start by helping a child learn his name, his teacher's name, the name of the school, the names of his friends, and the like. Once several meaningful words have been learned, others can be learned more easily.

■ If the meanings of words are stressed, a child responds more accurately when meeting the word again.

■ After reading a story or poem to children, a teacher discusses interesting words, word usages, or phrases.

■ Words need not always be introduced prior to reading. Especially at Level D, children learn more without the traditional word introduction activities.

■ Wide reading is by far the best vocabulary activity for children working at Levels C and D.

ISSUES IN VOCABULARY DEVELOPMENT

As in other areas of reading, certain problems seem to reoccur in vocabulary development. A review of several of these problems will help the teacher when he comes face to face with them in teaching situations.

Should Reading Be Taught Using Materials Which Are Designed Around a Controlled Vocabulary?

The term *controlled vocabulary* refers to the selection of words and the rate of introduction of words in reading materials, usually basal series. Words are introduced gradually in a controlled manner. Once a word is introduced, it is used repeatedly to provide children with opportunities to see and use it in many different contexts. The authors select words which they feel are essential for children to know in order to be able to read materials other than basal texts. The words are usually easy to learn and often come from a standard word list based on frequency of occurrence at the different grade levels.

However, there is no single sight vocabulary since no two basal series introduce the same words. Sometimes differences in word selections are extensive. Dolch prepared a list of 220 basic sight words which he claims "make up 50 to 75 per cent of all school reading matter."[3] However, a study by Olson showed that "there is only minimal agreement between the words common to five or more of the [basal] series studied and the Dolch list."[4]

Teachers who use basal materials can extend the vocabulary in many ways. Several suggestions to that end have been made in this chapter. By using the language experience approach for initial reading instruction, the child selects words which he uses in his speech. Therefore, the vocabulary is controlled not by outside authors but by a child's oral language, which is more extensive than the vocabulary of commercially prepared materials. By using words which represent objects in the room (such as *door, desk, window*), children's names, and places, the teacher assists chldren to learn words beyond the controlled vocabulary. He also introduces social studies, science, and arithmetic words when appropriate. In each of these ways the teacher can help to expand the controlled vocabulary of the basal reader. An example of this type of effort was recorded by Story, who found that her first grade children learned 2,124 words which had not been included in the basal texts.[5] She introduced words appropriate to holidays, words analyzed through simple word attack techniques such as initial consonant substitution, and words expanded by the common inflected endings. Of course, she was alert to the many opportunities to expand children's sight vocabulary through varied activities.

In answer, then, to the question, "Is it wise to use materials based upon a controlled vocabulary?" the answer is a qualified "Yes." Yes—if the teacher uses all opportunities to stimulate growth of reading vocabulary from other available sources. All of the major basal series' authors support and encourage teachers in this effort. No one today can justify an approach which uses controlled vocabulary approaches alone. If a teacher limits his vocabulary work to words in the controlled vocabulary, he is indeed limiting opportunities for vocabulary development. Recall Stauffer's urging, that "At no time should a basic reader program, even in jest, be referred to as 'the reading program.' "[6]

Should Word Introduction Prior to Reading Be Discontinued?

The question of word introduction relates to a practice which is advocated in many basal manuals: words are placed in context on the board, on a chart, or word card holder and discussed, pronounced, and studied prior to the reading of the story.

No standard use of this approach can be advocated. Some children need this type of help in a reading group, while others do not. Beginning readers are likely to need more word introduction and repetition than experienced readers. The teacher must be flexible. When he feels a child can read a story without word introduction, he encourages the child to do so; however, if he knows in advance that a child needs new words introduced first, he uses that approach.

Those children who need more visual exposure to word forms to remember them may be deprived of opportunities to see words in situations in addition to the text, if vocabulary is not presented prior to silent reading. In the introduction of words for children needing repeated exposure, the teacher may use the techniques of having children underline, circle, frame, or match word cards. The introduction of vocabulary can be done in such a way as to foster the application of word attack knowledge, instead of simply telling children words. The teacher may say, "You know the beginning sound in this word. What word beginning with that sound makes sense in this sentence?"

If a teacher lets children read a story without first introducing new words, he is not relieved of the obligation of teaching vocabulary. In such cases, a discussion of word pronunciation and meaning should follow the lesson. It continues to be important for a teacher to know how a child handles new words. Some teachers and most basals advocate reviewing a skill needed for word attack prior to the lesson and encouraging a child to use that skill when reading new words. In any case, it is advisable to break the routine of always introducing new words first, so that a child can gain experience in reading independently and in applying word attack skills.

Is There Value in Introducing Words Out of Context?

Closely related to the previous question is one concerning how words should be introduced. Some manuals suggest printing words on the chalk board for discussion. A child looks at the words, pronounces them, discusses their meanings, and then reads a story in which the words are used.

However, the precise meaning of any word is found only in context, and the impact of a word in context is different from that in isolation. Of course, many words such as *and, it, there, here,* are meaningful only in context and are difficult to define separately. Words which surround the unknown new word help with the attack on the new word. Many children can read words at the board when they are in isolation, but cannot work with them when encountered in their reading. The transfer from group work at the chalkboard to independent reading will be enhanced by starting with the word in context.

It is therefore advisable that new words first be introduced in context. The word should be used in a sentence and the discussion centered around its meaning in that sentence. The word can be framed, underlined, or listed in isolation as the lesson proceeds. Just as the lesson should start with the word in context, it should also end with the word in the context of the story or in a sentence of the child's own creation. By stressing the communication value of word study, teachers can help children learn sight words more readily.

How Can Vocabulary Be Taught to Children Who Do Not Speak Standard English?

Standard English is an issue of concern to any teacher who is involved with teaching reading vocabulary. Many children come to school with language patterns and dialects which are quite different from those expected to be used in school. Their names for concepts and objects may be quite different from those used by the authors of the books they are expected to read. However, since standard English is always changing and since the English used by many of these children is structurally complete and communicates quite well, it is important that their language be accepted. When a child feels his language is unacceptable to the teacher, he also feels he is personally unacceptable and rejected.

At the same time, it is essential that children develop concepts for words which are similar to the concepts used by most authors. A teacher is then in a position of accepting one language and, at the same time, teaching another form of it. Children can be encouraged to discriminate between their language and standard

English. First, they can be asked to indicate awareness of differences such as, "I am a good boy," and "I be a good boy." Second, they can indicate which is "school language." Third, they can translate from one language to the other. In each step mastery should be developed before proceeding to the next step.[7]

Children speaking nonstandard English can often read standard English, although, they may paraphrase what they read in their own language. A teacher must see the difference between such paraphrasing and errors in oral reading. He can stress the part of any reading lesson where a class develops concepts appropriate for words in a given story. Culturally different children need to develop listening vocabulary so that encounters with print can have communicative value.

How Can a Teacher Make Use of Maximal and Minimal Configurations in Words While Teaching Vocabulary?

Because of the emphasis on configuration in the development of sight vocabulary, the question of whether children learn best from maximal (*look, run, jump*) or minimal (*cat, rat, sat*) differences is raised. Initial instruction is probably easier when configuration of words is unique (maximal). However, later instruction is usually easier when a child has some grasp of minimal configuration differences.

It would seem prudent, therefore, for a teacher to use maximal differences in initial instruction of sight vocabulary, but to quickly introduce the idea of minimal changes. For example, if *look, run,* and *jump* should appear first, the teacher can direct children to examine *book, sun,* and *pump,* compare them with the words already known, and use them in sentences.

Teachers will find materials available which stress both maximal and minimal clues in initial reading. It does not seem to be necessary to make a choice. Instead, both types of configurations can be used to assist children to learn as effectively as possible and to extend knowledge of word patterns.

Chapter Review

Developing a reading vocabulary is essential for success in reading. It is approached with varying emphases and techniques in each of the four levels of reading. The ultimate goal is to instill in children the desire and the skills for wide, independent reading. Commercially available materials are making the teaching of vocabulary easier. These, in combination with a teacher's attention to individual children and their problems, can make reading a pleasant, successful experience for all children.

NOTES

[1] Irving Lorge and Jeanne Chall, "Estimating the Size of Vocabularies of Children and Adults: An Analysis of Methodological Issues," *Journal of Experimental Education* 32 (Winter 1963): 147–157.

[2] Marjorie Seddon Johnson, et al., *And So You Go* (New York: American Book, 1968), p. 28.

[3] Edward William Dolch, *The Basic Sight Vocabulary Cards, Instructions for Using* (Champaign, Illinois: Garrard, 1952).

[4] Arthur V. Olson, "An Analysis of the Vocabulary of Seven Primary Reading Series," *Elementary English* 42 (March 1965): 264.

[5] Suetta B. Story, "Does Johnny Know More Words Than Ivan?" *The Reading Teacher* 20 (November 1966): 131–133.

[6] Russell G. Stauffer, "Time for Amendment," *The Reading Teacher* 20 (May 1967): 685.

[7] Irwin Feigenbaum, "The Use of Nonstandard English in Teaching Standard: Contrast and Comparison," in *Teaching Standard English in the Inner-city* (Washington, D.C.: Center for Applied Linguistics, 1970), pp. 87–104.

SUGGESTED ACTIVITIES

1. Read Lesson Plan 4 in chapter 11. Develop a plan for working with multiple meanings of words using whatever materials you prefer.
2. Examine a basal reader at the pre-primer or primer level and one at an intermediate grade level to note how vocabulary is introduced. Prepare several alternative types of vocabulary introduction.
3. Visit a classroom where individual word banks are used for developing reading vocabulary. How were they used? What advantages did you note?

SUGGESTED READINGS

Betts, Emmett. *Foundations of Reading Instruction.* New York: American Book, 1946.

> See chapter 24 for a scholarly presentation of the problems of vocabulary instruction. Particular attention is given to concept development.

Cutts, Warren G. *Modern Reading Instruction.* New York: Center for Applied Research in Education, 1964.

Chapter 5 presents a short coverage of vocabulary development and is of particular interest for references to specific research studies.

Dechant, Emerald V. *Improving the Teaching of Reading.* Englewood Cliffs: Prentice-Hall, 1964.

See chapter 12 for a thorough examination of word meaning. Specific teaching techniques are suggested along with ideas about vocabulary reinforcement.

Deighton, Lee C. *Vocabulary Development in the Classroom.* New York: Bureau of Publications, Teachers College, Columbia University, 1959.

Chapter 6 treats the development of word meanings and is useful for sight vocabulary, as well as for word attack.

Hall, MaryAnne. *Teaching Reading as a Language Experience.* Columbus: Charles E. Merrill, 1970.

See chapter 5 on vocabulary development in the language experience approach for a detailed description of the format, development, and use of both individual and group word banks.

Russell, David H. *Children Learn To Read.* Boston: Ginn and Co., 1961.
Chapter 9 of this popular, easy to read, practical, and complete book deals thoroughly with vocabulary development.

CHAPTER SEVEN

WORD ATTACK

Advance Organizer

Following close upon the beginnings of a sight vocabulary are the challenges posed by the unfamiliar words a child encounters. How does he perceive them? What can his teacher do to assist him both in any given problem situation and in the long-range objective of preparing him to learn new words independently? The skill of coping with words not recognized at sight is called *word attack* and it forms the subject of this chapter. Although much remains to be learned in this area, five branches of word attack are generally acknowledged: configuration, context, phonics, structural analysis, and dictionary study —all of which the elementary teacher will find useful, regardless of the grade level of the children being taught.

Because independence in reading is a major goal, the teacher encourages the individuality with which each child successfully attacks unknown words.

THE CONTENT AND METHODS OF WORD ATTACK

One of the thorniest aspects of elementary school reading is that initial point at which a young reader encounters a word that makes no sense to him. This instant is charged with potential for either sound reading growth or a negative experience which may affect the reader's development in a permanently adverse way. Because of the critical importance of the young reader's encounter with an unfamiliar word, an extensive body of theory, practice, speculation, and even heated debate has grown up around the problem of word attack.

It is difficult to determine the exact procedures used by a child as he attacks an unknown word. Many children appear to rely heavily upon the use of context clues. Others clearly use phonics. Still others report that dividing words into syllables is useful. However, most children use a combination of skills in a personally developed approach and the most effective readers use any of several word attack strategies when a given situation demands. It therefore, seems desirable that each child should have the opportunity to employ all the skills of word attack so that he can evolve his own attack approach using those skills which seem most appropriate. For this reason, the effective elementary school reading program includes instruction in all word attack skills. Effective combined approaches do not develop by mere chance.

Chapter Glossary

Following are key word attack terms used in this chapter and in related professional material:

Word attack The process of identifying an unfamiliar word through one or a combination of techniques such as configuration, phonics, structural analysis, context clues, and the dictionary.

Phonics The application of phonetics, the science of speech sounds, to the teaching of reading. Phonics involves using knowledge of sound-symbol relationships to analyze words.

Configuration The shape or outline form of a word and the unique appearance of certain combinations of letters.

Structural analysis The analysis of a word according to meaningful structural units within the word, such as compounds, roots, prefixes, and suffixes.

Phoneme-grapheme relationship The relationship between a speech sound (phoneme) and its representation in print (grapheme).

Context clues Meaningful clues in the passage surrounding an unfamiliar word.

Closure Supplying the missing element in a sentence through knowledge of the rest of the sentence. Closure is closely tied to the use of context clues.

Consonant blend A combination of two or three consonants, such as *bl* in *blue* or the *spr* in *spring,* in which the letters retain their distinctive sounds.

Consonant digraph A combination of two consonants which represent one sound. For example, the *ch* in *chair* represents only one sound, and not a blend of the sounds usually associated with *c* and *h.*

Vowel digraph A combination of two letters which represent one sound, such as the *ea* in *each.*

Diphthong A combination of two consecutive vowels within one syllable in which both vowels are sounded, producing a blended sound. An example is the *oy* in *boy.*

Let us now examine each of the categories shown in table 3.

Ways of Attacking a Word

The area of word attack can be examined in detail by levels and categories. Table 3 serves as a quick reference to the overall area. Lines have been deliberately omitted between levels or between skills, in order to emphasize the interrelationship of the levels and the skills. Looking horizontally, the reader can grasp the entire content of the word attack at any level; vertically, he sees the progression from very early to advanced stages in the area of skill development being studied. Since table 3 is only a guide, it is obvious that children will not fall neatly into its classifications. They may well become especially interested in structural analysis, or in the dictionary, so that they actually develop skills in one area appropriate to Level D before developing other skills at Level B. Neither do children follow the outlined sequence within an area. A child may well learn to use clues for vowel sounds before he has developed skill in using consonants. Such individual learning characteristics are healthy and should be encouraged. In all cases, the teacher's role with any child is to know his strengths and weaknesses and to provide needed instruction.

TABLE 3 Ways of Attacking a Word

Level	Through Configuration	Through Context	Through Phonics	Through Structural Analysis	Through Dictionary Study
A	Visual Discrimination	Picture Clues Listening Closure	Auditory Discrimination	Oral Closure of Inflected Endings	Letter Names
B	Basic Sight Vocabulary	Reading Closure Context Clues	Consonants Initial Final Blends Digraphs Context and Phonic Clues	Inflected Endings Compound Words Contractions	Oral Definitions Alphabetical Order Location Skills in Dictionaries and Glossaries
C	Extended Sight Vocabulary	Review of Word Attack in Context Generalized Types of Context Clues	Vowels Long Short Digraphs Diphthongs Vowel Generalizations Syllabication	Prefixes Suffixes Structural Changes Root Words	Reading Skills in Dictionaries and Glossaries Use of Pronunciation Keys in Dictionaries and Glossaries Discrimination Among Multiple Entries
D	Advanced Sight Vocabulary	Systems for Using Configuration, Context, Phonics, Structural Analysis, and Dictionary Study			

Configuration

Starting with the skills of visual discrimination and moving through the development of reading sight vocabulary, configuration clues are useful in word attack. Remembering how unknown words look similar to and different from words which have previously been learned is a basic word attack skill. The larger the sight vocabulary, the more likely the child will be able to use configuration clues when he attempts to decode unfamiliar words. While many approaches to reading suggest the use of configuration as the basic initial tool in word attack, teachers have found that it is most useful when employed with other word attack skills. For example, if a child reads the sentence, "May I have a cup of c____?"—*coffee* being the unfamiliar word— he uses the general configuration plus context plus the initial letter in the word. Combining configuration with other word attack skills lessens the possibility of errors obtained by guessing.

Teachers find many opportunities to explain unusual configurations to children. Selected words taken from context (such as *look, see, Halloween,* and *February*) are frequently taught by having the child examine the peculiarities of the word. Generally the teacher will show the word, pronounce it, ask the children to look at it, and then pronounce it again. By calling attention to certain features of the word which are notable, the teacher assists the children in using configuration clues. An activity of this type is usually followed by reading selections in which the word, or words similar to it, are found.

Numerous opportunities also exist for teachers to help children recognize how words like *cat, bat,* and *sat;* or *ran* and *run;* or *car* and *can* are alike and how they are different. Attention to common endings or common word elements also helps the child to recognize small differences in words. By paying close attention to similarities and differences in words in initial instruction, the child is more likely to respond accurately to a word when he sees it again. By using the words in context, attention is drawn to how minimal changes in configuration change meaning as well as pronunciation.

Context

Awareness of the value of context clues is brought about at pre-reading levels when the teacher provides picture clues and listening closure situations to supply a missing word. It is natural for a child to attempt to complete the unfinished, using meaning clues to aid pronunciation. He tries to think about the words which he knows and about which word best completes the meaning and becomes aware of the language structure used. Context usage is also taught directly by showing children how authors provide obvious and helpful clues. Many authors use definitions, synonyms, or examples in order to communicate meanings when presenting new words or new concepts. For example, "An elephant is an *enormous* animal. It is very large." Teachers find it useful to help children search the pages for clues which the author has provided. As children become aware that these clues exist, they also become more skillful at using them. In certain types of books, particularly science and social studies texts, authors tend to provide explanations of technical terms which are being used for the first time. Synonyms, definitions, examples, and mood clues are meaning clues designed to assist the reader with difficult terms, but not necessarily with pronunciation. Once a term has been explained it is usually used without further explanation. Children need to become alert to such clues while reading, since missing them may make subsequent reading more difficult than necessary. One must keep in mind that like configuration, context clues may lead the child to unsupported guessing if used without the aid of other types of word attack skills.

Recently much has been written about the use of closure as a system for testing and for teaching comprehension skills. However, it lends itself to word attack in context as well. Most books designed for independent activities contain numerous closure exercises and the teacher can supplement these easily. For example, when introducing the new word *jungle* (which is needed for a lesson), the teacher writes on the board, "Tigers live in the _____." The children may be able to read the first four words; if not, the teacher reads them to the children. He attempts to use words which the children already know. Suggestions concerning the word that completes the sentence can be accepted, and when the word *jungle* is given, the teacher writes the word as the children watch. Closure activities are as appropriate for Level D as they are for Level B, but are best started orally in Level A and presented with printed sentences as soon as the child begins reading. An alternative to the type of closure used in the example above is for the word *jungle* to appear in print even though it is unknown. The technique is the same except that the word is already written. The teacher calls attention to the word, underlines it, and discusses it.

Several other types of context closure can also be used effectively.

The following is an example of forced-choice closure in a lesson on initial consonant sounds.

The dog had three little $\frac{\text{guppies}}{\text{puppies}}$.

The child should pick the correct word. An example of open-choice closure is a sentence such as,

The dog had three little _____.

In both cases, the clue comes from context. Several answers are possible in open-choice closure and more clues are needed for absolute accuracy. Partial closure is also helpful:

The dog had three little p_____.

Here the child uses the context and the first consonant to determine the missing word.

Exercises constructed using various types of closure are very useful because they stress word attack in context, which is the precise place where it should be stressed. With the aid of some elementary word attack techniques, the closure technique is not only valuable, but it is easy for the child to apply since it helps him concentrate on the part of the word stressed in word attack. One must be certain that the child is not discouraged by too many blanks or unknown words. He must have ample clues (known words) or the exercises quickly become too difficult. An illustration of the use of closure in many word attack situations is the set of materials prepared by Cynthia Dee Buchanan titled *Programmed Reading*.[1]

Phonics

Auditory discrimination taught in Level A is followed by phonics in Levels B and C. This extension of auditory discrimination is extremely important. At Level B in phonics, a child is usually working with consonants (initial consonant sounds, blends, digraphs, silent consonants, and medial and final consonant sounds). In some materials, authors advocate the teaching of vowels before consonants; however, the use of consonants before vowels is more common. Most likely, the child will learn some consonants and some vowels very early. As he works with initial consonant substitution, the child combines what he has learned at Level B about context clues with what he has learned in phonics to develop an effective technique for attacking unknown words. It is useful to present the initial consonants early and fairly rapidly in Level B. At the same time, some children need extensive experience with auditory and visual discrimination prior to developing phoneme-grapheme relationships. In such instances, teachers are not usually in a hurry to present the phonics content. At Level C the child moves into a study of vowel sounds. He studies long sounds, short sounds, *r* controlled vowels, vowel digraphs, and diphthongs. In addition to these, he learns generalizations and their exceptions concerning the situations that create long or short vowels, the division of words into syllables, and the relationship between syllabication and the pronunciation of words. At Level D the child combines all his phonic knowledge with other word attack skills into a system for attacking unknown words. Performance at Level D assumes that the child has learned effectively the content of phonics at Levels A, B, and C.

Most instruction in establishing a particular phonic learning follows this sequence:

- Developing the ability to hear the sound and distinguish it from other sounds.

- Developing an understanding of the phoneme-grapheme relationship.

- Presenting situations for application and overlearning.

One exercise in developing the ability to discriminate between sounds starts with the teacher's saying a word like *big* and asking the children to respond every time he says a word that starts the same way. For example, "Which of the following words begin like *big*? *Boat, bad, dog, butter, cat.*" A listening exercise follows in which the child listens for words beginning with *b* in context. (Discrimination activities suggested in chapter 5 can be reviewed for more ideas.)

Establishing a phoneme-grapheme relationship simply means that the child is taught to see the relationship of sound to print. Following the example just cited, the teacher concentrates on the letter *b* and tells the children that this is the letter that represents the sound heard at the beginning of *big, boat, bad,* and *butter.* Additional exercises through which the child firmly establishes this relationship usually follow. The teacher may ask the child to hold up a card with the letter *b* printed on it when he says a word that starts with that letter. Known words beginning with *b* can be written as children are asked to note how they are similar.

Another type of exercise begins with the teacher's placing several sentences on the board. Known words containing the letter *b* in the initial position have been underlined. The teacher and the children read the sentences. Then the teacher asks the children to read the sentences again—this time paying close attention to the sounds in the underlined words. After the reading the teacher asks, "How are all of the underlined words alike?" Children's responses tend to be that they all begin with *b* or they all begin with the same letter. The teacher can then show the letter card for *b* and provide contextual material so that children can find *b* words.

Many reading materials supply the teacher with a word chart for phonics. It is likely to have a key word for each sound accompanied by a picture clue for the sound. For example, *b* might have the word *boy* and a picture of a boy. Such a chart can be placed in the room for children to use as clues after instruction in a given sound.

Application exercises ideally follow these procedures. Now the children are placed in situations which call for the use of the phoneme-grapheme relationship awareness just developed. Sentences can be provided in which the child reads several words and then uses a combination of closure and phonics to complete them. For example, "The dog buried his b_____." or "The dog buried his
                                    bone
_one." or "The dog is burying his done." The point is for the child
                                    gone
to use his newly developed phonic skills to decode words in sentences.

Situations for use in overlearning are easily developed, but are often overlooked. Such activities are needed for those children who do not understand the learning when it is first presented. For example, a teacher can develop games using the sounds of the letters. He can also permit children to work in teams using exercises with letter sounds, and encourage them to find words that start with the new letters and then attempt to say them.

Because of the various sounds one vowel can have, additional complications arise when teaching vowel sounds. For example, clues to long and short vowel sounds are taught when the relationship is taught. In teaching the short sound of the letter *a*, the teacher may follow the steps above. Then, while looking at the words *cat, back, band,* and *can,* he helps the child to realize that each word contains one vowel followed by a consonant. When such a situation occurs, the child should attempt the sound of the short vowel first. Another short vowel is then taught, and the same generalization made. If approached in this manner, the child not only learns the sounds but also understands when the vowel is long or short. Three clues to the long sound of a vowel need to be taught as well: 1) a word or syllable ending in a vowel (*go, be/gin*), 2) a vowel digraph (*boat, meat*), and 3) a word ending in *e* preceded by a single consonant (*hope, ate*). In these situations, the child tries the long vowel sound first. The teacher explains that these generalizations are not absolute rules, for there are numerous exceptions. They are simply clues for starting word attack efforts. As the child learns sounds and generalizations, the teacher provides him with systems for using this knowledge.

After developing the ability to attack small words using his phonic skills, it becomes necessary for a child to develop skill in dividing longer words into syllables in order to be able to pronounce and decode them easily. He then applies the same phonic skills learned in connection with shorter words. When *picnic* becomes *pic/nic,* pronunciation is simplified. Since a vowel is followed by a consonant in each syllable, the child tries using the short sound first. For teachers who are not familiar with the various phonic and syllabication generalizations, the programmed exercises by Wilson and Hall can be consulted.[2]

Botel advocates the use of the discovery technique for teaching syllabication, in which children analyze specific visual clues as the basis for stating a generalization. He recommends the following steps:

1) Teacher provides accurate sensory experiences.

2) Students examine the structural pattern with teacher guidance.

3) Students collect words that fit the pattern.

4) Students and teacher generalize the pattern.[3]

Following is an example of this technique:

1) This teacher writes the known words on the board (*pencil, picnic, window, and index*) and asks the children to pronounce them. He may also ask the children how many syllables they hear.

2) The teacher directs the children to divide the words into syllables and to place a *v* above each vowel and a *c* above each consonant, starting with the first vowel and proceed-

   vc cv
   ing to the last. Example: *pen/cil.* He then asks specific questions about the number of consonants between the vowels.

3) The children collect words which fit this pattern.

4) The teacher helps the children develop the generalization that, in such situations, the word is usually divided between the two consonants.

Steps 3 and 4 can be interchanged without affecting the discovery technique (See Lesson Plan 3 p. 250, which illustrates the discovery technique.

Structural Analysis

Level B of structural analysis assumes that the child can clearly hear and orally supply the inflected endings which are needed for different sentence structures. For example, in Level A the teacher reads the sentences, 'Here is a girl. There are two _____." The child is expected to supply the missing word with the inflected ending which would also make the sentence linguistically correct. In Level B this idea is applied to reading situations where a child sees the difference between *girl* and *girls* in print. He relies upon his oral language experiences to read accurately. The study of the other common inflected endings, *ing, er, est, ed,* and *es* is also included, as well as initial instruction in the use of compound words and contractions. The content of Level B should be reinforced and continued in Level C, in addition to the study of common suffixes and prefixes and some study of base words. Starting in Level C and extending into Level D, structural word form changes are encountered. Doubling the final consonant and adding *ed* to *hop* to form *hopped* is one of these complicated changes. In Level D the child will be given opportunities for putting his knowledge of word structure into a system for independent word attack.

Structural elements such as root words, suffixes, prefixes, and compound words are important clues to word attack. The individual sounds of the parts are not as important, for these parts are often taught as whole pronounced units. In the case of a word having an inflected ending (*starting*), the child should see the ending *(ing)*, be able to remove it *(start-ing)*, pronounce the base word, and then add the ending and pronounce the full word *(starting)*. As children learn the common inflected endings *ing, ed, er, est, es,* their knowledge of words will expand rapidly. It is important for children to realize that the addition of suffixes to words often changes the spelling of base words *(hoping* equals *hope* plus *ing)*. A pattern approach and discovery procedure stressing visual clues are useful here. First, the teacher asks the children to read *hoping, writing,*

"Structural elements such as root words, suffixes, prefixes, and compound words are important clues to word attack."

and *making*, then to provide the base word of each *(hope, write,* and *make)*, and finally to determine how the base word was changed to add the inflected ending (the *e* was dropped before adding *ing*). The children can then learn to apply these structural generalizations when reading and spelling.

Suffix clues are often ignored since some children do not look closely at the endings of words. Inflected endings, a type of suffix, do not have specific meanings; rather, they change the function of the word. For example, adding *ing* to *run* forms the present participle *running*. Other types of suffixes such as *ful* and *ment* do carry meaning clues. Teachers ordinarily point out the difference between inflected endings and suffixes which carry meaning. Both carry important decoding clues.

Prefixes are easier to teach than suffixes because they occur at the beginning of words, carrying no change in the spelling of the base words, and because they usually have a precise meaning. In a typical activity for this subject, the teacher asks a child to use *happy* in a sentence and then to substitute the word *unhappy* for it in the same sentence. After listening to and looking at these two sentences, the child tries to find the difference between them. He isolates the words, and explains what *happy* and *unhappy* mean. The teacher finally asks him to define *un*. This activity is repeated with three or four different words until the child sees that *un* means *not*. Then the teacher goes on to another prefix, allowing occasionally for review of *un* along with other prefixes.

The ability to recognize and decode compound words is also a part of structural analysis. The child learns that for a word to be considered a compound, two complete words must be seen with both parts contributing to the meaning of the new word. Therefore, *father (fat her)* is not a compound word, nor is *together (to get her)*. Some children confuse the idea of compound words when they look for little words in bigger words. To see *cow* and *boy* in *cowboy* and *air* and *plane* in *airplane* is useful in identifying the compound words, but to see *to, get,* and *her* in *together* is not. The difference must be explained so that the children concentrate only on compounds for the purpose of determining pronunciation and meaning. Use of the discovery technique is recommended for study of compound words.

Contractions, another part of structural analysis, are used in the speech of children. Words such as *can't* and *don't* are more common than word combinations such as *cannot* and *do not*. Commercial materials are now using contractions where many of them previously used only stilted structures. Instruction starts with the use of contractions in simple sentences. Children are helped to generalize the meaning of the contracted form. Since contractions are common in their speech, such generalizations are easily developed. However, some children must be helped to realize that the contractions they use are abbreviated combinations of two words.

Dictionary Study

Dictionary study stresses the use of dictionaries to discover and/or check meaning, pronunciation, and spelling. As a child is learning letter names and learning to define words from context in Level A, he is in the readiness stages of working with dictionary skills. At Level B a child begins to become aware of alphabetical order. He uses his knowledge of the alphabet for the filing of word bank cards. This activity leads directly to the skills needed in dictionary work. Pupil-made and commercial picture dictionaries also permit early introduction of dictionary skills. The latter contains a picture definition for each word. If the child encounters the word *elevator* but does not know how the word is pronounced, he looks for the word and finds it next to a picture of an elevator. It is hoped that the picture clue will facilitate pronunciation of the unknown word. After locating words in picture dictionaries, the child progresses to books which have glossaries. Basic instruction concerning guide words, pronunciation keys, and multiple meanings is necessary. Most books that have glossaries include explanations for their use in the teacher's guide.

As the child moves on to Level D, he finds that word attack techniques often do not result in the identification of unfamiliar words. Instruction with elementary dictionaries is usually withheld until this time. The programmed publication titled *David Discovers the Dictionary,*[4] designed to help children use the dictionary, effectively provides detailed instruction and may be of help. At this point, the child is fairly independent of the teacher for word identification. He uses the study books that come with most dictionaries. They provide exercises in the use of the various features of the dictionary such as entries, guide words, and pronunciation keys. Using guide words for quick location of words on a page is a skill which depends upon refined alphabetical skills. To stress the use of guide words, the teacher can devise games and reward speed for location of a given word. Another item that needs to be stressed is the choice between multiple definitions of words in dictionaries. Teaching children to select the definition which fits the context which they are using is helpful because their most common error is to use the first entry and not look at others. When using a dictionary to determine how a given word is pronounced, the pronunciation keys are important aids. Directed instruction in the use of these keys and practice in using them with unknown words is an essential portion of dictionary instruction. Dictionary skills are reinforced if the child applies them when he comes to unknown words. As these skills improve, the teacher's help in spelling, pronunciation, and definition decreases.

ISSUES IN WORD ATTACK

There are probably more questions to be discussed in word attack than in any other aspect of reading. A study of them assists the teacher to consider each, to see advantages and limitations of different viewpoints, and to decide which stand to take. With some questions, teaching experience and exposure to various methods are necessary before making a decision. In any case, it is important for each teacher to be as informed as possible.

Is Balance Important in a Word Attack Program?

While most authorities in the field of reading stress the importance of balance in the word attack program, many teachers continue to place the major or entire emphasis on one or another of the word attack skills.

For example, some teachers place undue stress on configuration, particularly in beginning reading. In such cases the child must rely upon his memory for the configuration differences in words and finds it difficult to read any word which the teacher has not presented. Other teachers prefer to use picture and context clues as the major word attack skill in beginning reading. The child thinks about what he has read and tries to supply the unknown word through closure. Often, with a sentence such as "We had a big _____." the child is forced into a pure guessing situation if he uses context alone. Bond and Wagner state that "context clues are practically always used with other methods of word recognition. . . ."[5] Still other teachers believe that it is desirable to place the major stress on phonics. They present nearly all of the sounds before permitting a child to do much reading. However, since many English words cannot be understood completely through phonics, a child using only this system is not able to attack many unknown words. *Come, gone,* and *the* are but a few of the common words containing phonetic inconsistencies.

At present few authorities recommend one approach to word attack to the exclusion of the others. This is especially valid because the exact process that a given child uses is not known. For example, some children can hear sounds very well and blend them easily; to them phonics is useful. Others find it easy to use a combination of initial consonant substitution and context clues. Still others remember words from configuration with amazing accuracy. If a child is to develop his own system for attacking words, it is vital that teachers provide instruction in all aspects of word attack at the proper levels and permit the child to use those which are most effective for him.

Is the Synthetic or the Analytic Method Preferable
in Word Attack Instruction?

The teaching of word attack skills can be divided into two basic approaches, synthetic and analytic. The synthetic approach, popular with some teachers for a long time, calls for the teaching of sounds or word parts and then the building of these parts into whole words. *C-a-t* can be blended into the word *cat; un-happy* into the word *unhappy.* Such a system builds from parts to wholes. There are some basal reader programs that advocate synthetic instruction, and also several supplementary word attack programs that encourage teachers to approach reading from this viewpoint.

When using the analytic approach to word attack, the child first learns a core of sight words. For example, once several words which start with the letter *b* have been introduced, the teacher shows the children that these words begin alike. As they listen to the words and talk about them, the children usually are able to make generalizations about the sound of the letter *b* as it appears at the beginning of words. Soon thereafter they are encouraged to apply this generalization to new words and to use it as a part of their word attack techniques. The analytic approach starts with the whole word and centers on the parts being studied.

Both systems have their advantages and limitations. Following are some of the advantages of the synthetic approach:

- The sounds of some letters are easier to establish when presented in isolation. For example, some children may have trouble hearing the *t* sound in *toy,* but hear it well when isolated.

- As a rule, the synthetic programs are well structured and organized into a day-to-day sequence involving review and reinforcement.

- A child does not first become dependent upon the whole word memorization method. He learns from the beginning that the sounds of our language can be systematized, organized, and developed into a usable word attack technique.

- The synthetic approach can be merged with any other system the teacher is using. Programs of this type exist which do not require the teacher to have a complete knowledge of the skills being taught, but to simply follow the guide and provide the essential instruction. A basal reader or language experience program can be conducted at the same time with little interference.

Research shows that many children using the synthetic approach successfully learn to attack words independently. Reseach by *Sparks*[6], *Durrell*[7], *Wollman*[8], *Harris*[9], and *Chall*[10] would indicate that this is a satisfactory method for children to learn to attack words, to spell, to perform accurately in oral reading, and to read. A slightly different opinion is stated in a study by McDowell[11] which shows that children learn well by the synthetic approach in the first grade, but by the fourth grade, those children using the analytic approach are superior readers.

There is no synthetic approach presently advocated that does not acknowledge the need for the child to learn words at sight. Words such as *come, gone,* and *the* have to be learned at sight because they contain phonic irregularities. However, proponents of the synthetic approach usually prefer to withhold irregular words until the child has developed skill in attacking those that are regular.

The advantages of the analytic method are also many:

- Whole words are easier to learn than letter sounds because they have meaning.

- Many initial sounds (*b, d, g*) cannot be isolated without slight distortion. In isolation, *b* usually sounds like *buh,* but in *big* or *bad,* there is no *buh* sound. It is surely better to learn the word without distortion. In fact, many children have difficulty blending sounds which have first been learned in isolation, that is, saying *buh-ih-guh* for *big.*

- Dealing with whole words first helps a child concentrate on meaning as well as on pronunciation. Supporters of the analytic approach claim that getting meaning is the ultimate aim of reading and that instruction should start there.

- The analytic approach allows the learning to proceed from the whole to the part, that is, from the word to the sounds in it.

- A sound can be introduced whenever needed once a core of sight words has been established. In this way, the analytic approach is appropriate for all material designed to teach children to read.

Research to support the analytic approach is plentiful. Some examples are the studies by Miller[12], Gates[13] McDowell[14], and Tensuan[15]. Elaborate programs are also available for instruction with this approach. They are generally written with explicit directions which assist the inexperienced teacher. A teacher ideally introduces a principle when a child needs instruction, not only when a teacher's guide suggests it, and therefore he tries to keep informed about both the content of word attack and how to teach it.

The analytic approach is well suited to help children learn by guiding them to make generalizations and discover systems for independent word attack. These aspects tend to give it an advantage over the usual rote learning procedures used in the synthetic approach.

It is not uncommon to find children referred to reading clinics with decoding skills intact. They often feel that they are reading well; however, when called upon to discuss or interpret what they have read, they are completely baffled. Too long a period of synthetic word attack instruction introduced at too early a time in the school program is an important contributor to reading deficiencies. The opposite situation is also true—most children are referred with serious deficiencies in decoding words.

It is necessary to remember, however, that not all children respond to the analytic approach or to the synthetic. Therefore, the best procedure seems to be for the teacher to study the two methods and plan teaching techniques which will help him avoid the limitations of both. For example, when the teacher asks children to check their word attack attempts in context to determine whether their answers makes sense, meaning is stressed regardless of the approach.

Should Decoding or Comprehension Be Emphasized in Word Attack?

While the obvious answer is to teach both decoding and comprehension in word attack, it is not simple to practice. Most word attack drills stress decoding, but associating the written form with meaning is equally as important. It is not uncommon to find children attempting the decoding of a word that they have never heard. When they pronounce such a word, they have no clue as to whether they are correct, for the word is devoid of meaning.

Following are several suggestions to assist the teacher in making word attack a system for decoding while stressing meaning.

■ When initiating instruction in word attack, it is best to start with words in the child's listening or reading vocabularies.

In this way, the child can see from his previous knowledge what is being stressed, and he will not be preoccupied with the meaning of the word. When he completes the task, he will have pronounced a meaningful word, and he will know that he is correct and that he has learned something useful.

■ Teachers often use nonsense words to check a child's ability to decode. If the child has learned the ideas behind syllabication, he can follow directions such as "Divide *sogtep* into syllables." However, it is necessary for him to know that he is practicing with nonsense words. These words should not be used beyond such a practice period, since the ultimate aim of all reading activities is to help a child communicate with the author.

■ It is best to start a word attack exercise with the word in a sentence. If a child must take a word out of a sentence to attack it, he should return to the sentence to check the word for meaning. It is usually preferable to place a group of sentences on the board, rather than a list of words. When one approaches word attack in this manner, the children learn that thinking of the word in context helps them read for meaning more accurately.

■ The teacher can supplement activities suggested in teacher's guides by stressing the meaning of words in context, the meaning of word parts such as prefixes, and dictionary definitions.

■ When a child decodes a word but does not know what it means, it is important that he learn the meaning. The teacher can tell him or, if he knows how to use a dictionary, he can check the meaning there.

Because the ultimate objective of reading instruction is communication, the isolated decoding activity over an extended period of time is not recommended.

How Much Should a Teacher Tell Children?
How Much Should They Discover for Themselves?

Teachers frequently find themselves having to choose between telling children answers and letting them undertake the discovery by themselves. Such circumstances occur in both incidental and planned situations. Because no definitive choice is possible, both ideas deserve consideration.

A teacher can start a lesson by telling the children, "When you divide a word that has two consonants between two vowels, first try dividing between the consonants," and follow immediately with several examples:

$$vc\,/\,cv \quad vc\,/\,cv \quad vc\,/cv$$
$$pic\,/nic \quad win\,/dow \quad pen\,/cil$$

The children then practice the generalization with appropriate exercises. They can look in their books for words that fit it or fill out a work sheet which the teacher corrects to assess those faulty learnings that need to be retaught. The children are in the position of understanding the teacher's generalization and then putting it to use. On the whole, this procedure is easy and efficient for the teacher. However, for the pupils, the learning activity is often passive.

Many times the teacher finds that it is best to start with the discovery technique and to end by telling the children the objective if they are unable to complete the discovery accurately. In some cases, the children may not be able to state the appropriate generalization, and in order to provide accurate learning and to save time at this point, the teacher may tell them. Some children, however, have been told so often that it is difficult for them to assume the role of discoverers. In these situations, combinations of techniques are advisable.

It is common for a child to ask a teacher how to pronounce a word. Instead of telling him, the teacher can help with statements such as "You'll need a dictionary to attack that word, John." Or "Why don't you try to think about the word that might fit there, and remember it begins with the sound of 't' " (context clue plus initial consonant). Working with words in this manner provides an excellent chance of developing the habit of using previously learned word attack skills. There is also a good chance that a child will know the word when he encounters it again.

As the child assumes more and more responsibility for his own learning, there are more situations in which a teacher can help him discover meanings and generalizations. Discovery fosters active learning because the child is forced to think and to act. He is likely to remember a generalization he put in his own words, and because it is self-expressed, the teacher knows that it is understood and that the child is not merely parroting what he hears in class.

It is necessary for the teacher to remain alert to those situations which are best suited to self-discovery and those which are best suited to informing. Unfortunately, it is too common to see teachers laboring to help a child try to discover something which is not discoverable or which takes too long to discover, or something which the child is not yet ready to discover. When a teacher knows that a child has no means of attacking a word, he usually tells the child. There are times when a child comes to a word which he ought to be able to attack, but does not. If he is reading orally for the purpose of communication, it is not wise to ask him to sound it out or to look it up in the dictionary. Telling the child the word helps him communicate best in that particular situation. However, the teacher reintroduces that word in a word attack lesson and straightens out the problem then by analyzing the nature of the mistakes. He tries to find out if the word was new for that lesson, presented previously, missed by one child or by several members of the group, or completely foreign to the child's background of experiences. He then plans future instruction accordingly.

When informing a child of a word or word attack generalization, the teacher does not know whether the child knew or understood the generalization before he told him. Therefore, the type of activity that follows may be as important as the decision to tell the child. By using discovery techniques when they are appropriate and by giving children words when appropriate, optimal learning situations will result.

When Should Word Attack Be Taught?

Some teachers prefer to teach word attack in every reading lesson before the actual reading takes place. They feel that this system permits children to use the word attack technique in the reading that follows. Others prefer to teach the word attack skills after silent reading. By using words from the reading, the teacher helps the children understand the word patterns of the language with meaningful words. Other teachers do not like to teach word attack in connection with the reading lesson but at another time. They feel that reading lessons should stress discussion of the author's meaning. These teachers claim that there is often too much time spent on word attack drills rather than on reading and that children learn to attack words better as they read more.

No one answer is correct in this matter. In early reading, some of the lessons must provide vocabulary introduction and word attack instruction prior to reading. However, as children gain reading skills and can read on their own, it makes sense to have the word attack lesson after the reading. In the majority of cases, word attack lessons and drills can most effectively be conducted at a time separate from the reading lesson itself. Word attack can often be included in a spelling lesson where spelling aids are also stressed. Many teachers schedule a word attack period in conjunction with spelling.

An alert elementary school teacher will find numerous opportunities to provide word attack instruction within any subject area and whenever children need it to work successfully. By using all opportunities to stress the value of word attack, children see reading as a skill necessary for work in all other areas, not as a subject to be studied by itself. Opportunities also exist for grouping children according to their word attack skill strengths and weaknesses. For example, one group of children can work on their consonant sounds while another works on syllabication and another on vowel sounds. Such groupings have little relationship to reading grade level and are established only for the period of time that specific instruction is needed. In this way, the teacher can focus on actual reading, on discussion, and on the functional use of learned word attack.

How Can the Teacher Help Children Who Do Not Respond to Word Attack Lessons?

Every teacher has children in his class who do not respond to lessons in word attack. The reasons are many. The children may be inattentive, distracted, or confused by instruction which is too difficult. They may be bored because they already know what is being presented or because the teaching is poor. For the child who is not responding, the teacher uses diagnostic teaching techniques. He considers all possibilities and then makes adjustments accordingly.

Of special concern is the child who acts as though he is responding but is not. He sits quietly and says "yes" at the appropriate moment but is not really paying attention. Such children are hiding from learning and are able to do so because teachers have put them in completely passive learning situations. For use in phonics lessons, Durrell has developed an "every-pupil-response" technique which makes it possible for every pupil to respond during a teacher-directed learning situation.[16] Prior to a lesson, cards with the letters to be stressed are distributed to each child. For example, a child may have *b, c, s,* and *t* cards. The teacher asks the pupils to show the card which represents the first sound of words on a list which he reads. If a child is inattentive or unresponsive, he will not show the card, and can be easily identified by the teacher. The teacher can also notice when instruction appears to have been misunderstood and then adjust it. This system works with amazing efficiency and can be used with many adaptations in other subjects. When a child's response is observable by the teacher, the child tends to become more accurate and attentive as new learning is being presented.

Why Do Children Who Seem To Know Word Attack Skills Fail To Use Them with Unknown Words?

This question is asked by teachers and parents alike. It is clear that if a child knows word attack skills but fails to use them, learning has not been complete. Many children come to reading clinics with knowledge of letter sounds and a list of rules but cannot apply them. This is due mainly to the teaching of word attack without giving the children systems for its use. Direct teaching of word attack does not stop with the development of sound-letter associations and the learning of generalizations. Provision needs to be made for application in situations similar to those a child meets when he sees an unfamiliar word in reading.

While it is desirable for every child to develop his own system of word attack, there is a need for them to start with efficient systems from which modifications can be made according to their needs. For example, if children already know that there are as many syllables in a word as there are vowel sounds, it is necessary to develop a system for determining the number of syllables in a word.

- First, the teacher asks the child how many vowels are in the word.

- He counts them and perhaps even marks them.

- Then he asks how many vowel sounds there are and whether any situation exists that would cause a vowel to be silent.

- Next the teacher asks, "If there are ＿＿＿ vowel sounds, how many syllables are there?" The child has a system for using the generalization. From such an introduction, personal modifications can be made to develop efficient word attack usage.

Systems of word attack depend upon the child's ability to use visual clues to aid him with pronunciation, that is, to see letter combinations and patterns which signify particular generalizations and then accurately apply them. The alert child learns to shortcut this technique very rapidly, but it is best to provide him with the steps of the most accurate procedure so that he can continue from there.

Is Phonic Learning of Value in Attacking Most Words?

Several years ago, when Clymer presented the results of research concerning the utility of phonic generalizations which are taught in the various basal programs in the primary grades,[17] he seriously questioned the idea of teaching rules which have little utility and nomenclature which appears to have little value. Subsequently, both Emans[18] and Bailey[19] examined the utility of phonics in grades one through six and arrived at about the same conclusions. Before embarking on a program of phonic instruction, it is helpful to examine these sources closely.

While these studies caution us about the pitfalls of teaching rules, many word attack generalizations are useful when worded accurately and when viewed as part of a system that always ends in checking for accuracy in context. For example, the generalization stating that small words ending in a silent *e* usually have a first long vowel is now held in disrepute. However, other generalizations are usually helpful, such as the one which maintains that a final *e* affects the vowel sound when it is preceded by a single consonant. When the final *e* is preceded by two or more consonants, the preceding vowel is short (*fence, fringe*). Words such as *gone* and *come* are exceptions and have to be learned at sight and checked for contextual sense when attacked.

The well-advised teacher instructs children that generalizations usually work but are not always applicable. In the above example, he would suggest that the children try the long sound of the vowel first. If it does not give the correct pronunciation, then the short sound is probably the right one. Such directed efforts are better than pure guesses.

Can Modified Initial Approaches to Reading Help Children Attack Words More Effectively?

Since the English language does not have a one-to-one relationship between the phonemes and their graphemic representations, phonetic attack of certain words becomes complicated. For example, in the word *come* the *c*, the *m*, and the final *e* are phonetically consistent, but the sound of *o* is neither long or short. In *great*, the *gr* and the *t* are regular, but the *ea* combination is not. As a result, such words are usually introduced as sight words and are accompanied by special explanations. Some sounds are represented by more than one letter, such as the *j* sound in *jump* and *giraffe*. Some letters may have several sounds, as in *ate, at, father,* and *far*.

One answer to such confusion is to develop a system which will clue the child to the sound of any letter in some artificial manner. The Initial Teaching Alphabet does this by presenting a different letter for the forty-four major sounds. In ITA *ate* appears as *æt*, *hate* as *hæt*, and *fate* is *fæt*. There is no spelling change in words such as *at, hat,* or *fat*. As the child gains skill in reading and writing with ITA, he is gradually transferred to the traditional alphabet with its confusions. The idea, of course, is to make the initial teaching as consistent and easy as possible. Other alphabet revisions have likewise been tried. Research on the effectiveness of such altered alphabet systems is conflicting. Studies by Fry[20] and Hayes[21] show that they do not help children learn to read better. However, studies by Chall[22] and Mazurkiewicz[23] indicate that children do learn better with these techniques. Ohanian suggests that factors other than alphabet modification could be causing research confusion in ITA studies.[24]

Linguists have also attempted to provide regularity between sound and symbol by controlling the words which the child first reads. For example, all of the short vowel spelling patterns would be introduced first. Others have attempted to color-code the sounds with each phoneme represented by a designated color, regardless of the grapheme used to represent the phoneme. Still others have attempted to mark the words diacritically.

Although the systems differ, each attempts to help the child as he first encounters the confusions of English. It is important that teachers keep an open mind toward these systems, examining both pro and con studies carefully. Learning to read is a long-term process and before adopting major changes in systems, all possible long-range effects of such systems ought to be considered. If an alphabet system in initial reading produces a better reader by the time a child is in the fifth or sixth grade, then favorable reactions are probably warranted. If, however, a child becomes confused by learning two systems, such special efforts are wasted.

Chapter Review

Of the many techniques for word attack that have been developed, no one stands out as being adequate for all children at all times. Children's abilities are quite varied—some respond to context clues, others to phonetic clues, and still others to structural clues. The same children may respond better to one type of clue in one grade and to another the following year. Also, some types of clues are helpful with one type of word problem and other types with other word problems. The best approach to word attack seems to be an introduction of all the basic kinds of attack. Each child can assimilate them according to his abilities, add new techniques he has invented, and eventually develop his own system of word attack. The goal is to have each child learn to successfully rely upon himself rather than upon the teacher when he encounters difficulty with words. This type of independence in word attack leads to independence in reading.

NOTES

[1] Cynthia Dee Buchanan, *Programmed Reading* (St. Louis: Sullivan Associates, McGraw-Hill, Webster Division, 1963).

[2] Robert M. Wilson and MaryAnne Hall, *Programmed Word Attack for Teachers* (Columbus: Charles E. Merrill, 1968).

[3] Morton Botel, *How To Teach Reading* (Chicago: Follett, 1963), pp. 40–43.

[4] *David Discovers the Dictionary* (Tempe, Arizona: Learning Incorporated, 1963).

[5] Guy L. Bond and Eva Bond Wagner, *Teaching the Child To Read* (New York: Macmillan, 1960), p. 138.

[6] Paul E. Sparks and Leo C. Fay, "An Evaluation of Two Methods of Teaching Reading," *Elementary School Journal* 58 (April 1957): 386–90.

[7] Donald D. Durrell, et al., "First Grade Reading Success Study: A Summary," *Journal of Education* 140 (February 1958): 1–48.

[8] Walter A. Wollman, "A Comparison of Two Methods of Teaching Reading," Ph.D. dissertation, Western Reserve University, 1961.

[9] Theodore L. Harris, "Some Issues in Beginning Reading Instruction," *Journal of Educational Research* 56 (September 1962): 5–19.

[10] Jeanne Chall, *Learning To Read—The Great Debate* (New York: McGraw-Hill, 1967).

[11] Rev. John B. McDowell, "A Report on the Phonetic Method of Teaching Children to Read," *Catholic Education Review* 51 (October 1953): 506–519.

[12] Donald L. Cleland and Harry B. Miller, "Instruction in Phonics and Success in Beginning Reading," *Elementary School Journal* 65 (February 1965): 278–282.

[13] Arthur I. Gates and David H. Russell, "Types of Materials, Vocabulary Burden, Word Analysis, and Other Factors in Beginning, Part II," *Elementary School Journal* 39 (October 1938): 119–128.

[14] McDowell, "A Report on the Phonetic Method."

[15] Emperatriz S. Tensuan and Frederick B. Davis, "An Experiment with Two Methods of Teaching Reading," *The Reading Teacher* 18 (October 1964): 8–15.

[16] Donald D. Durrell and Helen A. Murphy, *Speech-to-Print Phonics* (New York: Harcourt Brace Jovanovich, 1964).

[17] Theodore Clymer, "The Utility of Phonic Generalization in the Primary Grades," *The Reading Teacher* 16 (January 1963): 252–258.

[18] Robert Emans, "The Usefulness of Phonic Generalizations Above the Primary Grades," *The Reading Teacher* 20 (February 1967): 419–425.

[19] Mildred H. Bailey, "The Utility of Phonic Generalizations in Grades One Through Six," *The Reading Teacher* 20 (February 1967): 413–418.

[20] Edward B. Fry, "First Grade Reading Instruction Using Diacritical Marking System, Initial Teaching Alphabet, and Basal Reading System—Extended to Second Grade," *The Reading Teacher* 20 (May 1967): 687–693.

[21] Robert B. Hayes and Richard C. Wuest, "ITA and Three Other Approaches to Reading in the First Grade—Extended into Second Grade," *The Reading Teacher* 20 (May 1967): 694–697.

[22] Chall, *Learning To Read.*

[23] Albert J. Mazurkiewicz, *The Initial Teaching Alphabet in Reading Instruction,* Fund for the Advancement of Education (February 1967).

[24] Vera Ohanian, "Control Population in i/t/a Experiments," *Elementary English* 43 (April 1966): 373–380.

SUGGESTED ACTIVITIES

1. Read Lesson Plans 2 and 3 in chapter 11. Develop one plan for teaching letter-sound association and another for following the discovery procedure. Use any materials which you prefer.
2. Prepare for a class discussion on Jeanne Chall's book, *Learning To Read—The Great Debate.*

3. Observe a word attack lesson in a second or third grade. Which elements of the lesson would you keep and which would you change?
4. Take the test at the end of *Programmed Word Attack for Teachers* (see Suggested Readings). If the questions present difficulty, study the contents of the book.

SUGGESTED READINGS

Botel, Morton. *How To Teach Reading.* Chicago: Follet, 1963.

A brief review of the most common word attack content is presented along with a carefully prepared explanation of the discovery technique. Lists of useful words with examples for the various concepts are also included.

Chall, Jeanne. *Learning To Read—The Great Debate.* New York: Mc-Graw-Hill, 1967.

An extensive review of research on decoding in learning to read and recommendations for current reading programs are major concerns in this book. Chall presents a strong claim, based on her survey of available research, for the early introduction of phonics in a systematic manner.

Dechant, Emerald V. *Improving the Teaching of Reading.* Englewood Cliffs: Prentice-Hall, 1964.

Especially valuable is the detailed account of word attack instruction with an emphasis on the philosophy of the topic.

Heilman, Arthur. *Phonics in Proper Perspective.* Columbus: Charles E. Merrill, 1968.

Presents the major theories of phonics instruction with specific teaching suggestions and word lists.

Spache, George D. and Spache, Evelyn B. *Reading in the Elementary School.* Boston: Allyn and Bacon, 1969.

See chapter 12, for an accurate review of the literature and research on word attack and for the authors' fully developed system for attacking words from an experience and research base.

Wilson, Robert M. and Hall, MaryAnne. *Programmed Word Attack for Teachers.* Columbus: Charles E. Merrill, 1968.

Designed for the teacher who needs a review of word attack, this book is programmed for self-administration and self-correction.

CHAPTER EIGHT

COMPREHENSION AND THE THINKING PROCESS

Advance Organizer

Just as language provides the means for reading, so thinking itself is basic to all reading activity. This chapter, drawing from recent theory and research in thinking, establishes a conceptual framework for viewing the types of thinking that occur during reading. From a discussion of three levels of thinking and four stages of reading comprehension, the chapter moves to suggest how the elementary reading teacher can use these general categories as guides to the selection of specific instructional strategies. Certain universal elements in comprehension are also treated. Throughout, comprehension is viewed as an active process, involving the reader, the material to be read, and the interaction between the two.

READING AND THINKING

Along with decoding, one of the requisite steps in all reading activity is good comprehension. It is a basic expectation of teachers and a likely topic in conversations with parents. But what is good comprehension? What skills must a child use in order to attain it?

"The child who comprehends is mentally active, anticipating, and thoughtful."

What processes does a teacher employ in order to help children comprehend better? A glance at some tests which reportedly measure
comprehension might lead one to believe that good comprehension
involves the reading of certain material followed by a quiz on
details and specifically stated facts remembered from the reading.
Or one might listen to teachers checking comprehension orally
after a reading exercise and conclude that good comprehension
involves how well children remember sequences and reiterate de-

tails. Clearly, to understand how a child comprehends, a teacher must first understand how a child thinks, for comprehension cannot occur without thinking. The child who comprehends is mentally active, anticipating, and thoughtful. The better a teacher understands how children think and how thinking skills develop, the better he effects the teaching of comprehension. But what is the actual relationship between thinking and comprehending? Schindler has noted that "thinking during reading varies with purpose and materials."[1] Stauffer has gone so far as to suggest that "reading may be an obstacle to thinking" in addition to its possibilities for developing habits of clear thinking.[2]

Three Levels of Thinking

A theoretical hierarchy of thinking skills has emerged from educational research during the past two decades, as authorities such as Stauffer, Russell, Bloom, and Sanders have written extensively in the area. For the following discussion, we have developed three levels of thinking as they can be applied to reading, drawing from the thinking of these four writers.[3] Table 4 illustrates these three levels, together with four stages of reading activity which we shall discuss subsequently.

TABLE 4   A Reading Comprehension Framework

		Stage of Reading Activity			
		1 Oral Language	2 Easy Reading	3 Instructional Reading	4 Independent Reading
Level of Thinking	1 Literal Under- standing		Carla ⟶		
	2 Interpretation		↓	↑	
	3 Problem Solv- ing		⟵——Mike		

Using the framework in table 4, an example of instructional adjustment is easily illustrated. If Mike, or Mike's reading group, has been given an activity at level 3 in rather difficult material and cannot respond, the teacher has two options: 1) to stay in difficult material and move back to level 2, or 2) to stay with problem solving and move to easier reading. On the other hand, Carla or her group may be responding well in level 1 to simple material. The teacher can now move Carla either to level 2 or to stage 3 with material for instructional reading.

Using such a framework, the teacher can adjust instruction in comprehension in a logical, systematic manner.

Level 1: Literal Understanding of the Author's Message As a child receives a message, through either reading or listening, his first thinking task is to understand the message literally. This level involves the understanding of specific details, the awareness of sequences, and a feeling for the general tone and setting of the message. Most teachers spend large quantities of time helping children become proficient at this level.

Questions which trigger literal understanding are easily constructed and evaluated. Appropriate types of questions include:

- What was the boy's name?

- How old was the boy?

- What did the boy do after the policeman chased him?

- Did the story happen in the summer or in the winter?

The child's response requires little more than remembering the words and ideas of the author.

Level 2: Interpretation of the Author's Message in Terms of Self At level 2, the reader can place the author's ideas into a perspective based on already developed concepts. Here, perhaps, the most common type of thinking activity results in paraphrasing, which requires a child to recast a message he has received into his own words, reflecting his interpretation of the message. Another type of interpretation involves understanding the main ideas of the speaker or writer and noting the relative importance of them. Also to be considered are the pupil's interpretation of the reading in the light of his experiences, and his ability to associate them with what has been said. Finally, interpretation involves the ability to make predictions, to estimate, and to determine implications inherent in the message.

Proceeding from level 1 to level 2, we move to a type of thinking generated by carefully thought-out questions which may not call for one correct answer. Although teachers generally provide fewer opportunities to develop thinking and comprehension at level 2 than at level 1, thinking in terms of one's own experiences must certainly become an integral part of the reading process if communication is to take place. The following are types of questions appropriate for this level:

- In your own words, tell what is meant when the author says . . .

- What would be a good title for this story?

- How did the story make you feel?

- Summarize the events on page 3.

Level 3: Problem Solving Problem solving includes the higher-order thinking skills. At this level a child applies what he is able to think about in levels 1 and 2 to solving a problem. In other words, he can use the information he has obtained in order to get results as he approaches unique situations. Problem solving includes the child's ability to think in an analytical way so that he can grasp an idea, establish criteria against which the idea can be evaluated, test that idea, and come to a conclusion. This conclusion then can be retested, reevaluated, and reconsidered; it is not an end in itself. The reader sees the organization of the author, restructures it, perhaps tests one author against others, and compares this view with his previous knowledge of the problem. After he tests what the author has said against his own experiences, he reacts to the printed message. He is setting up a dialogue with the author: he is accepting, challenging, rejecting, and thinking reflectively and critically.

A second aspect of problem solving involves creating solutions through divergent thinking. Here, a child starts with an idea and radiates his thinking to many possible solutions, each of which may be accurate. To think creatively in reading, therefore, the reader must go beyond the words of the author. He is on his own as he creates and stretches his mind in a desirable manner and as he formulates ideas. That comparatively few opportunities for creative thinking are made available to children is unfortunate. That creativity is often stifled because many teachers always ask questions for which they have the correct answer in mind is also unfortunate. That no other solution or answer is accepted as correct, regardless of its merit, is tragic. Suggested questions are:

- If you had been in that situation, what would you have done? (creative)

- How could what you have just read be applied to our problem of . . . ? (critical)

■ Can you find a source which disagrees with the article you just read? (critical)

■ Write a different ending for the story. (creative)

As we have noted, the types of thinking necessary for interpretation and for problem solving are encouraged far less often than the type needed for literal understanding. Yet every reading class, regardless of grade, provides teachers with many opportunities for questions and activities which promote thinking in each level. It is suggested, in fact, that teachers plan their lessons to provide activities which require children to use their capacity for operating at each thinking level.

As one reflects on the three levels of thinking, it becomes clear that a child moves from a relatively low level, literal understanding, to very high levels of thinking culminating with creative thinking. Although literal understanding is a lower-order thinking skill, it is vital for it provides the base for all other thinking. Interpretation is also vitally important, for the reader's ability to interpret the author's message and relate that message to his own experiences establishes the first essential of true communication through reading and sets the scene for problem solving. Another way to conceptualize these levels is to view literal understanding as a type of thinking which involves the ability to obtain a message accurately; to view interpretation as involving the ability to take that message and relate it to one's own experiences; and to view problem solving as using both levels 1 and 2 either critically or creatively in an application situation.

Certainly these types of thinking do not in actuality fit snugly into three distinct categories. Teachers will encounter situations in which it is difficult to distinguish one phase from another. When a child is making predictions in level 2, for example, he is very close to a problem solving task. For the most part, however, classifying thinking into three levels helps the teacher provide specific activities in all types of thinking through a balanced program.

Four Stages of Reading Comprehension

Let us now consider some key techniques which help children relate the thinking skills discussed here to the author's messages obtained from the printed page. The bridge from thinking to independence in reading comprehension may be viewed as a four-stage process:

1) thinking based upon oral discussion appropriate to the child's point of reference;

2) thinking based upon printed material at very easy levels;

3) thinking based upon printed material at the child's instructional level;

4) the type of thinking determined by printed selections which the child uses independently.

We shall consider each stage in turn.

Stage 1: Thinking and Oral Language The best way to involve a child in thinking situations is in terms of his point of reference, that is, when he has enough information about and experience with a topic to handle a discussion at any of the levels—literal understanding, interpretation, and problem solving. Even preschool children can and do think at all these levels. Refining and developing thinking skills can be carried out from the very beginning of the child's formal schooling by using situations in the room, community, or school with which children have had experience (or even by providing experiences at times) and then discussing them through listening and speaking activities. For example, a fifth grade class may be asked to develop rules of classroom conduct which will protect the right of other students to study. Based upon four years of schooling, most students will quickly formulate reasonable rules for classroom behavior, and will probably be more willing to follow the rules when they are developed in this manner. In stage 1 thinking activities start with the experiences of children, not with printed passages.

Stage 2: Thinking and Easy Reading After a child develops skill in the type of thinking used in stage 1, he is ready to be placed in situations where he can do the same type of thinking using the printed page as his source of information. Naturally, at this stage of the process, there is no desire to have him frustrated by the printed page. He should simply be engaged in thinking based upon printed material at an easy level. In other words, it is best for him not to encounter words he does not know and concepts he does not understand. The main idea is to have as little confusion from the printed page as possible.

Two things have changed in passing from stage 1 to stage 2. First, the child decodes the printed word and puts it into speech so that he can think about it. Secondly, the child relates to another person's ideas. He may or may not be able to make the associations the author hopes he will make. Therefore in stage 2, the teacher presents the same type of thinking developed in stage 1, but through relatively easy material in order to minimize the difference between a listening-speaking activity and an easy reading activity. In other words, the reading and the printed material do not interfere with the child's knowledge of how to think when purposes are set.

A natural technique for the transition from oral discussion to thinking based upon easy material is the language experience approach. Concept load difficulties are avoided inasmuch as children use their own oral language, based upon experiences, for the written material. Interference due to difficult words is also reduced because children find their own stories easy to decode. This approach is useful in situations where children find the printed word interfering with their thinking.

In stage 2 it is especially important for the teacher to help children understand the purposes of their reading and to motivate them so that there is interest in the reading task before them. It is helpful to form the purposes of reading in terms of the phase of thinking the teacher wants the children to do in their comprehension exercises.

When the teacher sets purposes prior to reading, he is, in fact, directing the children's attention so that they practice a specific type of thinking—thus, the term *directed reading activity.*

If the teacher wants to stress thinking that involves literal understanding, he states the purposes in reference to that type of thinking. For example:

- Reread the story to find a specific fact.

- Read the story and tell what happened after . . . .

- What reason does the author give for . . . ?

On the other hand, if the teacher is asking the children to read to make interpretations in light of their own experiences, the purposes for which they read are different. Some examples are:

- Read the story and write a brief summary of the major points.

- After reading the story, divide it into three parts which might make three scenes for a television program.

- After reading this story, tell in your own words what the author is trying to say to you.

When the purposes are set for problem solving, the teacher poses a problem. The children then apply their thinking skills to it, using the printed page. Several examples follow:

- In this story Joe is trying to solve a problem. After reading the story, let's decide whether Joe was wise in making the decision he did.

- After reading this story, compare what the people did with what the people in our city do. If they are different, try to decide which behavior is better.

- After reading this story, find three occasions when you think John broke the law.

Purpose-setting helps the children gear their thinking to a certain type of comprehension activity and therefore contributes to their becoming active, anticipating, thoughtful readers. Each child learns to react to his reading reflectively in terms of the purposes the teacher and/or pupils set originally.

Many activities can be planned to reinforce reading comprehension. Some suggestions designed to involve literal understanding include:

- Relate the facts of the story to a discussion in another subject.

- Draw a picture to show the sequence of events.

- Use recall exercises two or three days after the story to develop long-term recall techniques.

Examples of activities to follow reading for interpretation in terms of one's own experiences are:

- Ask children to draw pictures of their interpretation of the main character, the main scene, or a specific scene in the story.

- Ask children to present a brief oral report of an interesting book they have read.

- Help children learn to write brief, concise summaries of materials read.

Activities following reading for problem solving can include:

- A group of children present a play from a story they have read, using their own words instead of referring to the book.

- Compare a book from another subject with a book now being read.

- Help the children write brief stories or books after reading a certain type of literature (tall tales, for example).

After the children have read, thinking about the purposes that have been set for them or which they set for themselves, they respond, demonstrating either ability or inability to think in terms of the author's message. In thinking activities that follow reading, the child is very close to stage 1 in developing thinking skills. At this point he will discuss or attempt to discuss the printed page in terms of a common frame of reference. The teacher then proceeds as he did during the discussion stage (stage 1) of developing thinking. For children who cannot respond, he establishes experiences or relates the author's ideas to experiences the children can understand; that is, he reestablishes each child's thinking skills at a lower level of thinking. This may be necessary if the teacher has required too high a thinking level, or if the children were not successful at a lower level of thinking. In any case, the teacher has conducted a lesson in which the children have 1) been helped to establish purposes for their reading, 2) read thoughtfully and meaningfully, and 3) responded to the purposes for which they read.

Stage 3: Thinking and Instructional Reading   At this point, it is desirable to encourage thinking based upon printed material designed for the child's instructional level. The teacher first introduced thinking through easy material and now goes ahead with opportunities for thinking activities in more difficult material. As we discussed before, the difference between oral discussion and thinking while reading is twofold. First, in thinking as he reads, a child has to decode print; then he works with the ideas of the author. A child encounters more difficulty on the printed page in stage 3 than in stage 2. He is able to decode the print but may find some words that are not as familiar to him as those in the easier material. However, the teacher attempts to keep him from the extremely difficult task of going through complicated word attack techniques for numerous words while he is trying to think. Providing the child with material that is too difficult can create serious comprehension problems because he focuses all his attention on attacking words rather than on thinking about what he has read.

Now the children have progressed from discussing concrete, real experiences, to thinking while reading on a relatively easy level, to thinking with the author at advanced levels. For example, at an easy level, an author tells a story about a boy and his dog and about how the dog saves the boy from a dangerous situation. Reading this story may cause children to think of experiences they have had, not necessarily in a dangerous situation, but with a dog they have seen or owned. As they move to more difficult stages of thinking activities, the children will need to struggle a bit. If the message involves history, they have to imagine the situation from what the author has said. They must make inferences and hypotheses. Because they have not ridden horses in full armor, the children can only grasp this concept of the Crusades through their imaginations. They are going to have to use a considerable amount of mental energy and all their thinking skills in a very challenging manner. Teachers can help by providing background information to assist the children at this stage.

Certain special considerations need attention in stage 3. It is not advisable to put any child in a frustrating situation for a long period of time. However, challenging the child, as opposed to frustrating him, stretches the mind. The teacher must help him stretch and reach out in his thinking toward realistic objectives. To this end the teacher can create the types of activities that the child can achieve with some mental stretching. He can place the child in many situations in which thinking is done rather easily, as in stage 2, and also in occasional situations where he cannot achieve and where he realizes that there will be learning explorations for him in the future. Learning must be made challenging, but also enjoyable and successful at the same time.

Another important point for the teacher to consider is that all children do not have to read the same material in order to be involved in the same discussion. Suppose that the teacher picks a story about the world series for several children to read. Others in the class can read similar baseball stories at both easy and difficult levels. They all can bring to the discussion their own interpretation of the authors' ideas. In this way, the children gain the ability to compare one author with another, to react critically to each other's thinking about the authors, and to do some problem solving. Also advantageous is the fact that the poorer readers participate in the same discussion as the better readers. Often a child who cannot read well is a good thinker, and is very receptive to teaching through this type of activity. Therefore, if the child can think, he ought to be permitted to engage in thinking activities with all types of readers.

Stage 4: Thinking and Independent Reading Developing independence in comprehension is the ultimate objective in developing a child's thinking reactions to print. From the very beginning, the teacher stresses ways to help children move from reliance upon him to independence in reading activities. For example, he guides a child to select materials which interest him and to become aware of self-motivating techniques, such as glancing through a story, looking at pictures, reading captions, changing statements that he sees into questions, and contemplating what is going to happen. The child learns to ask himself, "Why did the author write this story?" "What does he have to say to me?" "How does what he is saying compare with what I've read on this topic previously?" Provided that the teacher has helped him develop the necessary skills in stages 1, 2, and 3, the next step for the child is to set his own purposes and then read. The teacher can reinforce independent reading even after the child has experience in it by aiding him with difficult passages or ideas. Following are several suggested activities that help children to develop independent comprehension skills at various levels:

- A group of children discuss their reading without teacher involvement in setting goals or in reacting to the discussion.

- Children prepare summaries of what they have read in notebooks which the teacher does not evaluate.

- Children in groups formed on an interest basis help each other learn within the area of interest.

- Paired children can tell each other the exciting parts of a story they have just read. No teacher evaluation is necessary.

- Children voluntarily develop displays of books they have read. Such displays are not evaluated by the teacher.

Thus, we have seen that the teacher has two basic considerations in mind: the level of thinking and the stage of comprehension in which the child is working. If the teacher places a child in a situation in which he does not respond, there are two opportunities to adjust instruction. One is to reduce the level of thinking to a simpler form—for example, from problem solving to interpretation. The other is to move down a stage or two in the type of activity involving the material being used. In these ways a teacher always has alternatives for adjusting instruction for children who do not respond.

UNIVERSAL ELEMENTS IN COMPREHENSION

Not only are the levels of thinking and the stages of comprehension interrelated and difficult to divide, but certain other factors cut across all levels of comprehension and instruction. They include memory, motivation, and length of material, and must be considered in all aspects of reading instruction.

Memory

A child with a good memory can operate better in thinking activities than a child who has difficulty remembering what somebody has said to him or what an author has tried to communicate to him through print. Clearly, if the child cannot remember what he has read, he cannot possibly make interpretations or solve problems based upon those passages. Since forgetting starts immediately, the later the discussion activity or the comprehension exercises follow the actual reading, the more possibility there is that forgetting will become a factor in the child's ability to think about what he has read. It seems logical then, for the teacher to start comprehension activities immediately after the reading in the initial stages of teaching. In this way he will place forgetting in a minimal position. Once a child can make appropriate responses immediately after reading, the teacher helps him develop the idea that memory is important by holding a discussion an hour later and one the next day, and by relating it to a discussion from the past week.

It may help the teacher to recall that once a child has learned to respond, he never completely forgets. When considering the problem of whether forgetting really occurs, Bugelski states, "The fact that we cannot recall material does not prove that it is completely gone or that it had no effects upon us."[4] Although it may appear that the child has completely forgotten what has been taught, the information can be retaught or recalled much more easily the second time. Through reteaching, more permanent impressions can be made on the memory banks. Bugelski maintains that all learning is stored in the brain and that proper stimulation is needed to revive it.[5]

Memory can be enhanced in three basically different ways:

1) *Impact* If an event has impact, we are very likely to remember it. The memories are there, and we can recall at will. Other activities which might have been as important but which did not have as great an impact are more difficult to recall. With help or in a similar situation, those memories sometimes return. Even if this is not the case, a new situation is easier to handle because of the previous experience in one similar to it.

2) *Recency* Another factor that affects memory is the recency of the learning. We remember things that happened last week better than those that happened last month; and we remember the latter better than events of last year. For example, there are probably complete years in a person's early life which he cannot recall at will. He may not remember anything that happened in second grade. However, he can probably remember many things that happened in his senior year in high school. Forgetting starts immediately after learning, and the more time that lapses after the occurrence of events, the more a person tends to forget them.

3) *Repetition* The greater the number of times we encounter a certain type activity, the greater the possibility is that we remember it. Repetition makes a strong impression upon our memory banks. There are probably many things we remember that did not have a great impact upon us or are not particularly recent, but which we remember basically because of repetition. For example, most men remember their service serial number for the rest of their lives because they had to use it again and again. Teachers often rely on repetition for teaching and helping children to remember. Repetition activities which call for the use of the new learning are usually more effective than those which call for rote drill. The child is more interested and impact is added at the same time as repetition. In reading, some teachers feel that repetition in and of itself is needed for a child to learn new skills. It would seem, however, that a combination of the three factors of impact, repetition, and recency is necessary for satisfactory recall at a later date.

Motivation

Running through each level of thinking and stage of reading comprehension is motivation. Opportunities to evaluate the child's interest and attitude toward his reading are necessary. In a study of reading attitudes, Healy found that "favorable attitudes produce significant achievement and more reading."[6] A child who reads without interest or with a poor attitude is in serious difficulty. Initially, teachers attempt to create interest and attitude through their own enthusiasm, by relating what is read and thought about to the child's previous experiences, by providing the child with stimulating material, by placing each child at a reading stage he can handle without extreme difficulty, and by caring about children themselves. It is expected that a child's interests increase in some areas and wane in others. However, the child who remains interested in school in general is the child who is successful in school. The child who loses interest in school may be suffering from boredom, lack of purpose, or constant frustration from the activities he is expected to perform. To stimulate favorable attitudes, efforts to motivate the child prior to reading activities are well spent. Basically, a teacher's enthusiasm for a story, his tone of voice, or his reaction to the child's responses to a story affect how well the child responds. Hopefully, self-motivation is created so that the child will want to continue to read and to engage in reading activities.

Another important consideration in developing motivation is the selection of materials. Many teachers have found it useful to permit children to select much of what they are to read. Such a technique utilizes the motivation the child brings to the reading session and enhances his committment to the completion of that reading. Some teachers feel awkward and out of control if they do not select all the material for the child to read. In such cases it is suggested that the teacher start by permitting a limited amount of free selection. He will tend to feel more comfortable with it as he watches the reaction of the children and sees the results. He will also find this technique to be extremely effective with seriously handicapped readers.

Length of Material

Another important factor in each level of thinking and stage of reading comprehension is the sheer quantity of print to which the child is expected to respond. The quantity can vary from a word to phrases to sentences to paragraphs to groups of paragraphs to larger units of print, such as stories and books. In most reading programs, a child is first approached through words or simple sentences. His ability to literally understand words and simple sentences is first assured before moving to groups of sentences and paragraphs. Teacher's guides for basic materials usually suggest that first graders read one sentence at a time, discussing it to assure correct comprehension of the material. The opposite idea exists in the language experience approach, which, we recall, starts with ideas in sentence and story form and places word study after reading with meaning.

The teacher is always concerned about the quantity of print to which he expects the child to react. Quantity in itself can create problems with memory, motivation, and confused thinking. It can also promote fatigue, discouragement, and forgetting. It does not always affect the reader negatively, however, for sometimes a large quantity of print helps by providing clues to the author's mood and tone. Also, as the story develops, it usually becomes more interesting, and the child becomes more interested in it.

It is now obvious that comprehension is no simple matter. A teacher must focus his attention in several different directions simultaneously. If he does not have a working knowledge of the skills involved in thinking, the stages of teaching comprehension, the part memory plays in reading, the attention needed to develop motivation, and the difficulty some students have in dealing with large quantities of print, the teacher is likely to be ineffective in teaching comprehension. Children may not respond, and he will be unable to evaluate the reasons. The more attention a teacher gives to these factors of comprehension, the better teacher he will be. It is through comprehension activities that the reading act is completed in terms of communication. Therefore, to help a child effectively communicate with an author, a teacher needs to initiate instruction, based upon his understanding of the above factors, which will ultimately develop independent readers.

ISSUES IN READING COMPREHENSION

Several questions involving important issues in comprehension need the attention of teachers. A discussion of these issues will help the teacher with his instruction and his planning for better reading activities featuring the thinking-comprehension skills.

What Is the Role of Questioning in Comprehension?

Questioning is used to motivate children to read for answers, to keep attention focused appropriately, to check comprehension, and to further stimulate thinking activities. Generally, questioning starts with the teacher's direct involvement in the formation of questions and the acceptance of answers and proceeds to the formation of questions by the pupils themselves. It is necessary for the teacher to consider the purpose of the questions he asks and to recognize the kinds the pupils ask. In a study of twelve randomly selected classrooms, Guszak found that 56 percent of all questions in reading were recall questions, while 13 percent involved recognition.[7] Therefore, 69 percent of all questions asked in reading were at the first stage of comprehension—literal understanding of the author's message. He further found that .6 percent of all questions were involved interpretation and 15 percent treated evaluation. The study can be interpreted to conclude that .6 percent of the questions were at the second stage of comprehension, interpretation, and that 15 percent were at the third stage, problem solving. The Guszak survey is convincingly representative of most teaching and shows basically that teachers focus their questions on literal understanding at the first stage of comprehension. Perhaps the reason for this is that answers are easier to formulate and evaluate, for they are either right or wrong; there is no need for subjective evaluation. It is not surprising then that students are more equipped to handle questions at this stage than at the other two. The solution to overemphasis of one stage of comprehension is for teachers to become aware of the three stages and of the kinds of questions appropriate to each.

The procedure of classroom questioning presents several difficulties. For example, children usually respond to a teacher's questions by raising their hands, and the teacher usually selects one of them to answer. At that point, the teacher knows only the response of one child. He does not know the answers of the other children who raised their hands but were not called on, or of those who did not raise their hands. As a result, the teacher operates on the assumption that because one child knew the answer, the others did, or that when one child answers, the others are listening and their learning is reinforced. However, this is not always true and teachers do well to capitalize upon every opportunity to have every pupil respond. One idea that can be used in stage 1 of comprehension is for the children to flash cards with *yes* or *no* written on them in response to the teacher's questions following a reading. Five or six such questions will be very enlightening to a teacher. The children who do not respond can be temporarily grouped for re-reading experiences finding passages which support literal understanding. Such techniques are efficient ways of checking literal understanding without using a large amount of instructional time.

Another difficulty arises in questioning when a child cannot provide the correct answer. The teacher can either stop the lesson and work with that child or go on with the lesson and come back to him. The teacher has a responsibility to the total group, as well as to that individual child, and since circumstances vary, he has to decide which approach seems most efficient at the time. In most cases, a teacher will probably find it useful to obtain an appropriate response from another child, proceed with the lesson, and then work in a small group with those children who were unable to respond to the questions. The teacher must consider several possibilities:

- Is the material too difficult for the child? Is there a chance that he can understand it? If the child finds the material difficult, he may be focusing his attention on decoding words.

- Are there concepts in the material that the child has not encountered before and that therefore are strange to him?

- Is this an unnatural response for this child? Can he usually respond to these kinds of questions, or is he, in effect, blocked by a specific kind?

- Does the child need to reread the selection? Many children find it difficult to think and remember accurately during a first reading. On a second reading, they can concentrate more fully on the understanding involved.

- Is the child able to respond to that level of question? If he cannot, the teacher tries to make sure that the child can respond to the next lower level of questions. He then tries to build understanding so that the child will be ready for the more difficult level questions.

In lessons that involve questioning, teachers may be placing pupils in uneasy positions. Some children become anxious and have difficulty responding in group situations; yet, in effect, they are able to respond. A teacher can make it easier for these children to respond by any of the following guidelines:

■ The teacher tentatively ignores incorrect responses instead of commenting upon them. For example, when a child makes an inappropriate response, the teacher says, "Does anyone have another opinion?" instead of saying, "No, that is wrong. Didn't you read your story?" Children gather from teacher responses to their answers that sometimes it is not wise to *try* to respond.

■ The teacher's attitude toward the questioning is very important to the children. Many teachers make children feel that they are genuinely interested in their answers to the questions. Others make children feel that they are merely being tested. The former approach is preferable, because enthusiasm, a smile, or a little laughter help children feel involved during the questioning period.

■ Most questioning following reading is overdone. Children are questioned to death and grow to feel that they must remember every detail, main idea, and possible inference. While children should be thorough readers, many teachers analyze a story to the point at which reading is no longer enjoyable. Three or four well-chosen questions usually provide adequate after-reading questioning. A few carefully developed questions are far superior to ten or twenty carelessly developed and meaningless ones.

■ It is valuable to concentrate on the purpose of a question. Sanders sees three basic purposes in asking questions: to motivate interest, to instruct, and to evaluate.[8] By thinking about the purpose for which he is asking a question, a teacher formulates better questions. Sanders also believes that there are three elements in good questioning: precision, clarity, and close connection to the material which has been read.[9] Clearly, the more the teacher thinks about the question he is asking, the greater possbility he will have of getting appropriate answers from the children.

One pitfall involved in answering questions designed to elicit responses in a particular level of thinking is the fact that a child's response to a given question might well reflect thinking at a level higher or lower than was intended. The teacher accepts such responses and if he wants further response, he can rephrase the question to encourage the student to think again. For example, if a question is asked to which a child is expected to answer by paraphrasing information in the book, but instead he uses the words of the author, the teacher can say, "Yes, now tell me the same thing in your own words." Another factor that becomes important is the time between the question and the answer. If the child senses that he must answer immediately, he is likely to respond on a lower level of thinking than is intended. Thinking about what has been read is truly a reflective process, and teachers must allow children time to reflect before appropriate responses can be made.

We have seen, then, that questioning plays a major role in teaching comprehension. Care and attention to the purpose and types of questions, care in obtaining responses from children, and care in reacting to the responses of children are necessary considerations of the teacher.

Why Is it Important for Children To Think About What They Read During the Initial Stages of Reading?

Few would contest the fact that reading does not take place unless the child is thinking. Although Chall can be quoted as contending that a decoding emphasis is needed in initial reading instruction, a careful reading of her research reveals that attention to comprehension is also considered important.[10] However, there does not have to be an either/or solution to the problem of the place of thinking in the reading process. If a child is started in reading with attention to the decoding process and to the ideas he gets from decoded words, he will see reading as a form of communication from the beginning. Clearly, if a child cannot decode, he cannot possibly communicate, for he will not understand the message. On the other hand, if he decodes but does not think about what he has decoded, he will not understand that reading is a communication process. Reading is best presented by providing a child with optimum opportunities to benefit from both aspects of the process. Only when a child is not permitted to focus too long on one aspect of reading to the exclusion of others can a balanced reading program be developed.

What Is the Relationship Between Speed of Reading and Comprehension?

The efficiency with which a child handles printed material is of vital concern to all teachers. When children are given reading assignments to work on independently, certain amounts of time are usually blocked out for the completion of the assignments. Teachers know, however, that all children do not work at the same rate—some finish before the allotted time and others do not. As a result, many teachers attempt to help children read more rapidly.

It does not seem reasonable for large amounts of time to be spent helping children read faster in elementary school programs. For most young children, fast reading means careless reading and skipping over ideas. They may not choose to reread and mull over ideas, and the possible result may be poorly developed reading habits.

At the same time, it is advisable for all teachers to stress efficiency, for there is a great deal of time wasted in many classrooms when children do not work consistently or efficiently on reading material. Exercises which help children set purposes and read specifically to satisfy them are extremely useful. Their stress is on successful completion of the assignment within reasonable time limits, not on the number of words per minute the child handles. The rate builders in the SRA Reading Laboratory are typical of these exercises. A child is expected to read a page and answer the questions in a three-minute period. Fortunately, the child is always working at his instructional level, because the exercises are graded according to his ability to handle them. In any classroom some children can work on very difficult materials, and others on very easy material with all of them doing the work in the same time period. In such situations, children learn to adjust their reading rate to their purposes for reading.

A useful technique that can be taught early in a child's reading career is skimming. It is generally taught by giving children a specific idea to look for in the print. They read for that idea only, going quickly from topic sentence to topic sentence. The teacher explains that they are not responsible for the other material on the page and that skimming is a skill which is taught for an expressed purpose, not for reading in its traditional sense.

The exact relationship between speed and comprehension is somewhat uncertain. However, it can probably be said with some degree of certainty that a child who reads very slowly or word by word does not have the same opportunities to see the relationship between ideas in various paragraphs as the child who reads more rapidly. As ideas come to the mind faster, there is a better possibility of seeing the relationship between them. There is also a better opportunity to complete a reading in a given sitting. If the reading is completed in several different sittings, the child may not be able to closely relate the ideas of the author gained in one sitting to those gained in other sittings. Therefore, a teacher usually provides children with material which can be handled in one sitting so that comprehension can take place at that time. He does not make a blanket assignment to a large group of children and expect each child to be equally capable of comprehending it, whether he completes it in one, two, or three sittings.

Generally stated, speed is of minor importance in the elementary grades and is best reserved for attention in junior and senior high school programs.

How Can a Teacher Develop Diversification of Comprehension Activities?

Diversification of comprehension activities is achieved through planning. The teacher sets objectives of comprehension for each lesson prior to the reading and varies them. He gives the children opportunities to consider various objectives within a given lesson. For example, a child can read part of a story for the purpose of recalling as many specifically stated facts as possible. Then he reads the remainder of the story for the main idea which he can state in his own words. Finally, he reacts critically to what he has read or creates his own continuation of the story.

Diversification enters into comprehension activities not only within a given lesson, but also in a flexible day to day program. It is not uncommon to see these activities become stereotyped with the same kinds in evidence at the end of each session. Children find this boring and tend to become sluggish in their responses. The key is for the teacher to consider comprehension the most enjoyable part of the reading activity and to provide games, discussions, and engrossing independent activities. A comprehension activity that is extremely interesting should not be worn out with repetition, but instead savored on an intermittent basis.

What Does Linguistics Offer to Comprehension?

Many of the current articles about the relationship between linguistics and reading focus upon the decoding aspects of the process. However, a careful examination of the ideas of the linguists provides valuable insight into their contribution to the thinking aspects of reading. The work of Goodman in analyzing the reading process has led to his definition of reading as the reconstruction of an author's message.[11] Wardhaugh defines reading as the processing of language information.[12] Both these writers stress the comprehension dimension of reading and call for attention to syntactical patterning and semantics in examining the relationship of thought and reading. Lefevre presents four major language devices that signal and shape the larger patterns of American English. These are intonation, functional order in sentence patterns, structure words, and word form changes.[13] Lefevre maintains that each of these language devices is incompletely represented in writing and in print, because what we say and hear cannot be completely represented graphically in ordinary English print. Let us examine each of these areas briefly and see which writing clues are available to the reader to better understand the signaling devices available in our language.

Intonation   As an author writes, he is aware of the intonation of the words and phrases that he uses. Since words on a printed page do not have intonation, nor its elements of juncture, stress, and pitch, it is necessary for the reader to supply them in order to fully comprehend the ideas that the author is trying to communicate. Juncture involves the pauses between words. For example, the difference between *a name* and *an aim* is a matter of juncture. In writing, these differences are indicated by spacing and spelling. Stress can be represented in writing through punctuation, such as question marks and exclamation points, by underlining or italicizing important words, and at times by sentence order. The reader uses these written signals to further help his comprehension. In oral reading, pitch enters into play. Pitch refers to the highness or lowness of a child's reading voice. On one end of the continuum is the monotone reader and on the other end the reader who uses highly variable tones to express the author's message.

Functional Order in Sentence Patterns   As we listen to someone talk, we obtain clues from the order in which he presents words to us. With some direction from the teacher, a child can be taught to see this order in written material. Lefevre states that "our basic sentence order is rigid and arbitrary,"[14] and "normal sentence order involves the basic functions of subject first, and verb second, and possibly a completer third . . ."[15] It is helpful for a child to anticipate this order when reading. Such anticipation enhances active, thoughtful reading and reduces the chances of error in word calling. Closure activities, previously discussed, are excellent ways of helping children use language structure clues.

Structure Words   Some words in our language can be considered *full* words, such as *dig, cat, house,* and *people.* Other words such as *when, and, or,* and *about* are structure words. Lefevre estimates that there are only about 300 structure words in a 600,000 word dictionary.[16] However, those 300 words are extremely important, for they are repeated again and again in all printed material. They are quite often the helpers which aid greatly in comprehension. Some assist nouns, while others assist verbs. Some are phrase markers, some clause markers, and some question markers. For example, the words *who, why, when,* and *where* are clues to a forthcoming question. Words such as *up, in, out,* and *of* are clues to a forthcoming phrase. A teacher who is interested in helping a child with structure words will find it useful to consult Lefevre's ideas on linguistics.

Word-Form Changes   A given word with slight changes can be a noun, a verb, an adjective, or an adverb. The beginning reader easily uses differences in word forms in his speech. The teacher can help him to become aware of his use of the words in speech and then to find the same uses in written composition.

Heilman discusses linguistics through the use of the term *melodies.* He believes that "if a child reads word by word, he treats each word as an utterance . . ."[17] This habit will eventually destroy the melody of spoken English and thus preclude reading for meaning. It may be helpful for the teacher to think of the area of melody as one of the major contributions of linguistics to the field of reading in terms of comprehension. Children ought to think of a piece of written material as something that they can produce orally with melody and fluency, so that it is a piece of communication, not a large collection of single utterances which, by themselves, carry little or no meaning.

How Can a Teacher Help Slow Learners with Comprehension?

The slow learner operating in discussions based upon written material is likely to be slow in responding and inaccurate when he does. The teacher has two basic alternatives for helping this particular type of child. First, the child's level of material may have to be adjusted so that he can better handle the decoding of the print. If the child is reading material which is so difficult that on every tenth word or so he has to stop and use an elaborate word attack technique, he is going to have difficulty concentrating on the meaning of the material. The second alternative is based upon a continuous awareness of the level of thinking which is required of the child. The teacher may be asking the child to do higher levels of thinking in interpretation or problem solving before he ascertains whether or not the child truly understands the ideas of the author in a literal sense. It is also possible that the child has never had much opportunity to participate in discussions involving the various levels of thinking. And we would certainly advocate that when a child shows difficulty in comprehension in any particular exercise the teacher give consideration to the level of material and the level of thinking which the child is able to handle.

Even in situations in their clinic, the authors have found few cases in which a child is not able to think in terms of literally understanding someone orally, interpreting someone's speech or using his thinking skills in simple problem-solving situations. However, there are many children in the clinic who cannot use these same thinking skills in reading. They can be helped by instruction in reading which focuses on the types of thinking skills presented in this chapter—especially those stressing the oral situation first. Game-like activities are also helpful for these children. For example, the teacher can use a comic strip, removing the words from the pictures. The children can be asked to place the pictures in order and to make up stories to go with them. Likewise, the use of headlines from newspapers, accompanied by the articles which go with them can be used for matching type games. The game feature makes comprehension enjoyable and tends to stimulate the children's thinking.

How Does Oral Reading Affect Comprehension?

Functional oral reading is an effective means of demonstrating communication through reading. It is one technique a reader can use when he wants to share a written message with the rest of the class. Oral reading can also be used as a tool of evaluation (see chapter 13).

When reading orally to communicate with others, stress is placed on fluency. Children need good models which present oral reading that sounds as though someone is talking to them. Before reading orally, it is recommended that the child always read the passage silently. He can read faster silently and is not concerned with how his reading sounds to others. He can concentrate on meaning and on how the author conveys it.

Teachers need to attend to the reader who is not reading meaningful phrases, but simply words in a monotone. First, the teacher determines whether the material being read is too difficult, a common word-calling symptom. The child then practices, perhaps by listening to himself on a tape recorder. During the reading itself, the teacher sees that the children who are listening are attentive and that they do not follow in their books. The material read orally has to be worth listening to and should not be a story that the listeners have already read. It is often useful to have children choose reading selections which have interested them and which they feel they would like to share with others.

The following suggestions may be helpful to the teacher planning oral reading activities:

- For children reading at the first and second grade levels, there is more oral reading in the classroom than for children at higher levels of reading. In the initial stages, children vocalize words when looking at the print, and even though they need to pronounce the words in order to associate the form with a meaning in their speech, the teacher directs them to observe a line of print silently before reading aloud. As children advance in reading, the quantity of print to be read silently before it is rendered orally increases to paragraphs, pages, and entire stories.

- A class can develop standards for oral reading and use them for self-evaluation. The following chart of standards was developed in one second-grade class:

  When We Read Aloud
  We try to sound like people talking.
  We group words together.
  We change our tone of voice as we read.
  We remember to look at the . , ? !

- Children enjoy taping their oral reading and using the tapes for self-evaluation. Tapes of favorite stories and of individual creative stories can be used as material for a listening station.

■ Sharing favorite parts of literature provides another meaningful situation for oral reading. Occasionally small groups of pupils can be formed for this type of sharing through reading aloud.

■ Stories which have a lot of action or conversation can be presented effectively through oral reading. A group of pupils preparing a story for presentation to another group is a purposeful use for oral reading.

■ Perhaps the most interesting manner for conducting oral reading is to have children form pairs and read orally to each other. All children in the room can be reading at the same time while the teacher moves from pair to pair to offer help.

■ In regular reading lessons, some oral reading can be used for finding the sentence, paragraph, or page which answers a question or proves a point.

■ The teacher's model of expressive oral reading is also important. As he reads literature aloud to pupils, he tries to demonstrate fluent and expressive reading.

■ When experience charts and plans are read with children in the pre-reading and beginning reading stages, the teacher avoids unnatural stress on individual words and demonstrates reading in thought units.

■ Direct instruction in the part intonation plays in oral reading is included. For example, a sentence can be read more than one way with stress changed to convey various meanings. "Come to dinner now." can be read by children as their mothers might say it when first calling them. Then they can read it as their mothers might after calling them several times.

For pupils who have difficulty reading orally in a smooth manner additional experiences with very easy material can be provided. Oral situations can illustrate the relationship between spoken language and the reading of print with the intonation of speech. For example, a teacher may ask questions such as, "Johnny, what are you going to do after school?" "Ann, what do you see on my desk?" "David, what did you have for breakfast?" He writes the answers on the chalk board or on a chart, and asks the children to read them. If the lack of smoothness is still evident, he can ask the children to repeat the sentence they said previously. They should then realize that as they read the printed words, they need to supply the inflections of speech.

A teacher must be alert to the numerous opportunities for incidental oral reading which occur in language arts, social studies, and science activities. Reading of new articles, reports, creative dramatics, and choral reading can also encourage expressive oral reading. While too much stress on oral reading, with or without silent reading preparation, may be detrimental to reading comprehension, oral reading with a purpose can demonstrate communication through reading.

Chapter Review

Comprehension is one of the most important aspects of reading. Without comprehension, a child merely reads words and does not realize that they are a means of communicating the ideas, thoughts, and feelings of an author. Instruction in comprehension is one of the most enjoyable aspects of teaching reading. To watch a child develop his abilities to think about what he has read and to see him stretch his mind and tackle various types of problem situations through thinking is truly remarkable. The teacher hopes to see every child in his class develop in this way. However, when a child has difficulty in progressing with the rest of the class, the teacher acts to discover the reasons. To help the situation, he makes adjustments in the level of thinking and the stage of comprehension the child is handling. He makes sure that the elementary levels are fully grasped before advancing to the next level of difficulty.

The information now available concerning how to help children improve their capacities of thinking, interpreting, and solving problems with the materials that they are reading is in the infancy stage of development. In the coming years materials will be available that will greatly assist children in developing specific skills in the various areas of comprehension. To this end many schools are providing professional libraries and are subscribing to the journals which report the latest research in thinking in the area of reading.

NOTES

1 Alvin W. Schindler, "Developments Which Are Needed for Improving Teaching of Comprehension and Study Skills," in *Speaking to the Issues* (College Park: University of Maryland, 1967), p. 63.

2 Russell G. Stauffer, "Language and the Habit of Credulity," *Elementary English* 42 (April 1965): 369.

[3] The presentation in this chapter has relied heavily on Bloom's work, but in the interest of stressing the practical application of the development of thinking to reading, we have narrowed the range of thinking levels from six to three. See especially, Benjamin S. Bloom, ed., *Taxonomy of Educational Objectives* (New York: David McKay, 1965).

[4] B. R. Bugelski, *The Psychology of Learning Applied to Teaching* (Indianapolis: Bobbs-Merrill, 1964), pp. 176–177.

[5] Ibid., p. 177.

[6] Ann K. Healy, "Effects of Changing Children's Attitudes Toward Reading," *Elementary English* 42 (March 1965): 272.

[7] Frank J. Guszak, "Teacher Questioning and Reading," *The Reading Teacher* 21 (December 1967): 229.

[8] Norris M. Sanders, *Classroom Questions* (New York: Harper & Row, 1966), p. 1.

[9] Ibid., p. 3.

[10] Jeanne Chall, *Learning To Read—The Great Debate* (New York: McGraw-Hill, 1967) pp. 137, 234, 275.

[11] Kenneth S. Goodman, ed., "The Psycholinguistic Nature of the Reading Process," in *The Psycholinguistic Nature of the Reading Process* (Detroit: Wayne State University Press, 1968), pp. 13–27.

[12] Ronald Wardhaugh, *Reading, A Linguistic Perspective* (New York: Harcourt Brace Jovanovich, 1969).

[13] Carl A. Lefevre, *Linguistics and the Teaching of Reading* (New York: McGraw-Hill, 1964), p. 8.

[14] Ibid., p. 9.

[15] Ibid.

[16] Ibid., p. 119.

[17] Arthur Heilman, *Principles and Practices of Teaching Reading* (Columbus: Charles E. Merrill, 1967), p. 247.

SUGGESTED ACTIVITIES

1. Examine Lesson Plan 5. Develop a plan for teaching a comprehension skill in an oral and in a reading situation, using any materials which you prefer.

2. Selecting a newspaper story as a basis, prepare two questions requiring literal comprehension, two requiring interpretation in terms of self, and two requiring problem solving. Using them, practice with some children or, second best, with your classmates. Were you specific? What types of responses did you expect and what types were given?

3. Compare the definitions of comprehension found in the Suggested Readings. Prepare your own definition and apply it in the lessons which you are preparing.

SUGGESTED READINGS

Bloom, Benjamin S., ed. *Taxonomy of Educational Objectives*, handbook 1, *The Cognitive Domain*. New York: David McKay, 1965.

This reading must for the student of thinking treats the development of the taxonomy with great thought and care. It is helpful to start with the Appendix and then to study the contents of the book.

Lefevre, Carl A. *Linguistics and the Teaching of Reading*. New York: McGraw-Hill, 1964.

As a linguist, Lefevre feels that the major contribution to reading from his field is in the area of comprehension. See chapter 1 for a statement of the case.

Russell, David H. *Children's Thinking*. Boston: Ginn, 1956.

A high priority book for the student who wants to know more about thinking. See chapter 4 for a discussion, definition and specific suggestions for the improvement of thinking.

Sanders, Norris M. *Classroom Questions*. New York: Harper & Row, 1966.

An interesting and easy to understand treatment of what good questioning is and how it can be implemented in more classrooms.

Stauffer, Russell G. "Language and the Habit of Credulity." *Elementary English* 42 (April 1965): 362–369.

One of many discussions by the author concerning the area of comprehension, this article arranges the hierarchy of thinking differently from the one presented in this text. The thoughtful discussion is coupled with specific suggestions for the teacher.

CHAPTER NINE

READING FOR STUDY: A NEGLECTED AREA

Advance Organizer

This chapter reviews the common study skills needed in most study situations, as well as others which pertain to the specific context of the content area and textbooks used in the area. Not all study skills need be taught in connection with the teaching of other reading skills; however, they must be taught early and continuously in the school's program. Ultimately, the child should develop independent techniques with which he can handle any assignment and pursue independent study.

The Need for Study Skills

It has been said that a major weakness of elementary schools is their failure to develop effective and efficient study habits in young children.[1] In fact, many elementary school teachers may be so preoccupied with teaching the mechanics of reading skills, that they overlook the necessity of teaching techniques for the use of those skills in various types of study situations. Clearly, techniques designed to assist children to study successfully are an essential part of a comprehensive elementary reading program.

The overall goal involved in reading for study is to develop a reader who is not dependent upon the teacher for learning. From the broadest viewpoint, the goal of helping students learn *how* to learn is really the ultimate aim for all learning both in and out of school.

THE READING OF TEXT MATERIALS

Since schools are still largely textbook oriented, it is a necessity to find appropriate texts. However, this need presents a problem. Williams has found that many text materials are too difficult to promote effective learning.[2] Even the easiest encyclopedias, according to Liske, are too confusing for the average elementary school student and are appropriate only for the better readers.[3] Too often, when it comes to reading textbooks in subject areas, the assumption is made that the pupil is automatically able to perform at the grade level for which the text was written. Such assumptions, research tells us, are invalid.

Because all subject teachers teach *through* reading, it is necessary for them to know and to practice directed reading activities, to know how to evaluate the level of difficulty of all material they assign to children, and to be informed about study skills —especially which skills are appropriate for which types of assignments. As Schindler has written, "A major responsibility of the teacher is that of surveying reading materials, to identify situations in which skills can be applied, and to stimulate application of this skill with question and discussions."[4] Yet while these critical tasks remain unattended to in many classrooms, children continue to flounder about in inappropriate reading materials, unaware of study skills that would simplify their task. Ultimately, many leave the elementary school with all interest in study gone, destroyed by years of frustration and failure.

A direct relationship appears to exist between a child's reading ability and his chances of success in school. Some research indicates that progress in the content areas parallels progress in reading.[5] Others suggest that improved reading performance results in improved grades earned in other academic areas.[6] Although these studies connect good reading with academic effectiveness, they by no means preclude the necessity for specific study skill instruction in the various content areas.

A major limitation of textbook-oriented classrooms is that the materials which the child may read and understand in a fifth or sixth grade classroom have little or no relevance to the world he will face when he leaves formal schooling. As Heilman has noted, "The time lag between research and publication and the adoption of textbooks in the various content areas causes the most recent textbooks to be somewhat inadequate."[7] It therefore becomes all the more important for pupils to learn to use materials in the specific content areas independently, in addition to mastering the content of specifically assigned textbooks. As a child learns to read in the humanities, science, and mathematics areas, he should learn to use relevant materials, not merely to study within the scope of a single school year or a given curriculum.

It is by now a cliché to remark that society faces an unprecedented information explosion, and that what is learned today may be inadequate for survival tomorrow. Yet the fact of escalating amounts of knowledge remains, coupled with a "materials explosion" in which more textbooks, more visual aids, more materials of all types are available to teachers than ever before. It appears that single text instruction is as out-of-date as a reading program which relies solely upon a single basal series for all children. However, using multiple materials will present new problems. The retraining of teachers to learn to group children effectively and to utilize the many materials available, has, in fact, created a need for an entirely new continuing teacher education process.

Selecting Among Multiple Materials

In selecting materials appropriate for children in the classroom, the teacher has two basic obligations. First, he must assess the difficulty of materials which he expects children to handle. Then, he must select instructional alternatives for materials which are too difficult for some children to read but which represent what he considers essential content.

Assessing Difficulty   In assessing the difficulty of material relative to each child's ability to handle it, the teacher analyzes several aspects of the difficulty of the material. First, the concepts may be foreign to the student. In such cases, the teacher develops these concepts through real or vicarious experiences such as field trips, discussions, films, and pictures. Second, a teacher is alert to specific vocabulary difficulties in assigned text materials. Proper nouns, technical names, familiar words used with a new meaning, and words for which concepts have not been developed cause particular difficulty. A survey of all material prior to assignment allows the teacher to identify such words so that he can present them in such a manner that they do not disrupt the pupils' study. Third, the teacher is aware that text material differs in difficulty from page to page, and from chapter to chapter. For example, one study of textbooks found fluctuations of several grade levels of difficulty within many of the texts.[8] Thus the teacher cannot assume that, because a child can read the first chapter in a text, he will find the following chapters equally readable.

Finally, in any subject, the teacher has an obligation to acquaint the child with the particular format of any materials he is expected to read. Perhaps headings in a particular book are unique in their structure, or questions at the ends of chapters would help the children prepare for purposeful reading. Perhaps the book has a helpful glossary or a table of contents that permits children to survey a chapter before reading it, thus preparing them to read with greater purpose and meaning. Perhaps the book has a foot-note arrangement or suggested related assignments which could be useful to students having trouble with the material. Preparation of this type prior to assigning specific material for independent reading is profitable for many students.

Instructional Alternatives with Difficult Material   After assessing text materials, the teacher will realize that, regardless of what he does to adapt it, certain material is not appropriate for particular children. In such situations, a teacher has several alternatives. First, he may ask other pupils to read to those students for whom a book is too difficult. Second, he may decide that instruction should take a form other than reading, in which case he will tend to rely more heavily on pictures, film strips, and discussions than on independent reading. Third, he may locate alternative materials which cover the same content more simply, making it possible for children to learn the content without being frustrated by reading difficulty.

Finally, in some cases, a teacher may find it useful for students to write their own texts. In this case, he would follow the steps of a modified language experience approach.[9] Language would be stim-ulated through discussion of a concept with the teacher or viewing a film strip or motion picture, watching a television performance, conducting an experiment, or taking a field trip. After the experience is concluded, a discussion of it—an *oral* expression of what happened—can be stimulated by questioning. When the teacher is satisfied that the children are thinking actively about the activity, he can ask various students to contribute their ideas orally. These contributions in turn can be recorded and duplicated, providing the first pages of their book for one of the content areas. As a teacher continues to provide experiences through stimulation, developing oral language, and duplicating dictated material, a textbook is created which can then be reread, studied, and used for specific types of reference activities. After several stories have been dictated, a table of contents can be constructed, an index developed, cross-references added from other material which children recall reading on similar topics. Specific words unique to the content of that area can be identified and filed in word banks.

Through this technique, a teacher accomplishes two objectives. First, the children are placed in learning situations where they can learn through reading, for they can read their own stories. Second, the children are learning skills necessary for reading in that particular content area: they are, in other words, learning the vocabulary, the concepts, and the methodology necessary for further learning through written materials in the subject area.

GENERAL STUDY SKILLS

Several skills have been identified as essential for children's growth toward independence in reading and learning. Not every teacher is equally well prepared to teach all study skills, but all teachers should be prepared in those skills most relevant to the areas of instruction which they explore with children. Following is a discussion of the most important study skills a child learns in the elementary school grades.

Locating Information

Locating information is essential in all subject areas in all grades. One skill necessary for proficiency in locating information is the use of the table of contents and the index. Many teachers find it useful to start lessons not by asking everyone to turn to page X, but by having children locate the page through the table of contents or the index. Awareness of the place and function of these text tools is useful to all pupils throughout their school years.

Young children enjoy mastering the card catalog and being able to locate books, reference materials, dictionaries, and periodicals.

Also important is the skill needed to locate information in sources outside text materials. Instruction in locating such material involves use of the library, periodicals, newspapers, and trade book materials.

Using the Library   Instruction in the general functions of the library can be handled by the school librarian, if one is on the staff, by the classroom teacher, or by the reading specialist. Whether the library is within the classroom or centrally located, students need to learn to locate books, reference materials, dictionaries, and various periodicals that they are expected to use, as well as additional materials of their own selection. They also must learn what specific materials are appropriate for certain subjects. Thus a teacher making a social studies assignment, for example, should be familiar with all social studies reference materials available in the library in order to assist the children in finding them.

Using the card catalog is an essential skill. If a school library is not available for instruction in this skill, a public library may be used. There is probably no better training for pupils in general library skills than assisting the librarian with some of the clerical work of the school library. If this is not possible, meaningful activities involving searching for specific information in the library can be developed for groups of children. As they work cooperatively, they learn from each other and grow in their capacity for independent study. The more children become acquainted with the library and know where materials are and how to use them, the more they tend to regard the library as a useful and habitual resource.

Using Trade Books Informational trade books for children, which have increased in quantity in recent years, offer a valuable source of information for those who desire to go beyond the instruction provided in text materials or for those who do not respond to the content area texts provided in the classroom. In both cases, the teacher's awareness of their availability and his estimate of their level of difficulty are necessary and useful in directing children to appropriate learning materials.

Using Periodicals and Newspapers Periodicals, and also newspapers, can be useful sources of study in the elementary grades. Teaching children to locate and apply information in periodicals to primary classroom learning is an especially important instructional emphasis in today's world full of newspapers, magazines, and journals.

Many schools subscribe to commercially prepared newspapers designed to provide experiences similar to those which children will eventually have in reading regular newspapers. In the upper elementary grades, many children are able to locate valuable material in local newspapers. At that point, studying the location of material in newspapers—and their advantages and disadvantages as a source of information—is a significant part of any instructional program. (See Lesson Plan 6 on newspapers in chapter 11.)

In many elementary schools, pupils produce a newspaper which reports the news of their room or school. All of the children contribute to the production of such a home newspaper. The features can be the same as those of the local paper, so that students become aware of the construction of a newspaper and of how articles are written. The class discusses styles of writing found in news reporting, in editorials, in sports stories, and in feature articles, and the use of headlines to convey a main idea in a succinct form. And, in effect, by making their own newspaper, children learn to use other newspapers more efficiently. Many commercial papers provide class copies upon request.

Most periodicals contain a concept load more difficult than most elementary school children can handle and have a vocabulary which restricts their use to only the more able pupils. Such restrictions do not preclude the use of magazines as valuable sources of information, however. Since many parents subscribe to various types of periodicals on a regular basis, information in them is readily available to their children. The use of pictures, charts, and graphs can be explained so that the children can work within the structure of many of these publications.

Research Activities In recent years, problem-centered units and so-called inquiry or discovery approaches have become popular in the elementary curriculum. Research activities which result in mere "busy work" are considered more damaging than useful. It is preferable rather, that teachers construct activities which coordinate with learning activities normally in progress, so that children will learn to view available resources as truly useful. If a child were to challenge an author's statement, for example, he might be given an opportunity to go to reference resources for verification. If he shows special interest in a regularly scheduled activity, he might be given library opportunities to pursue that interest on his own. Or he might find opportunities to use the library as a source of information concerning a project growing from a unit in history or science.

The point is that it is unnecessary to assign "busy work" in order to take full advantage of opportunities to develop the use of reference materials as independent study skills. The purpose of unit activities involving research should always be clear to pupils, as should the awareness that information gained through independent study can often be used to contribute to other unit activities. In oral sharing situations, children can realize the value of such organzational skills as note-taking and outlining.

Using Maps, Graphs, Tables, and Pictures

All children need to be exposed to the skills of interpreting maps, graphs, tables, and pictures accurately. Because these types of material represent techniques of communication which are not usually cluttered with words in paragraph form, many students who have trouble reading the texts of some books may find it useful to have systems which permit them to use tables, graphs, maps, and pictures effectively.

Each teacher who uses books which contain visual aids needs to study them fully. When initially presenting the book to children, the teacher provides directed experiences in the use of these aids. For example, if a particular book uses bar graphs repeatedly, such a graph is explained in detail the first time it is presented. Discussions following the explanation demonstrate whether children are able to interpret the graphs accurately. Likewise, map reading, table reading and picture interpretation are valuable learning skills in the content areas. The inclusion of these types of visual aids in textbooks is costly; authors do not include visual aids unless they consider them to contain vital information. Therefore, time used in their interpretation and their understanding is well spent.

A helpful procedure is to ask children to compare a table presentation with a presentation of the same information in regular prose form. For example, first and second grade children can keep a record of the temperatures at specified hours for a month, developing a table such as the following:

NOVEMBER TEMPERATURES

	9:00	12:00	3:00
Nov. 1	40°	52°	56°
Nov. 2	45°	55°	59°
Nov. 3	32°	40°	41°

If the same information is then compiled in prose form, pupils quickly discover that the table form is an efficient means of presenting and quickly locating specified types of information. The same procedure can be followed in functional classroom situations such as charting heights and attendance.

Boys and girls in the intermediate grades often respond with interest when shown the efficiency of tables in finding specific information through the use of box scores for baseball games. The teacher may ask pupils to find the number of hits or runs scored by a particular player. Pupils realize in this way that certain information is included in the box score that cannot be included in the prose report.

Tables and graphs are also important in teaching the use of skimming as a means of efficient reading to locate only desired information.

Skimming and Scanning

Early in school, it is appropriate to instruct children in techniques for surveying material quickly in order to locate information once a specific purpose has been established. In practice exercises, children should not be impressed with the speed of their operation, nor with the number of words per minute at which they function. The purpose is to stress efficiency and flexibility in finding specific information. Skimming and scanning are activities which even children use when they begin reading newspapers. As they read a headline, they determine whether that article is one which they wish to pursue further. Similar activities can be provided for children in school. The purpose can be set by the children or the teacher, following which all members of the class read to meet that purpose. The use of material previously read is an excellent means of refining skimming and scanning skills.

Following Directions

A skill essential to success in future study situations is the ability to follow oral and written directions accurately. From the time of earliest pre-reading instruction, a teacher provides opportunities for children to respond to various types of directions orally: first, to simple directions expecting accurate execution; later, to sequential directions which involve compliance in a particular order. At all levels of reading, instruction in following oral and written directions should be a routine part of the reading program. Specific instructions which are found in most texts seem appropriate and useful for this end. Encouraging children to write directions for the activities of other children is also a good technique. Here, as in the language experience approach, the child is placed in an author's situation.

Methods of Sustained Study

Students need special instruction to develop techniques in preparation for extended periods of study. One such study system, the SQ3R approach, has received especially wide support. Following is a summary of this study procedure.

- Survey—to glance over the matter, look at pictures, read a sentence or two, and look at the table of contents to get an idea of what is to come.

- Question—to translate the material surveyed into questions which will become objectives for study. At times the student is expected to change the title of the story into a question. At other times he looks at the picture and questions what will happen next.

- Read—to answer the questions. As the child reads and answers his questions, he is encouraged to formulate new questions on the basis of the information he has read so far. Reading becomes an active, inquisitive process.

- Recite—to feed back the understanding of the read material to the teacher or to another child or to the reader himself. Quite often recitation takes the form of a discussion which the teacher leads. Other times children may be asked to do certain written assignments or to discuss the material with each other. The children are deciding whether their reading has satisfied the original questions they developed.

- Review—to study the material at another time. Here the child can check on items which are unclear. He may put the book aside and review it again another day. Periodic review is suggested because it reinforces what is learned.[10]

The SQ3R method (Survey, Question, Read, Recite, and Review) seems a logical way for a child to organize his own study. That children may study with different techniques and be successful goes without saying, for there is no single method which all children should use to study. Yet, independence in study seems fostered by techniques initially presented systematically. Maxwell, for example, found that, of the college students whom she surveyed who had heard of the SQ3R method, few used it.[11] Her conclusion was that the technique was taught too late for them to develop it as a habit. Although able students continue to evolve independent study approaches as they progress through school and college, experience suggests that instruction in specific study techniques early in school helps many children to "start off on the right foot" by supplying opportunities to practice study techniques under teacher supervision.

Transition from these directed reading activities to independent use of approaches such as SQ3R can be planned to some extent. For example, purposes set by the teacher give way to purposes set by the children (SQ steps). SQ3R activities can be developed with newspaper articles or with prepared reading materials at a very early age. As a child gains maturity in study, he may find that he would like to modify the technique presented and that, for him, a shortcut or an extension of the technique is particularly useful.

Such modifications and adaptations of a given study technique are not only appropriate but should be encouraged.

STUDY SKILLS PARTICULAR TO SPECIFIC SUBJECT AREAS

Each content area has specific study skill requirements. Teachers alert to these needs will reinforce the general study skills mentioned above in terms of specific activities appropriate for reading in the humanities, social studies, mathematics, and science areas. Authorities in these areas write differently and make different assumptions concerning the previous learning of students in their particular area of content specialization.

Specialized Subject Area Vocabularies

Perhaps the most unique area needing the attention of content teachers is that of specific vocabulary development in which technical words and words most appropriate to a given subject are emphasized. Words such as *divide, product, area, equal, compare,* and *average* have meanings in arithmetic which are different from those which the child ordinarily associates with them. The teacher, therefore, would be mistaken to assume that when a child can recognize these words, he understands their use in a specific content area. Discussions about word usage prior to asking children to perform with written material in that area are particularly worthwhile. The techniques used for developing general vocabulary are also appropriate for specific vocabulary in the content fields.

Aside from words that denote distinct concepts, there are a mass of technical words which a child must learn and master in order to be able to work in a content field. This is particularly true in the area of science. With such words, the teacher can make no legitimate assumption about previous learning or previous instruction in them.

Format

The format of books in language arts, social studies, arithmetic, and science may also differ considerably and, as a result, cause certain confusion for children. For example, in a science book, the format may be designed so that a child is expected to operate at a problem solving level. As noted in chapter 8, problem solving involves a high level of comprehension and thinking, and for a child to operate on that level, understanding and interpretation must have taken place. If the child has difficulty with a book designed for problem solving, the teacher will find it worthwhile to look toward a lower level of thinking to be certain that the child has successfully mastered the tasks required at that level. Likewise in arithmetic, the child's problem solving might be quite different from the problem solving assigned to him in a science text. The teacher always analyzes those differences and helps the child develop the skills that are necessary. With a language arts text, a child might be taught to summarize, to take notes, or to outline. Although these are the skills eventually needed in all subject areas, they can be introduced first in language arts textbooks. The teacher is encouraged to remain alert to the many possibilities during the instructional period for teaching reading and study skills using the books which serve as texts for other areas. The teacher who is aware of such instructional possibilities will find that children learn more easily and that study skills which serve the ultimate goal of independent learning can be developed. Sheppard presents specific ideas for studying science and social studies in two separate books.[12]

Organization

Teachers will note that authors in the various content areas organize their materials differently. Social studies materials may be organized by time periods or geographic areas, while science materials are likely to be organized by units or topics of scientific study. By helping children become aware of such organization, the teacher helps a child read and study the materials. Particularly useful for instruction in this area is the table of contents. Reading and discussion of the book's organization from the table of contents is usually a valuable study skill.

The compact nature of the content of some texts adds to the complexity of the reading task. One history chapter might cover fifty years, while another chapter might cover two years. The reader must be made aware of the techniques employed by authors to use space to designate importance as well as time.

For the teacher to provide instruction in the use of textbooks, he must first be aware of the peculiarities of the specific texts he has chosen. No generalizations will substitute for the efforts of a teacher to determine how he might best aid students to study assigned texts.

ISSUES IN STUDY READING

Self-Direction

As stated at the outset, self-direction in study is the ultimate goal for all instruction in study skills. Holt, an exponent of the "open classroom," has reminded teachers that many children are not self-directed, that they do not understand why they are in school, that they fail to see why they must complete a certain assignment or participate in a certain type of activity.[13] Purpose for working in school is a topic which merits full attention. Some educators urge that the teacher be in the director's seat, supervising all learning from his vantage point of experience and know-how. Others maintain it is beneficial for children to determine what they want to learn and then to study those things that they have chosen. No doubt both points of view are well taken; however, students should not be forced to study in areas if purposes for study are unclear.

In other words, if a teacher cannot explain satisfactorily why pupils are studying something which has been assigned, they should not have to study it. Such explanations are pertinent for both teacher and pupils. They make the teacher think more carefully about his assignments and his explanations of the purposes. They force the student to think about the activities in which he is involved and encourage him to consider why he is doing a particular assignment. On occasion, every conscientious teacher will find it necessary to terminate an activity that he cannot explain to a pupil's satisfaction. Generally, upon reflection, those particular activities prove to be of questionable value. In their place, he substitutes activities which pupils understand more readily and for which more clear-cut purposes are evident.

Perhaps the most striking characteristic of an open classroom is the fact that the pupils are working enthusiastically and purposefully toward clearly outlined objectives, whether teacher-defined or pupil-developed. Such a classroom demands a flexible, creative teacher who is determined to design instruction which will place children in situations where learning is an exciting, searching process.

Learning Centers and Their Use in Content Area Study

Learning centers are in popular use today and feature activities which provide pupils with a degree of self-selection, self-pacing, and self-evaluation. Pupils are permitted to work individually or in small groups toward the completion of center activities. Teachers can gear the centers effectively for study in the content areas by 1) developing meaningful centers, 2) assisting children to work in the centers, and 3) conferring with children about their efforts.

Classrooms with learning center activities are by nature open classrooms. All of the advantages of open classrooms are also present in learning centers. However, some teachers find it difficult to use the learning center concept effectively. It is suggested that they start learning centers on a small scale, evaluate them with students, and make modifications as needed. Of course, all teachers should develop the skills needed to use learning centers so that they have the professional option to use them or not. (For further information see chapter 12 or the *Learning Center Handbook*.[14])

Chapter Review

The knowledge explosion continues to grow and study in school more and more involves multi-text study. To cope with these factors, children will need better developed study skills. One trend in reading instruction must be to teach study skills at all levels in a variety of materials—both for general use and for specific subject areas. By directing attention to such skills, teachers will help children become independent in their study techniques. As with other areas of reading, independence is the ultimate aim.

NOTES

[1] Miles A. Tinker and Constance M. McCullough, *Teaching Elementary Reading* (New York: Appleton-Century-Crofts, 1968), p. 205.

[2] David L. Williams, "Rewritten Science Materials and Reading Comprehension," *Journal of Educational Research* 61 (January 1968): 204–206.

[3] Wilfred W. Liske, "An Investigation of the Readability of Selected Juvenile Encyclopedia Material by the Cloze Procedure and a Comparison of Results with Readability Formulas" (Ph. D. dissertation, University of Maryland, 1968).

[4] Alvin W. Schindler, "Developments Which Are Needed for Improved Teaching of Comprehension and Study Skills," in *Speaking to the Issues, Position Papers in Reading* (College Park: University of Maryland, 1967), p. 68.

[5] Emmett A. Kinkleman, Relationship of Reading Ability to Elementary School Achievement," *Educational Administration and Supervision* (February 1956): 65–67.

[6] Robert M. Wilson, "Scholastic Improvement of Successful Remedial Reading Students" (Ed. D. dissertation, University of Pittsburgh, 1959).

[7] Arthur W. Heilman, *Principles and Practices of Teaching Reading* (Columbus: Charles E. Merrill, 1967), pp. 373–374.

[8] Marsha Wasserman, "An Analysis of the Readability of Six Publications for Tenth Grade Slow Learners" (M.A. thesis, University of Maryland, 1968).

[9] Robert M. Wilson and Nancy Parkey, "A Modified Reading Program in a Middle School," *Journal of Reading* 14 (March 1970): 447–452.

[10] Francis P. Robinson, *Effective Study* (New York: Harper & Row, 1961) pp. 13–35.

[11] Martha J. Maxwell, "Implications of Research on College Readings for the Secondary School Teacher," in *Speaking to the Issues, Position Papers in Reading* (College Park: University of Maryland, 1967), p. 52.

[12] David L. Sheppard, *Effective Reading in Science* (New York: Harper & Row, 1960); *Effective Reading in Social Studies* (New York: Harper & Row, 1960).

[13] John Holt, *How Children Fail* (New York: Pitman, 1968), pp. 73–74.

[14] Louise Waynant, ed., *Learning Center Handbook* (College Park: University of Maryland, The Reading Center, 1970).

SUGGESTED ACTIVITIES

1. Apply the SQ3R technique to one of the chapters of this book.
2. Read Lesson Plan 6 in chapter 11 and develop a plan for teaching another study skill using any materials you prefer.
3. Observe a teacher providing instruction in the use of maps, graphs, or charts. What are the reactions of the children? How would you teach this lesson?

SUGGESTED READINGS

Duffey, Robert V. "Reading in the Social Sciences," *New Perspectives in Reading Instruction*. Edited by A. J. Mazurkiewicz. New York: Pitman, 1968, pp. 481–492.

The author cites eight specific and worthwhile instructional suggestions for the purpose of helping the slow reader to read better in the social sciences.

Mahoney, Sally. "Basic Study Skills and Tools." *Elementary English* 42 (December 1965): 905–915.

An outline of study skills by grade level provides specific ideas for instruction in the various study skills.

Robinson, Francis P. *Effective Study.* New York: Harper & Row, 1961.

A useful primary reference for detailed information concerning the SQ3R technique of study.

Weiss, M. Jerry. *Reading in the Secondary School,* pt. 6. New York: Odyssey Press, 1961.

Although the text is written for secondary teachers, part 6 is useful for information pertaining to study skills. It presents opinions for teaching reading in science, English, mathematics, and social studies.

CHAPTER TEN

CHILDREN'S LITERATURE

Advance Organizer

The preceding chapters have been concerned with direct instruction and with the materials designed to teach pupils "how" to read. This chapter is devoted to another dimension of the reading program: developing a personal interest in reading through a planned program of recreational reading.

A good elementary reading program produces children who enjoy reading and who *do* read in their free time, not merely children who know how to read. To achieve this goal, a teacher must know his students, consider factors which influence children's reading interests, be acquainted with the qualities of good literature and with many examples, and be able to conduct a planned literature program as a part of the total curriculum. From pre-reading to the attainment of independence in reading, experiences with literature and opportunities for personal reading are essential elements of the reading curriculum.

LITERATURE IN THE ELEMENTARY CURRICULUM

Probably every parent, school administrator, and teacher feels that time spent on direct instruction in reading is vital. Yet, there are parents, school administrators, and even teachers who feel that time spent on children's literature is a nice "extra" but not an essential. Those who urge children to read independently but who do not provide time and materials that promote the enjoyment of books for pure pleasure as a regular part of the school experiences cannot expect children to develop real interest in reading.

The reading habit does not develop automatically; time must be allotted in elementary classes for the exploration and enjoyment of both prose and poetry. Because developing a permanent interest in reading is one of the primary objectives of elementary reading, the time devoted to literature and personal reading rates a high priority. Support for this dimension of reading must be evident in a strong school-wide elementary reading program.

We use the term *children's literature* to refer to those materials, both fiction and non-fiction, which were written primarily for the reader's enjoyment rather than for his direct instruction. This term can be too narrowly interpreted if great stress is placed on literary merit as the primary consideration. While literary quality is certainly one criterion for evaluating children's books, interest and individual choice must also be acknowledged.

Although schools do succeed in teaching most children the mechanics of reading, the "interest" side of the ledger is often shockingly bare. The amount of personal reading done by the general public reflects the schools' lack of impact in developing strong reading interest in many individuals. A number of factors seem operative. Emphasis on skills may overshadow the development of wide and enthusiastic reading. Elementary reading programs must provide both those experiences which build reading skills and those which build reading habits and attitudes. Nonexistent or ill-equipped elementary libraries take a further toll. The narrow reading programs of some school systems, which rely entirely upon basal textbooks for their pupils' total exposure to reading are another cause of lack of enthusiasm for reading. While some literary material may be part of their content, basals are primarily instructional rather than recreational in focus. These books cannot and were not intended to supply the extensive materials needed for a rich program of personal reading.

Detailed class analysis and discussion may also detract from the enjoyment and appreciation of literature. Requiring detailed written reports about independent reading often leads pupils to dislike reading. Selecting literature solely on quality rather than children's interest may add further unfavorable effects.

However, the outlook for literature as a desirable and enriching curriculum experience is bright. An expanding publishing industry annually supplies an abundance of literature for children, while federal funding has assisted the growth of elementary school libraries. Teachers have more resources from which to draw for an enriched literature program than ever before. Also, more parents are aware of a responsibility to encourage their children to visit public libraries and to read for pleasure at home.

The Value of Literature for Children

Literature belongs in the elementary curriculum because it possesses qualities and values which cannot be supplied by any other curriculum area or by direct instruction in the skills of reading. Fader has said that every individual

> . . . is impoverished if he does not read with pleasure, because if he does not read with pleasure, then he is unlikely to read at all. And the poorest man in the world is the man limited to his own experiences, the man without books.[1]

For children who have difficulty reading independently, exposure to literature will come primarily from hearing it shared in the classroom by the teacher and the other children. It is especially important for those children who have experienced frustration in reading to enjoy stories read aloud by others. The enjoyment offered by literature can lead to the development of a love of reading. The entertainment attraction of stories is probably the most significant factor in motivating children to read independently, thus furnishing a constructive and creative use of leisure time.

Literature can broaden children's knowledge as they explore other ways of living in different times and places through the eyes of characters both similar to and different from themselves. Books also can offer vicarious experiences which extend children's knowledge of the world in which they live. For those children with limited backgrounds, literary experiences can help fill the void of a restricted range of concepts and vocabulary.

Literature can lead to understanding of self and of others. As children read about child characters with problems, they can develop an awareness of causes of behavior. Often their ways of thinking about themselves and others will be deepened or possibly altered. The role of books in developing self-insight or as a means of guidance is a significant value of literature. Bibliotherapy—using books to help children understand their personal problems—has been discussed by some authorities. Anderson identifies bibliotherapy as functioning in two ways in most elementary classrooms.[2] First, a child reads a book in which the main character has a problem similar to one he is experiencing. Second, and probably a more common application of bibliotherapy, a child or a group of children read books dealing with problems which may not be personal for them but from which they can understand how a particular problem affected the lives of the characters in the book. For example, in reading *Strawberry Girl, Roosevelt Grady,* or *Blue Willow,* children who have never experienced poverty can understand how it affected the people in these books. Readers can admire how the heroes of *Door in the Wall* or *Johnny Tremain* gradually learn to live with their physical handicaps. Even at the pre-reading and beginning reading levels, understanding of others can be fostered by using picture-story books. For example, when kindergarten and first grade children hear the story of *Crow Boy,* they can feel the isolation of that character. Of course, a teacher must judge whether reading about a character with a problem similar to one a child is experiencing is desirable or whether the child wishes to direct his reading to other topics. (The booklist "Personal Problems of Children," listed in Appendix A, identifies books related to problems of children.)

Literature also stimulates creativity. As children become acquainted with the creative products of authors and illustrators, they can develop an awareness of language, writing styles, and imaginative ideas. This exposure establishes a foundation for creativity. Along with hearing and reading many examples of fine poetry and prose, children should be encouraged to create original stories and poems. Literature can stimulate creative efforts in other areas as well, such as art and dramatics, if children are allowed to interpret what they read through these media.

Literature can be interwoven with all curriculum areas. However, while fictional literature extends and enriches curriculum study, it is not designed specifically to teach content. For example, *Across Five Aprils* has merit as an imaginatively and sensitively written book, as well as a well-drawn account of the Civil War. That the book helps children understand this period of history is an added benefit, not the major reason for presenting the book. Books of historical fiction, biography, and regional fiction do correlate with much of the social studies content of the intermediate grades. A teacher will want to have these books available when they are appropriate. However, such use must not spoil the enjoyment dimension of literature.

Finally, literature can develop an awareness of language. The aesthetic experience with language which it provides cannot be duplicated elsewhere in the curriculum. It is often the language quality and the imaginative use of words which distinguishes the excellent from the mediocre book. Exposure to the distinctive language of literature is closely related to fostering creative writing because it provides excellent models. If children are to use language imaginatively in their personal writing, they should have many opportunities for hearing the language through good literature.

In summary, children's literature is generally acknowledged to have the following values for children: it provides a source of entertainment, extends experience, promotes understanding of self and others, stimulates creativity, enriches other curriculum areas, and promotes language awareness.

FOCUS ON THE CHILD

A teacher's first consideration in planning a literature program should be the children themselves. What motivates these children to read? What are the individual interests of each, as well as the general interests of children of their age and grade level? Although there will be common interests among any group, others will differ within any classroom group. Knowing pupils' interests, backgrounds, abilities, and reading levels provides the teacher with a basis for the selection and recommendation of books while he seeks to extend both the pupils' range of interests and their exposure to books.

Attitude, interest, and personal motivation are determinants of response in any learning situation. A child who experiences pleasure and enjoyment in reading will be more likely to develop favorable attitudes toward reading; he will be more likely to develop "the reading habit."

Personal reading implies personal preference and choice with strong elements of individuality determining what each individual selects to read. There are some intangibles in personal preferences; a teacher must acknowledge and accept these. His obligation is to make a variety of interesting books available and to present many types of literature in interesting ways.

Children's attitudes toward reading and their choices of reading materials are affected by a number of factors, some of which can be manipulated by the teacher in the learning environment. Others, while they need to be recognized by the teacher, cannot be controlled. Research has established that cultural background, social class, parents' interest, age, sex, and intelligence influence interests; none of these can be directly influenced by the teacher.[3]

Factors a teacher can manipulate are the accessibility of books and the manner in which they are presented. A teacher can also see to it that the general attractiveness and literary merit of books are such as to appeal to children's interests. The teacher must recognize, too, that a child who cannot read well will not choose to read in his free time.

Social class can have a bearing on reading attitudes and interest. Children from the middle and upper classes tend to read more widely than do children from lower economic levels. Many of the latter come from home environments devoid of books and magazines, and so reading activities are not a part of their background or value system. A dearth of literature portraying life situations of these children is another reason contributing to their lack of interest in reading. In the past the world of books has not seemed relevant to many of them. In seeking to promote reading with male delinquents who had formerly rejected books, the authors of *Hooked on Books* found that the basic questions "What does it mean to me?" and "Why should I?" had to be answered in very real terms if these boys were to view reading as worthwhile.[4] On the other hand, children from homes where reading is valued often take more naturally to it.

Interest Factors

Reading preferences among children are tremendously significant—and tremendously varied—although some commonalities have been observed. Animal and home stories are of interest in the primary grades, adventure stories in the upper elementary grades, and peer group stories at the junior high school level. Spache has reported that the interests of children of low, average, and high intelligence of the same chronological age are comparable except that children of high intelligence have a wider range of interests.[5]

As early as first grade, there are some differences in interests between boys and girls, but these differences become much more evident as children move through the elementary grades. Girls tend to read more widely than boys and will read stories with masculine main characters, while boys in the intermediate grades tend to reject books they label "girl's books." When choosing books to read to the whole class, therefore, a teacher must consider sex preferences. Once started, however, the remainder of a book that has adventure, an interesting plot, and life-like characters, regardless of the sex of the main character, will appeal to children of both sexes.

In a review of research on children's reading interests, Huus found that the most important single factor in children's reading preferences seems to be the adults in the environment.[6] The implication for teachers is obvious. If they provide a reading model and make appropriate books accessible, there should be a favorable effect on children's reading. Pfau, reporting on an experimental program in primary classes where an intensive effort was made to create a reading environment and to encourage recreational reading through a thirty-minute period devoted to activities with library books, concluded that reading achievement was increased and attitude toward reading improved when such a program was followed.[7]

In ascertaining pupil interests, a teacher may employ several tools. Probably the most widely used and most easily employed is observation of children in everyday situations. An alert teacher can find many indications of interests through observing the children's art, discussions, and play activities. Another tool is a questionnaire or interest inventory which indicates children's leisure-time activities, television and film preferences, and hobbies. Bond and Wagner have developed a brief questionnaire which can be readily adapted for a particular group.[8]

Another means of determining pupil interests is the interview or pupil-teacher conference. In an interview a teacher may wish to use the questionnaire or interest inventory orally, especially for those pupils who are not yet able to read independently and who would have difficulty completing the questionnaire individually. Other information regarding pupils' interests can come from talking with parents and checking school records. As pupils keep individual records of their personal reading, a teacher will have another source of information regarding what children like to read.

FOCUS ON THE LITERATURE

In planning literature experiences, teachers must seek to answer the questions, "What is a 'good' children's book?" "What types of literature should be featured in a planned literature program?"

"What about balance and quality?" The first step in finding answers, knowing children and their interests, has been explored. The next step is to examine the available literature and to establish some guidelines for selection.

What is a "Good" Children's Book?

A teacher needs some framework for answering the seemingly simple question posed in the heading. It is possible to fill a classroom library corner with highly recommended books and still not have materials which appeal to children. Each year brings an increase in the number of books published annually for children. Since the number of books available is large and since many are of poor or mediocre quality, standards for evaluation are important. However, meeting certain criteria of evaluation does not mean that a book will necessarily be popular. Children should not be required to read certain books merely because they are highly recommended. Arbuthnot offers a pertinent comment on judging books, when she states that "a book is not a good book for children, even when adults rate it a classic, if children are unable to read it or are bored by its content."[9]

Support for selecting quality material is presented through the argument that children, in actuality, can read only a small percentage of the available literature and that they need to be exposed to high quality materials. While free choice and self-selection by pupils are desirable, a teacher should choose materials high in *both* interest and quality to read to children. With the large quantities of children's books now available, the criteria of both quality and interest can be met.

In college courses for prospective elementary teachers, we have found that when students are asked to enumerate the qualities of a good children's book, they quickly name plot, theme, format, language quality, and characterization but are surprised when informed that they are only at the easiest and most routine level of evaluation. Of course, the importance of credible, lifelike characters, excellent craftsmanship, originality, arresting plot, and substantial content cannot be underestimated.

However, an even more important consideration is what books can do *for* children and how they can reach children with greater impact than just surface enjoyment of a story. Arbuthnot suggests examining books in light of their relation to children's basic psychological needs.[10] The need for achievement; for physical, emotional, and intellectual security; for belonging; for play; and for aesthetic satisfaction can add to the appeal and value of books for children. For example, in the picture-story book, *Swimmy*, the needs for belonging, security, and achievement are portrayed through the story of the fish. Books of humor, such as *Horton Hatches the Egg*, can fulfill the need for play even though they touch upon other needs also. Arbuthnot states that, "Themes built around the need to achieve and the need, both to be loved and to bestow love, are vital at every age to a child's dreams of himself as a competent and accepted person."[11] Reaching children at a psychological level is also basic to bibliotherapy. (See p. 219.) In other words, in selecting books for children, a teacher must look for quality books having themes relevant to children's lives.

What Types of Literature Should be Included?

The types of literature that should be included in a balanced literature program is another question for consideration. Examination of textbooks in college courses in children's literature shows books ranging from Mother Goose, ABC books, and very simple picture books in the pre-school years, to more involved content books with simple plots in the primary years, to simple novels and nonfiction books at the intermediate grades. Stories about nature, everyday experiences, holidays, and home and family life abound at every level. As children gain greater independence in reading, they will sample realistic fiction about children in situations similar to their own lives, folk and fairy tales, modern fantasy, myths and legends, poetry, biography, historical fiction, and informational books. Separate criteria for each of these types have been established, and the reader is referred to texts about children's literature for this information. (See *Suggested Readings*.)

Jacobs suggests three parallels for achieving balance in literature experiences.[12] He calls for a balance between the new and the old, between realistic and fanciful literature, and between prose and poetry. Some old literature which has stood the test of time and which has qualities of lasting appeal still belongs in today's program. Stories written about contemporary times also have great relevance in stimulating interest and in understanding one's way of life. Realistic stories are easy for children to experience through identification with lifelike characters. Fanciful literature can stretch the imagination and provide an escape into a different world. Although children will read considerably more prose than poetry,

poetry has a special place in literature experiences. Again, the qualities of interest, meaning, and language that draw children to prose also function in the enjoyment of poetry.

It is the teacher's responsibility to provide a balance in literature and personal reading through books he reads to children and selections he makes available. Requiring children to read a certain number of books of particular types is forcing reading and will probably not produce favorable reading attitudes. A sufficient balance in children's reading will probably be achieved if a teacher presents various types of books in an interesting fashion. Teachers are sometimes concerned about children who read exclusively about one topic. However, at least they are reading something! Teachers do well to let them choose their own reading but also to expose them to other types of literature and other topics through classroom book sharing.

Recent Developments in Children's Literature

The effect of the increasing number of books published annually and the federal funds available to purchase library materials for elementary schools have already been cited. An additional trend toward meeting the needs of multi-cultural pupil populations has exerted an impact on both the substance and availability of books for children. Among the developments which are significant for the elementary school teacher are controlled vocabulary trade books for beginning readers, books with characters from minority groups (particularly blacks), more realism in fictional stories with an effort to present some characters and situations which are not "model" ones, the use of children's paperbacks, and packaged sets or kits.

Books for Beginning Readers Books designed specifically for the beginning reader have flooded the market in the past decade. They are labeled "I can read," "easy to read," "beginners books," or "controlled vocabulary books." This development is both desirable and alarming.

For too many years, the only materials which a child in the initial stages of reading could use were the pre-primers and primers of basal series with their stilted language and diluted stories. The recent availability of easy materials with a variety of stories and topics has been welcomed by parents, teachers, and children. These books are valuable for encouraging independent reading, and parents and teachers should supply them for children who are learning to read.

However, the use of controlled vocabulary materials as the only constituent of a literature program is alarming. With their vocabularies and limited sentence patterns, this type of book lacks some of the qualities of good literature, especially distinctive language. For example, rain falling in *Rain Drop Splash* is described by such words as *splashed, splunked,* and *trickled;* in a controlled vocabulary book a less colorful word such as *fell* would probably have been used. Vocabulary control is supported in instructional materials but questionable in literature. However, because some controlled vocabulary books do meet the standards of good literature, each book should be judged on its own merit. While they do contribute material for independent reading, these books should not be looked upon as providing literature experiences. Since children can understand many books which they cannot read for themselves, teachers should select well-written and enjoyable picture-story books to read to them.

Books with Minority Group Characters Children's stories about minority groups are increasing in number and availability. In the early 1960s attention was focused on the lack of curricular materials to provide meaningful content for the multi-cultural school population and this national movement had an effect on literature as well. While books of this type are increasing in number, the number is still far too small. Writing in 1965, Larrick stated that, "Across the country, 6,340,000 nonwhite children are learning to read and to understand the American way of life in books which either omit them entirely or scarcely mention them."[13] If character identification is significant in attracting children to books, the need for books about children from many minority groups is obvious. It is also important for middle and upper class children to read stories about those with other social and economic backgrounds. There is a need both for books such as *The Snowy Day* and *Who's in Charge of Lincoln?* where there is no mention of the characters' being black and for books such as *North Town* and *Mary Jane* in which being black in modern America is an important consideration.

In a study of the inclusion and treatment of minority Americans in children's literature, Gast recommends:

The use of contemporary children's literature about minority Americans should be increased in supplementing reading and social studies textbooks in the public schools. This recommendation is imperative if a balanced and 'culturally fair' presentation of American life is to be afforded to school children.[14]

A beginning has been made with books containing nonwhite characters. Teachers, librarians, and publishers are aware of the necessity and value of such books. However, popular books with adventure, humor, and lifelike characters of any social class or any ethnic group have value for children from minority groups too since they also need to read about those different from themselves.

Increased Realism In realistic fiction for children in the intermediate grades, there has been an ever-increasing trend toward more true to life situations. An example of this is the book with minority group characters. The trend is also evidenced in the parent image and home situations in some of the more recent books. While it is not advocated that children's books depict the violence which abounds on television and movie screens, children reading about less than ideal home and family situations can gain insight concerning behavior. As they react to the alcoholic father in *Queenie Peavy* or the too busy parents in *Harriet the Spy,* they are more aware of various home situations which affect children's lives. The increase in realism in current books is one aspect which makes reading more personal for children.

Paperbacks The paperback book, while relatively late in coming to the elementary school, is now making an impact upon the availability of reading material and upon the reading habits of children. The obvious advantages are the low cost, the variety of titles, and the opportunity for children to acquire personal libraries. While the materials are not durable, a nominal expenditure stocks a classroom with an extensive array of books.

Many well-known and popular books are now available in paperback editions. Several book clubs for elementary pupils offer paperbacks for personal collections. A school book fair or exhibit can encourage children to purchase these inexpensive books. While not intended to take the place of a well-stocked library, paperbacks should be capitalized upon to increase personal reading. The significance of these reading materials is reflected by the establishment of the Media Commission of the College Reading Association, by the appearance of *Paperbacks in Education,*[15] and by the publication in educational journals of articles about the use of paperbacks.

Packaged Kits or Sets   Another development in children's books is the packaging of sets or kits of trade (library) books. The kits are available from a number of publishers and are of two general types. One type contains a collection of previously popular books; the other contains books written especially for that kit. Both types generally include a variety of topics and are designed to meet a range of reading levels. While kits do supply a variety of content, they do not furnish sufficient material for a recreational reading program for all reading levels and interests within a class. The books within any kit may vary in quality and therefore need to be judged on individual merit.

Kits are particularly valuable in schools without a central library and provide one type of classroom library materials. For teachers conducting individualized reading programs, the kits are helpful to start the programs. For teachers unfamiliar with children's books, the kits may be a starting point for building their knowledge of books which can be used for personal reading. The kits are to be regarded as only part of the material needed for recreational reading, and their use does not eliminate the teacher's responsibility of making many other types of materials available. If a classroom literature program is based entirely on books contained in kits, it is likely to be insufficient.

FOCUS ON THE TEACHER

The key to developing a personal love of books is a teacher who communicates enthusiasm and an appreciation of literature through his attitude and example. Knowing children and their interests, and knowing literature are of great importance in promoting personal reading. Significant as these are, however, the success or failure of the personal reading program in the elementary school rests with the classroom teacher. In those classrooms where teachers are enthusiastic about books, and where stimulating contacts with literature are an integral part of the school experience, children are more likely to become avid readers. The teacher's responsibility, then, is to provide motivation, time, and materials to stimulate personal reading.

Underlying all experiences with literature is acceptance of the goal of encouraging a positive attitude toward reading; every practice, technique, or experience with literature ought to contribute to or be harmonious with that goal. In other words, a teacher should employ only techniques which contribute to favorable attitudes toward reading. Literature is not a vehicle for teaching specific facts, for providing drill on skills, for providing practice in writing reports, for analysis of minute details, for plot-dissection. What Anderson deplores as the "F.B.I. approach" does not belong in the elementary child's experiences with literature.[16] The traditional, required book report frequently creates a distaste rather than an appetite for reading for large numbers of children. We are all probably familiar with the attitude expressed by a fifth-grader (a prolific reader) when she told her parents that she only wrote book reports on books she did not like because she did not want to spoil any of the good ones! However, it is possible and desirable to provide many voluntary and creative ways for pupils to share and enjoy their reading.

Principles for Working With Children's Literature

As a summary of points discussed in this chapter and as a guide for working with literature, the following principles may be considered in planning and implementing children's experiences with literature:

- Enjoyment rather than instruction is the prime consideration.

- The literature program must be *planned* rather than incidental.

- Free choice of reading materials is desirable, encouraged, and respected.

- Stimulation of wide reading is more important than stress on quality.

- Classroom time must be provided for recreational reading and sharing of reading.

- Exposure to a wide variety of easily accessible materials must be provided.

- Personal reading is not to be dissected, analyzed, or reported in detail.

- A teacher presents a model through his attitude and enthusiasm toward teaching.

With the preceding principles in mind and remembering that

pleasure, exposure, and appreciation are foremost concerns in using books with children, we now direct our attention to putting the literature program into practice. The following suggestions can serve as guides for recommended experiences with major emphases on oral reading by the teacher, independent reading by the pupils, classroom libraries, and book sharing activities.

Oral Reading by the Teacher The most frequently employed technique to expose children to good books is oral reading by the teacher. By this means a teacher can best convey his enjoyment of books and ensure that children are exposed to a variety of types, topics, and writing styles. Quality literature can be presented at the same time that children's interests are considered. Children are stimulated to continue to read the story independently after the teacher reads aloud only an incident, an amusing dialogue, or an exciting chapter. At other times a teacher may read aloud a complete book after which there may be spontaneous discussions of a character's reactions, a significant theme, or a situation that has some relevance to the students' lives. They may talk about the author's skill in making a setting or situation come alive, or they may read additional stories by that author, about that topic, or with the same general theme.

In choosing books to read aloud, a teacher may select stories that children can understand but which they cannot read independently. There are numerous books that children, especially those at Levels A, B, and C, can enjoy and should hear before they have the ability to read them.

Oral reading by every teacher should be a standard procedure every day in every elementary classroom. Although it is rightfully a part of the daily class experiences, primary teachers are more apt to read to children than are intermediate grade teachers. In some classrooms at the intermediate grades, oral reading by the teacher does not occur because it is felt that these children are able to read for themselves. However, because it often leads children to read, shows an appreciation of reading by the teacher, and provides the best means of enjoying literature, daily reading or storytelling by the teacher is strongly recommended.

Independent Reading Classroom time should be scheduled for independent recreational reading, and the teacher should be free to assist children with words or to confer informally with them about their reading. Teachers also can select a few of the good readers to assist other children. Free reading is more valuable than some seat work activities frequently used while teachers are occupied in teaching another group.

In encouraging independent reading, teachers do not have to require children to complete every book they start. As adults we do not finish every book we select for reading, and children should have the same privilege of rejecting a book they do not like. Teachers may find it helpful to tell children, "Try a book. If you don't like the characters or the story after the first chapter or two, put that book aside and select another. We don't all like the same stories."

Pupils should always have a library book to read when they have free time. However, this alone does not provide enough time for recreational reading. Often students who need this reading most will take longer to complete assignments and will have very little free time to read.

Pupil-Teacher Conferences   From time to time during independent reading periods, a teacher may conduct individual conferences. In individualized reading (see p. 272), pupil-teacher conferences are used for instructional purposes; in recreational reading such conferences are used to provide a more personal interaction with a pupil and his reading. The purpose is not for skill instruction but for discussion of books or for suggestions concerning future reading. A teacher can use the conference to discover reading interests and to determine the types and extent of independent reading.

Library Visits   From kindergarten through the sixth grade, time should be reserved on a regular basis for a minimum of one visit each week to the school library; children should also be able to visit the library when necessary during regular school hours. During the regular library visit, children can check out books for the week. If a librarian is available, a special activity such as story telling, library instruction, or book talks can also be included. Ideally, the library functions as an indispensible resource for the elementary school. In communities without a public library, the school library has an even greater function in providing materials and services.

Visits to local public libraries are also encouraged. Teachers will find that a field trip to a nearby library is worthwhile. Procedures for borrowing books and for obtaining library cards can be explained by the librarian. At the close of the school year, a field trip of this type is especially valuable to encourage children to read during the summer vacation. In schools where there is no elementary library, use of the public library is essential.

Classroom Library Corner   A focal point of every classroom should be the library or free-reading corner where there is concrete evidence of a dynamic reading program. Ideally, the library corner includes an abundant supply of frequently changed books and interesting book displays. Attractive bulletin boards, dioramas, mobiles, and other art objects can be featured in this corner. Also useful are a reading table where children can read and examine books, and if space permits, additional chairs and rugs. Book files and notebooks, copies of the class newspaper, and book reviews (described below) can be available to guide the students' selection. Children as well as the teacher assume responsibility for planning and caring for this learning center. The opportunity to display their work can motivate them to use books for stimulating creative art and writing projects.

Small Group Book Sharing   Small group activities related to books can be a successful means of informally sharing reading experiences and of stimulating further reading. Groups of five to ten children provide a comfortable, relaxed setting. Some children who would be uncomfortable talking in front of a class may be more relaxed in such a group. More children can do more sharing if groups are small. For example, if an entire class of thirty give separate reports, considerable time is consumed. However, if the class is organized into five groups, with each child given five minutes, thirty children in a class can share their reading in some form in only a half-hour of class time. It is recommended that most oral book sharing be conducted in small groups.

Personal Recommendations   For adults, one spur to personal reading is the casual but genuine recommendation by a friend or colleague of a book he thinks would be enjoyed. It is logical to capitalize on similar personal recommendations by children to stimulate others to read. A few minutes a week in the small groups described above can be utilized for this purpose. This practice seems much more meaningful than a rote oral book report given before an entire group with a child parroting, "I read _____. The author was _____. I liked it because _____." This type of report is often given before an audience that has little interest in such a routine procedure.

Group Notebooks or Files   Group notebooks or files can serve as a means of reacting voluntarily to books and as a source of children's recommendations for reading. A teacher places a notebook or file box in the library corner at the beginning of the year. In that notebook, he identifies twenty to fifty books which are usually popular with children of that grade level. Every time a pupil reads one of the books, he may write a comment about that book, feeling free to sign or not sign his name. Children then can read their classmates' comments to decide whether to read one of the books. Pupils may be asked to recommend other books that can be added to make the file an on-going project and one which is directly related to pupils' reading.

Book Reviews   Writing book reviews presents a practical experience with a specific writing style. A teacher can introduce book reviews through a local newspaper or through professional magazines which include reviews of children's books. He explains that a book review may cause a reader to want to read a new book and that it evaluates a book without giving a plot summary.

Reviews written by the children can help others decide whether to read a particular book. These reviews can be included in the class newspaper or a special paper consisting entirely of reviews. They can be duplicated and taken home to inform parents about the class's reading, distributed to other classes, and posted in the school and classroom libraries. In all writing experiences with books, however, teachers must be careful not to overdo formal writing or to make such activities dull and routine.

Class Newspapers   A meaningful language arts activity which integrates reading and composition skills is the creation of a class newspaper. Information about new books and displays in the classroom library or an interview with the school librarian can be included. Other possible features are original poems or stories as well as the book reviews described above.

Book Jackets   Writing a "blurb" similar to those found on the insides of book jackets is still another type of writing experience with books. The teacher provides examples by reading aloud blurbs from several books with which the group is familiar. Also, before reading a book to the class, he can read the blurb for that book. The style of writing is discussed as children note the characteristics. Then the children write their own blurbs for presentation in small group sessions or for model book jackets. The book jackets can be illustrated and used for display.

Character Sketches   Character identification is one of the strongest forces which propel children through a story, and it can be used as the basis of a type of writing which is an outgrowth of literature —the character sketch. The teacher usually presents a few sketches before asking children to write them. He might read one before reading a particular book saying, "Do you think you would like to know more about this person?" The riddle, or "Who Am I?" type character sketch is usually popular. After hearing the teacher's examples, children develop their own character sketches. These can be oral, written, or dramatized for added emphasis and enjoyment. Small group sessions can be used for sharing the sketches.

Other Creative Experiences   Activities with literature can provide a creative stimulus for original writing. Poetry, tall tales, fables, conversation, or incidents can serve as models after which children pattern their own stories or poems. Often these will be of a particular type or treat a special topic. In working with creative writing, ideas and content are more important than form. Frequently exposure to the language of literature can be the touchstone for developing language awareness and creativity.

Books can lead to creative expression through art and through dramatic experiences. For example, children usually enjoy illustrations, murals, mobiles, dioramas, and puppets which correlate with favorite books. They are enthusiastic about dramatic interpretations of a favorite incident or memorable conversation in a book, or the pantomime of a favorite character. Props and scenery are generally very informal and are kept to a minimum; the objective is not a finished production but rather self-expression through dramatic interpretation.

How Can Teachers Keep Informed About Books?

Selecting books for children and keeping informed about recent publications are continuing problems for elementary school teachers. Fortunately, a number of sources provide this type of information. Reviews of children's books appear in such educational periodicals as *The Horn Book, Elementary English,* and *Childhood Education.* Large-city newspapers, as well as some popular magazines such as

Saturday Review, also include reviews of children's books. For suggestions about new books which may be appropriate for his classes, the teacher always maintains contact with children's librarians of local public libraries and with school librarians. Appendix A contains an annotated list of references for selecting and evaluating children's books.

Chapter Review

The reading habit, if not begun in the elementary school years, may not begin at all. The true evaluation of the effectiveness of literature experiences for today's children will be evidenced in their reading habits as adults. Only if recreational or personal reading is made an integral part of the school experience and a meaningul part of children's lives will the teaching of reading be successful in producing children who are readers. The children's age, sex, background, and interests must be considered by the teacher in choosing reading materials. Also essential are enthusiasm and diversity of presentation and balance in materials. Improved elementary library facilities with qualified personnel to assist the teacher in developing rich programs of personal reading are needed. Providing experiences with literature and opportunities for personal reading remains the responsibility of every teacher in every elementary classroom.

NOTES

[1] Daniel N. Fader and Morton H. Shaevitz, *Hooked on Books* (New York: Berkley, 1966), p. 10.

[2] Paul S. Anderson, *Language Skills in Elementary Education* (New York: Macmillan, 1964), p. 281

[3] George D. Spache, *Good Reading for Poor Readers* (Champaign, Illinois: Garrard, 1970), pp. 3–7.

[4] Fader and Shaevitz, pp. 11–12.

[5] Spache, p. 4.

[6] Helen Huus, "Interpreting Research in Children's Literature," in *Children, Books and Reading*, Perspectives in Reading, no. 3 (Newark, Delaware: International Reading Association, 1964), pp. 123–127.

[7] Donald W. Pfau, "Effects of Planned Recreational Reading Programs," *The Reading Teacher* 21 (October 1967): 34–39.

[8] Guy L. Bond and Eva B. Wagner, *Teaching the Child To Read* (New York: Macmillan, 1966), p. 293.

[9] May Hill Arbuthnot, *Children and Books* (Chicago: Scott, Foresman, 1964), p. 2.

[10] Ibid., pp. 3–10.

[11] May Hill Arbuthnot, "Dawn Wind Stirring," in *Children, Books and Reading,* Perspectives in Reading, no. 3 (Newark, Delaware: International Reading Association, 1964), p. 5.

[12] Leland B. Jacobs, "Give Children Literature," *Education Today,* Bulletin no. 22 (Columbus: Charles E. Merrill).

[13] Nancy Larrick, "The All-White World of Children's Books," *Saturday Review,* 11 September 1965, p. 64.

[14] David K. Gast, "Minority Americans in Children's Literature," *Elementary English* 44 (January 1967): 21.

[15] Vivienne Anderson, ed., *Paperbacks in Education* (New York: Teachers College Press, 1966).

[16] P. Anderson, p. 290.

SUGGESTED ACTIVITIES

1. Prepare a display for a classroom library corner.
2. Visit the children's section of a public library. Observe a story hour and participate if possible.
3. Read one of the books cited in this chapter and analyze the reasons why that book would or would not appeal to children.
4. Prepare a stimulating book talk which would motivate children to read the book you selected.
5. Examine one or more of the book lists in Appendix A.

SUGGESTED READINGS

Arbuthnot, May Hill. *Children and Books.* 3d ed. Chicago: Scott, Foresman, 1964.

A comprehensive treatment of children's literature is presented as well as extensive bibliographies with every chapter and for every type of literature.

Fader, Daniel N., and Shaevitz, Morton H. *Hooked on Books.* New York: Berkley, 1966.

This paperback book describes a program for using paperbacks, magazines, and newspapers to stimulate delinquent and multicultural youth to read.

Huck, Charlotte S., and Kuhn, Doris Y. *Children's Literature in the Elementary School.* New York: Holt, Rinehart and Winston, 1968.

Chapter 1 is a basic introduction to children's books. The final three chapters contain practical suggestions for conducting a planned literature program with many activities using books.

Larrick, Nancy. *A Teacher's Guide to Children's Books.* Columbus: Charles E. Merrill, 1960.

Each chapter discusses a different topic relevant to types of literature and to using books with children. A helpful annotated bibliography is included.

Spache, George D. *Good Reading for Poor Readers*. Champaign, Illinois: Garrard, 1970.

The factors affecting children's interests and the psychological aspects of reading materials are discussed. The book lists included emphasize books which appeal to children who have difficulty with reading.

PART THREE

MEANS
OF
IMPLEMENTATION

CHAPTER ELEVEN

PLANNING LESSONS

Advance Organizer

Putting one's theory into operation is a challenge for all teachers, but particularly for beginning teachers. Daily instruction in reading must be an outgrowth of a clear understanding of the broad objectives of reading instruction and must be centered around the specific objectives for each lesson. For effective planning the teacher asks and answers many questions: Do children possess all the previous understandings for learning the content of this lesson? What are the objectives? What materials would clarify the presentation? What procedures will accomplish the objectives? What follow-up is appropriate? How can I evaluate each child's learning?

This chapter stresses the necessity of planning and provides a framework for developing plans for teaching reading. Six specific plans are presented for implementing the content discussed in Part Two. Each plan illustrates a different type of skill.

A Basic Format for Planning

Planning is one of the necessary components of effective teaching. The inexperienced teacher often has difficulty in planning lessons efficiently and thoroughly. Although commercially prepared elementary reading materials are usually accompanied by detailed teachers' guides containing thorough and helpful lesson plans, a beginning teacher may find it difficult to adapt that material to the needs of his particular class. Also, a great deal of reading instruction is accomplished with materials and in situations which the teacher himself has designed and for which there are no prepared guidelines. The lesson plans illustrated in the following pages are prototypes which teachers can adapt to much of the content and the situations in their particular classes.

A plan provides a guide for teaching that clarifies the presentation of material. It is not, however, an exact record of what will occur. Rather, a plan helps organize content into a sequence of activities and provides clues for evaluating learning and for indicating areas for future learning. Planning, of course, must be based on the levels, needs, and interests of the group for whom it is intended. Because pupil responses are of foremost importance in teaching and learning, any lesson must be altered on the basis of pupil-teacher interaction in each learning setting.

The plans which follow are intended for small groups working at specified levels on particular skills. In most classes, all children would not be at the same level of reading development; therefore, these plans would probably not be suitable for all groups within a class. Further, the plans contain only hypothetical suppositions about pupil responses; a teacher must be able to adapt all content and procedures in light of the pupil-teacher interaction that occurs in each lesson.

Although there are many possible formats for planning lessons, we have elected to use one basic outline in each of the lesson plans which follow because of its simplicity and adaptability to various content. In each example, the major headings are identical, but the *Procedures* section is developed differently as a result of the different nature of the skills to be taught and the difference in levels.

The sample outline described in each lesson, while it is not the only way to teach the content of that lesson, does emphasize one logical development for achieving the objectives. Other creative ways of teaching the content and a variety of materials and procedures are desirable and essential for effective, interesting teaching and learning. Teachers can use this basic planning framework to guide their thinking, although they will not necessarily find it practical to write plans in this amount of detail.

Format of the Plans

The outline followed in the illustrative plans consists of the following divisions: previous learnings assumed, objectives, materials, procedures, and evaluation.

Previous Learnings Assumed   The prerequisite knowledge for grasping the concepts of any lesson is an important aspect of planning. For a lesson to be appropriate for a given group of pupils, the necessary prior learnings should have already been mastered. In other words, the structure of every lesson is determined by the group's previous knowledge. As the teacher develops plans for teaching, he is, in effect, "programming" the learning sequence in light of pupils' backgrounds and levels. If he discovers that a necessary previous understanding is not known by several pupils, he must revise the original plan in order to teach or to reteach the missing concept. If only one or two pupils lack an essential previous understanding, the teacher will find it most efficient to work with them individually but probably not during the specific lesson.

Also, attention may be given to previous learnings in a quick review or "warm-up" as the first part of a lesson.

Objectives   Effective teaching must center around clearly stated objectives. In planning a reading lesson, the teacher identifies the general objectives of the reading program to which a specific lesson relates. (These broad objectives were discussed in chapter 2.) For each lesson it is also important to identify specific objectives for pupils, many of which can be stated in behavioral terms. A lesson plan states what children should be able to *do* as a result of that lesson. Procedures are therefore planned after objectives are identified.

Materials   All materials to be used by the teacher in a presentation and those materials needed by the children are listed in the lesson plan. If the teacher identifies beforehand specific materials which can be used to promote interest and facilitate learning, the teaching is more likely to be stimulating. Student teachers and new teachers are more apt to present lessons with originality and variety when asked to focus on the possible use of pictures, charts, objects, pupil-response cards, and audio-visual equipment within a lesson.

Attractive materials do not guarantee effective teaching and learning; but if the materials enrich and clarify, if they aid in accomplishing the objectives, and if they add to pupil involvement, their contributions are valuable.

Procedures   Procedures comprise the major part of a plan and should be written clearly enough so that someone else would be able to follow them as a guide for teaching. There should be a logical sequential development with attention given to motivation, pupil involvement, provision for questions and pupil response, and a summary of the major understandings covered.

The plans which follow utilize procedures for each skill which were recommended in the chapters on the instructional program for Levels A through D.

Evaluation   Evaluation is a vital part of teaching, as we have seen. It should be carried on continuously by the teacher in all aspects of reading instruction. Much evaluation in reading uses specific tools such as tests and inventories for assessing pupil achievement, but continuous evaluation in all reading activities is an integral part of diagnostic and developmental teaching.

The evaluation section of a lesson plan provides guides for evaluating pupil learning and the effectiveness of the teaching. These sections in the following sample plans are hypothetical but are included to point out the relationship between this dimension of planning and other dimensions. In evaluating a lesson the teacher considers whether each objective was achieved by each child. He then plans subsequent learning experiences on the basis of his evaluation.

LESSON PLAN 1:   PRE-READING AND BEGINNING READING "AN EXPERIENCE CHART" (LEVELS A AND B)

Previous Learnings Assumed

It is assumed that children have the ability to express ideas in oral language.

Previous handling of experience stories is helpful but not essential, as is previous experience in matching similar letters and words.

Objectives

General Objectives For children operating at Level A, pre-reading, the general objectives are to show a relationship between spoken and written language; to provide experience in left-to-right progression, in visual discrimination, and in auditory discrimination; and to develop interest in printed words.

For children operating at Level B, beginning reading, an additional objective is to develop sight vocabulary.

Specific Behavioral Objectives As a result of this lesson at Level A, children should be able to :

- Suggest and discuss ideas pertinent to the topic.

- Follow a line of print from left to right.

- Match letter, word, phrase, and sentence cards to letters, words, phrases, and sentences on the chart.

- Identify two or more words which begin with the same sound.

At Level B, children should be able to do all of the above as well as identify specific words which they can read.

Materials

- A stimulus object or an experience to motivate discussion—for this lesson, a turtle.

- Primary chart paper and a felt-tip marker.

- A chalkboard.

- Letter, word, phrase, and sentence cards to correspond with the content of the chart.

- Duplicated copies of the chart.

Procedures

Initiation The teacher presents a topic or stimulus for discussion. In this example, he has brought a turtle to class.

Oral Discussion The children are encouraged to talk about the turtle.

The teacher can ask, "How does the turtle look to you?" Or he can explain, "I found him in my yard. I thought you might want to decide how we can take care of him."

Recording of the Story As children talk, the teacher writes their ideas on the chalkboard or on the chart. One example is:

The turtle came from the woods and Mrs. Conner found him in her yard.
We will keep him in a big box.
The turtle has marks on his shell.

Children's ideas are recorded as spoken with no attempt made to control vocabulary, to use only short sentences, or to repeat certain words.

Reading of the Story After the story is developed, the teacher reads it aloud to the class. Then he may say, "I'll read it again. You might like to read it with me this time." As he reads, the teacher moves his hand from left to right. For further reading practice, depending upon the group, he may ask individual children to read either the complete story or single sentences with him.

Further Practice The story can also be recorded on chart paper for rereading. Again, the teacher reads the story with the children first, to build the feeling of success. After this, individual children can be asked to read the entire chart or separate sentences. The second day's activities include having children match letter, word, phrase, and sentence cards for visual discrimination practice. The teacher can ask children at Level B to find a word they know how to read, or to look for a particular word. "Find the word *turtle* as many times as you can," for example. In instances where there are two or more words beginning with the same sound, children can be asked to listen for the beginning sound as the teacher says words from the chart, such as *has, him, her,* or *big, box.*

Other Follow-up Activities A duplicated copy of the chart, to take home or to keep in a personal folder of experience stories, can be given to each child, who is then asked to illustrate it. Children can also be asked to underline words they can read. The teacher then writes those words on cards for their personal word banks. Additional rereading of the chart may also be desirable.

Evaluation

Each child is observed to determine whether behavioral objectives for this lesson were achieved. The teacher makes the following type of notes as he observes individual children:

Juan: needs more experience in expressing ideas orally.

Jack: had difficulty in matching words and phrases.

Joe: quickly identified specific words.

In planning future experience stories, then, the teacher has some indication of points to be stressed.

LESSON PLAN 2: A PHONICS LESSON (LEVEL B)

Previous Learnings Assumed

It is assumed that children have learned the sound and letter forms for the consonants r, m, and b. No value judgment is implied in this order; the lesson is merely structured in such a manner as to require the learnings listed below.

It is also assumed that children have three or four words beginning with w in their sight vocabulary which act as stimulus words, and that all words used in the sentences are in their sight vocabularies.

Objectives

General Objective The general objective of this lesson is to develop independence in word attack.

Specific Behavioral Objectives As a result of this lesson, children should be able to:

- Recognize the sound of w in spoken words by responding with the appropriate *yes* or *no* card.

- Attack the new words by applying context clues and the initial consonant sound of w.

- Attack new words by using consonant substitution.

Materials

- Magazine pictures to illustrate sentences in *Application* step.

- Every-pupil response cards for *w, r, m, b, yes* and *no*.[1]

- A chart for initial consonant substitution used in *Application* step.

Procedures

Auditory Experience Several activities can provide auditory experience with the sound of *w* in spoken words.

- The teacher may say, "Listen to the word *wagon . . . wagon . . .* Now I am going to say some words. Listen to see if they begin like *wagon*. I will say *wagon* and then another word. If the words begin alike, hold up your *yes* card. If they do not sound alike at the beginning, hold up your *no* card. Ready?"

  The word pairs might include *wagon/want, wagon/boy, wagon/rabbit, wagon/wonderful, wagon/watch, wagon/month.*

- Or, the teacher might announce: "You have already learned the sounds you hear when *r, m,* and *b* are the first letters in a word. Remember that *w* is the letter at the beginning of *wagon*. This time hold up the card which shows the first letter in the words I say. Ready?" The teacher then pronounces a list of words, for example: *monkey, watch, witch, rose, run, book, mark, with, big.*

- To provide practice with oral context, the following type of activity could be used. The teacher asks, "Can you think of a word beginning like *wagon* which could be used in these sentences?"
  You can _____ a sweater.
  There are pictures on the _____.

Development of the Phoneme-Grapheme Relationship *Visual presentation* of the phoneme-grapheme relationship might be accomplished in the following way. The teacher writes *we, will,* and *want* on the chalkboard and announces: "Here are some words you know how to read. What is the first letter you see in these words?"

After the children have identified *w*, the teacher asks: "Show me your letter card for *w*. Does *we* sound like *wagon* at the beginning? . . . What about *want* and *wagon*? . . . What about *with* and *wagon*?"

Association of sound and letter can be accomplished, again referring to the list of words, by the teacher's asking: "How are the words in this list alike? . . . That's right, they all begin with *w*. They look alike, and they sound alike at the beginning. You know that the letter *w* stands for the sound you hear at the beginning of these words."

Application Using magazine pictures which correspond to sentences containing a new word beginning with *w*, the teacher may say: "Now, let's see if you can figure out some new words which begin with *w*. You know all the words except the ones beginning with *w*. Read the sentence I write for each picture, and think of a word that makes sense in the sentence."

Examples might include:

The girl is looking out the *window*.
The street is *wide*.
The boy has a glass of *water*.
The family likes to *watch* T.V.

It should be noted that the purpose is not for all children to commit these words to their sight vocabularies but to provide practice in using both context and the phonetic clue to attack unfamiliar words.

Further Practice For additional practice in consonant substitution with the letter *w*, the teacher might write or display a chart containing the following list of words:

get	ball	make	ride	tent	pin
_et	_all	_ake	_ide	_ent	_in

He would also say to children: "Here are some words you know. If the first letter of the first word is changed to *w*, you have a different word." The teacher will write *w* as the first letter of the word in all the examples and will ask the children to read all the resulting words.

In future reading situations children should be asked to look for words which begin with *w*. In this way they can find words (and even pictures) to add to a *w* chart in the classroom.

Evaluation

The teacher determines through observation of individual pupils whether all objectives were accomplished by each child. He notes such reactions as:

Billy: could not remember the sounds of *b*, *m*, and *r* from previous lessons and did not seem to distinguish the sound of *w*.

Ana: could not respond in the auditory exercises but did very well with the context sentences.

Carol: needs more auditory experience.

As he evaluates, the teacher may decide that another lesson needs to be devoted to this content, or that children appear ready to proceed to learning another consonant sound, or that some children need more practice with the content application.

LESSON PLAN 3: DISCOVERY PROCEDURE IN WORD ATTACK[2] "VOWEL GENERALIZATION OF SILENT e" (LEVEL C)

Previous Learnings Assumed

It is assumed that the stimulus words are in the children's reading vocabularies, that children know long and short vowel sounds, and that they know all the words used in the application step except the words to be attacked which follow the pattern being studied.

Objectives

General Objective   This lesson is designed to strengthen the broad objective of developing independence in word attack.

Specific Behavioral Objectives   As a result of this lesson, children should be able to:

- Apply the generalization of the silent *e* to new words.

- State the generalization of the silent *e* resulting in a long vowel sound.

- Respond with individual cards to indicate which word fits the context.

Materials

- Transparency and overhead projector

  or

- A chart of sentences for attacking words in context.

- Every-pupil response cards for *long/short 1, 2,* and *3.*

Procedures

Providing Sensory Experiences The teacher will need to provide auditory and visual exposure to the pattern to be learned. This can be done through use of a transparency with an overhead projector, through display of a chart of words, or through a written list on the chalkboard. Examples might include: *ride, rode, make, use, like, ate.* The teacher may read the words or ask the students to pronounce them.

Observing the Pattern In this step the teacher asks specific questions to call the pupils' attention to the visual clues to word attack. Appropriate questions for this pattern are:
"How many vowels do you see in each word?"
"What is the last letter in each word?"
"Listen while I say the words. What letter makes the last sound you hear in *ride*?"
"In *rode*?"
The teacher does this for each word in the list and then asks:
"What can you say about the sound of the *e* in each word?"
"Listen while I say each word again. Listen for the vowel sound. Hold up your card for *long* if you hear a long sound for the first vowel, and hold up your card for *short* if you hear a short sound for the first vowel."
The teacher then says *ride* and emphasizes the correct response

by saying, "Yes, your *long* cards should be up because the *i* in *ride* is long."

This procedure is continued for each of the examples, after which attention is given to the number of consonants between the vowels:

"How many consonants do you see between the two vowels in the word *ride*? Yes, one."

With some groups the questioning might be shortened, but the teacher must be certain that children are aware of the pattern.

Generalization of the Pattern At this step pupils are ready to generalize the pattern of the silent *e* vowel rule. Here the inductive development of the generalization comes toward the end of the lesson, although some authorities prefer that application precede the generalization. The teacher decides which order he prefers. He may ask, "What can you say about words which have two vowels when one of those vowels is a final *e*?" The teacher should accept the children's wording as long as it is accurate:

"When there are two vowels in a word, one of which has an *e* at the end, the first vowel is usually long and the *e* is usually silent."

Application of the Pattern The transparency or chart of context sentences is now displayed. For example:

A _____ is a piece of money.
   dime   *dim*   *dip*
    1   2   3

You can _____ on the ice.
   slid *slow* *slide*
    1   2   3

The old man walked with a _____.
  camp *cane* *can*
   1   2   3

A _____ tree stays green all year.
  pin *pink* *pine*
   1   2   3

Children should be asked to identify the word that makes most sense in the sentence and to hold up their 1, 2, 3 cards to indicate their choice. Each answer should be discussed with questions and comments such as, "How did you know the first word was *dime*? What kind of vowel sound did the *e* tell you to expect?"

Magazine pictures can also be used in the application step, as in Lesson Plan 2 (page 249). For example, with appropriate pictures the following sentences could be used:

The man will *drive* the car very fast.

The *crane* will lift the dirt.

What will he *decide* to do?

Further Practice Children can collect examples of silent *e* words to add to their personal word banks or to class word banks.

Another lesson should be planned using words which illustrate this pattern that children find in their reading.

Evaluation

The teacher may make the following observations about each child.

Joan: The objectives were (or were not) accomplished, for she could identify the new word following the pattern of the long vowel and the silent *e* in the application step.

Bobby: needs more help with identifying long and short vowel sounds.

Marcia: needs more practice in attacking new words in context.

LESSON PLAN 4: VOCABULARY AND CONTEXT (LEVEL C) "MULTIPLE MEANINGS OF WORDS"

Previous Learnings Assumed

The words used in the examples are already part of the children's sight vocabularies, although some of the meanings may be new to them.

Objectives

General Objectives Plan 4 is an example of a lesson designed to increase independence in word attack through the use of context clues; to develop comprehension, with the context used to extend word meaning; and to increase reading vocabulary.

Specific Behavioral Objectives   As a result of this lesson children should be able to:

- State two or more definitions for selected words.

- Use the context of a sentence to determine the appropriate meaning of a word.

- Collect additional examples of words with multiple meanings.

Materials

- Group and individual word banks.

- Transparency and overhead projector

  or

- A chart of written context sentences.

- Every-pupil response cards 1, 2, and 3.

Procedures

Prior to this lesson the teacher will have surveyed both group and individual word banks, as well as the reading texts being used, in order to identify appropriate examples for this lesson. Many different examples can be used following the general lesson procedure.

Initiation through Oral Discussion   The teacher may ask, "Which of these two sentences would you most like to be true? 'You must be present at school seven days a week. . . . You will get the present you want for your birthday.'"

After children have responded, the teacher asks, "What word was used in both sentences? . . . That's right: *present*. When I say the word *present* by itself, do you know whether it means *to be somewhere* or *a gift*? . . . How can you tell which meaning goes with the word *present*?"

Children will discuss the two meanings and will generalize that meaning can be known only by how the word is used with other words in a sentence.

Application in a Reading Situation   Making use of an overhead transparency or a chart, the teacher may begin, "Here are some words you know how to read. I have used each word in two or three sentences on this transparency (or chart)." Each sentence is numbered so that pupil response cards can be used.

1) The man will park the car.
2) Children like to play in the park.

1) My watch says ten minutes until four.
2) The soldier was keeping watch.
3) Lots of people will watch the game.

1) John is at the head of the line.
2) The dog will head toward home.
3) Your head is a part of your body.

1) You can cross the street when the light is red.
2) The woman sounded very cross.
3) Do you ever cross your fingers?

The teacher asks the children to read the sentences and to select the word that is common to all sentences in each group. Again, the teacher may say, "When I say the words *park, watch, head,* or *cross* by themselves, do you know what I really mean? . . . No. Only if I say them in a sentence can you tell what the word means in *that sentence.* Let's try some sentences with these words. When I say the sentence with *park, watch, head,* or *cross,* show me whether the word means the same as it does in sentence 1, 2, or 3 on the chart. Show me your 1, 2, or 3 card."

The teacher can then use a variety of sentences such as "The people wanted to watch the ball game." He reinforces the correct response by saying, "Yes, your 3 card should be up because *watch* in that sentence means the same as it did in sentence 3 on the chart. Let's try another."

Summary To evoke generalizations about the importance of the context, the teacher may ask once again, "How can you tell what *park, watch, head,* and *cross* mean in any sentence since you know these words can mean more than one thing? That's right: the rest of the sentence will tell you the meaning."

The teacher can also ask children to get out their individual word banks or he can use a group word bank, saying, "Many of you have some of the same words in your word banks, but I wonder if you meant them to be used the same way." This will lead logically into follow-up activities.

Further Practice Pupils can collect other examples of words with multiple meanings for the class word bank or for their own word lists. A lesson might be developed from the teacher's selecting an example of a word with multiple meanings from among several word banks and asking each child, "How did you use this word?" Other children might respond with additional meanings. Children might also work in pairs, with one child holding up a word card and asking another child for two or more meanings.

Evaluation

As children respond with their number cards, the teacher can determine whether each child readily grasps the various meanings of the words utilized. He evaluates their application of this knowledge as they collect other words on the following days. He also notes how children use context to define a word.

LESSON PLAN 5: A COMPREHENSION SKILL (LEVEL D) "DISTINGUISHING BETWEEN FACT AND INFERENCE"

Previous Learnings Assumed

It is assumed that children can read the words in the advertisements selected, that they are able to read at the literal level, that they are able to interpret material in terms of their own experiences, and that they know the meaning of terms *fact* and *inference*.

Objectives

General Objective   The general objective of this lesson is to extend children's reading comprehension.

Specific Behavioral Objectives   As a result of this lesson, children should be able to:

- Identify a given statement as fact or inference.

- Read at the problem-solving level as they use information gained in reading to respond creatively in a new situation.

In this instance they should be able to apply knowledge of fact and inference as they critically evaluate other ads in magazines and on television and as they use their knowledge of fact and inference to write original ads.

Materials

- Magazine advertisements
- Every-pupil response cards 1 and 2
- Opaque projector (optional)

Procedures

Oral situations are used initially to present the type of thinking that will be required in the reading activity.

Initiation in an Oral Situation   The teacher may ask, simply, "Do *you* believe everything you read?" Then the children discuss the reasons for their answers. The teacher then asks, "Do you ever get ideas from your reading that the author didn't really tell you?" This question too can lead to pupil discussion ending in the realization that it is not undesirable to add one's ideas to those of an author but that the reader should be aware that he is doing this.

Oral Examples   These oral situations can be presented at earlier levels of reading development, with appropriate statements for a particular group, such as the following:

The teacher may begin: "I see that Bruce is absent today. Is that a fact?" Children respond, "Yes!" The teacher may continue: "Bruce is not here because he is on a trip. Do you know if that is a fact?" The children will probably respond that they cannot know that Bruce is on a trip solely from the fact that he is absent. "If I say to you that Bruce is ill, is that a fact, are you supposing, or are you only referring that he is ill because he is not here? What else could you infer from Bruce's absence?" The children will suggest other possible answers not definitely verified. The teacher may conclude, "I have a note from his mother saying that he is sick. Is that a fact?"

Several other oral examples are possible. "Sally brought her lunch box to school today. Is that a fact? . . . Is it a fact that Sally brought her lunch? . . . You can infer this, but is it possible that Sally may not have brought her lunch, that she may instead have carried something else in that box?" The children may suggest other inferences.

The teacher may also say, "There are some new library books on the reading table. Is that a fact? . . . Is it a fact or an inference if you think that you will look at or will talk about the books today?" The discussion may bring out the point that, in their past experiences, whenever new library books were available they did talk about and look at them. However, until the books are examined, the idea that they talk about them is an inference.

Application in a Reading Situation   Using an opaque projector, the teacher may say, "Let's look at some magazine advertisements. As you look at each one try to see what *facts* they give you and what ideas the reader can only infer."

The ad selected might use the approach that three out of four individuals use a certain product. After pupils have read the ad, questions designed to identify all facts stated in the ad are usually asked first. Next, questions such as, "Is this product better than another brand?" will help children understand that, although the ad writer hopes they will infer it is better, he does not directly state that it is better.

With another type of ad—one promoting some beauty product— pupils can be asked, "Did the ad writer tell you what (brand name) is, what color it is, etc.? Are these facts? . . . Did he say you would have cleaner or prettier skin as a result of using this product, or does he only hope the reader will make that inference?"

An ad for a food product might lead to the question: "What does the ad writer want you to think about his food? What facts did he give you? What inferences do you think he wants you to make?"

Several other ads may then be shown with the teacher announcing: "I'm going to make a statement after you read each ad. You should decide if the statement I make is a fact or an inference. Answer by holding up your 1 card if the statement is a fact and your 2 card if the statement is in inference." Time should be provided for children to discuss their answers.

Summary   The teacher guides the discussion to bring out the generalization: "When you read, look for the facts an author states, but also realize that you make inferences from the information you read."

Follow-up Activities   Children can be asked to write ads to sell a product and to think about the inferences they want their readers to draw. These ads can be used by the group in the next day's reading or language arts lesson.

Children can also be asked to listen carefully for facts and inferences in the television commercials they see that night, or the magazines they read that evening. They can collect examples of magazine ads for further discussion and for other comprehension activities, such as detecting propaganda techniques or studying word meanings.

Evaluation

The teacher evaluates each child's ability to distinguish between fact and inference by his responses. He also evaluates the child's ability to use knowledge of fact and inference in the ads he writes. He will note whether any individual children have difficulty in this type of comprehension, and he may plan additional discussion and reading experiences for them.

LESSON PLAN 6: A STUDY SKILL (LEVEL D) "USING AN INDEX"

Previous Learning Assumed

It is assumed that children know alphabetical order, that they are able to read most of the words in the headlines and index, that they have had some experience in using the newspaper for studying current events, and that they are able to classify ideas into main categories.

Objectives

General Objective   The overall objective of this lesson is to develop depth in comprehension.

Specific Behavioral Objectives   As a result of this lesson, children should be able to:

- Use an index to locate specific information.

- Use knowledge of alphabetical order to quickly locate a topic in the index.

- State the understanding that an index is an efficient tool for determining where specific information can be located.

- Classify ideas under more than one heading. For example, they should realize that movies might be listed under other headings such as theaters or amusements.

Materials

- Copies of the same newspaper for each child.

- Indexes from other newspapers.

- Content area textbooks with indexes for follow-up instruction.

Procedures

The efficient use of an index is pointed out effectively through a discovery or problem-solving approach, in which children are asked questions and are permitted to find the answers through a variety of methods.

Children bring the daily newspaper to class, or the teacher requests enough copies for each child from a local newspaper office. A sizable paper from a relatively large city will be better for most classes than a small local paper.

Initiation   Questions are important in the development of this lesson. After the papers have been distributed, the teacher may say, "Let's see if we can locate specific information in our papers." Being sure to make the questions applicable to his particular situation, he asks questions such as the following:

Can you find what is playing at the _____ theater tonight?
Can you find out the score of the game between _____ and _____?
Can you find the weather map?
Can you find the highest temperature in the nation yesterday?
Can you find the _____ comic strip?
Can you find whether there are any furnished apartments for rent?
Can you find the gain or loss for yesterday on the New York Stock Exchange?
Can you find out what is on TV at eight o'clock on channel __?

As children search through the paper for the answers, the teacher should observe each child's reactions. Some children probably will be using the index, while others will be leafing through the pages at random.

Discussion After a few questions have been answered, the teacher may ask, "How can you quickly find the information you want to know from a newspaper?" Some may answer that, because they know the sports news is always on the first page of the third section, they look for that section. Another child may say he looks until he finds a heading related to what he wants to know. Another may say that there is an index on the front page which tells on what page certain information can be found.

At this point it is desirable to discuss the question of which method was the fastest.

The same exercise can be undertaken in a book, with the children coming to the conclusion that use of an index is a quick method of locating information.

Classification of Ideas Here too, the teacher uses questions to stimulate response. He may ask, "If I ask you to find a baseball score, what do you look for in the index?" The children may suggest baseball or sports, after which the teacher asks: "What else would you expect to find under *Sports*? . . . If you are looking for movies and the word *Movies* is not listed, what else could you look for?" Or, "If I ask you to find a recipe, what would you look for in the index?" The point to be stressed is that, when we use an index, we may have to look for more than one way of labeling or classifying information. Examples of indexes from other newspapers and books which use different categories can extend this understanding.

Follow-up Activities Within the next few days application of the use of the index should occur in the content areas of, for example, social studies and science, with children being asked to find specific information by using the indexes in various books in these subjects. Additional practice with newspapers can be provided if necessary. If children are preparing group or committee reports, or if they have a class newspaper, they can develop indexes for their own materials.

Evaluation

The teacher might note the following for each child:

- Does he need additional practice in applying alphabetical

order so that he does not read the complete index when looking for a specific word?

■ Does he need more practice in classifying ideas?

■ Is he slow in applying the index to locate information?

The teacher should use all such observations in planning additional work with an index or with classification of ideas.

Chapter Review

Teachers must see planning as a means of translating theory into procedures for implementation of the theory. Any plan is a guide rather than an exact record of a lesson. It can contribute to effective teaching and learning but must be related to the needs and levels of the pupils. Until teachers of reading realize how objectives can be attained through careful planning of learning experiences, such objectives are likely to be removed from the actual classroom experiences with reading.

NOTES

[1] Donald D. Durrell, "Learning Factors in Beginning Reading," in *Teaching Young Children to Read*, ed. Warren G. Cutts (Washington, D.C.: United States Office of Education, 1964), p. 75.

[2] Adapted from Morton Botel, *How To Teach Reading* (Chicago: Follett, 1963), pp. 40–43.

SUGGESTED ACTIVITIES

1. Prepare a plan for teaching one reading skill following the outline of the plans in this chapter.
2. Examine commercial reading materials, and evaluate the plans included according to objectives, materials, previous learnings, procedures, and evaluation.
3. Observe children in a reading situation and try to identify the objectives of the lesson in behavioral statements. Evaluate the lesson in terms of those objectives.

SUGGESTED READINGS

Baker, Robert F. and Schutz, Richard E. *Instructional Product Development*. New York: Van Nostrand Reinhold, 1971.

Field-tested, entry-level guides to the fundamental skills and concepts in instructional product development, including all aspects from identification of the desired outcome, through the writing of objectives, to refinement of the finished material or teaching strategy.

Brown, Thomas J. and Banich, Serafina F. *Guiding a Student Teacher.* New York: Harper & Row, 1962.

See chapters 6–11 on planning for direction on how to develop and analyze plans for teaching.

Devor, John W. *The Experience of Student Teaching.* New York: Macmillan, 1964.

The student-teacher and the beginning teacher will find the practical discussion of planning and the specific examples in chapters 6, 9, 10, and 11 helpful sources.

Mager, Robert F. *Preparing Instructional Objectives.* Palo Alto: Fearon Publishers, 1962.

A paperback devoted to helping teachers develop clear, well-stated, and well-defined objectives for instruction. Attention is given to framing objectives in terms of observable behavior of the learners.

Perrodin, Alex F., ed. *The Student Teacher's Reader.* Chicago: Rand McNally, 1966.

See chapter 8, designed to help the student teacher understand the complexities of effective planning and to integrate content from methods courses with student teaching experiences in planning.

Walbesser, Henry H. *Constructing Behavioral Objectives.* College Park: Bureau of Educational Research and Field Services, University of Maryland, 1968.

The task of constructing behavioral objectives requires a technical competency which is explained in detail in this book in an interesting format.

CHAPTER TWELVE

INDIVIDUALIZATION AND GROUPING

Advance Organizer

Regardless of the instructional objectives, materials, approaches, and the pupils' level of reading development, the task of reaching the individual remains. The focus of this chapter is on individualization and types of grouping which best meet individual needs.

The topics of individualization and grouping are complementary because each individual must be recognized both as a unique learner and as a group member. Schools must seek efficient ways of teaching groups of pupils while also providing for individual differences. Even in this age of the computer and of educational technology, individual learners remain the most important concern of our instructional programs. Approaches, materials, and curriculum content demand major attention, but this attention is significant only when it promotes individual growth in reading.

INDIVIDUALIZING INSTRUCTION

Throughout this book we have viewed children's reading achievement in terms of developmental levels—in which individual children progress at different rates, requiring different amounts of time and repetition to master various learnings. Pupils differ in background, ability, interests, adjustment, and learning style. In individualizing reading instruction, therefore, it is essential that the teacher look at a child's total reading development rather than at a grade level standard.

Individualizing instruction is both necessary goal and a difficult task. Because each learner is unique, and because a teacher is responsible for a number of pupils, each of whom varies greatly from all the others, providing appropriate instruction for individuals presents a formidable challenge. Yet, the teacher of reading must be concerned with instruction for each individual at the same time that he employs efficient ways of teaching groups of pupils. Few educators today would dispute the fact that appropriate instruction can occur in both individual and group learning situations and that both individual and group settings must be provided in a balanced reading program.

How Is Individualization Defined?

Individualization of instruction involves the adaptation of curriculum to pupils' interests and levels. In the past, content and rate of learning received the greatest attention in planning instruction for pupil groups evincing wide ranges of ability. The graded school concept, departmentalization, ability grouping, acceleration, and retention were common devices for fitting children and curriculum content together. Today's concern with individualization moves beyond content and rate of learning toward a concept of each child as an individual learner. The contemporary view is that learning is "personal, unique, unstandardized."[1] Individualization of instruction is concerned with developing each child's potential to the fullest, while also considering him a group member. The *1964 Yearbook of the Association of Supervision and Curriculum Development*, for example, contains the following description of individualization:

> Individualization of teaching is, under the best of conditions, a difficult, easily misunderstood function. Individualization of teaching goes beyond the content of the curriculum and beyond standardized instruction. Certainly it goes beyond routine academic achievement, for individualization gives *personal relevance* to experiences which the individual learner shares with the other members of his group.[2]

Individualization should be an underlying principle of all reading instruction. It should, however, be clearly distinguished from "individualized reading"—which refers to one approach for organizing a reading program—although this approach certainly stresses individualization of instruction. Another point often overlooked is the fact that not all individualization of instruction denotes a teacher working with only one child but implies, rather, the planning and provision of experiences which are appropriate for a child's level of reading development. Such experiences can occur in a one-to-one relationship between pupil and teacher, in a small group, or in a large group setting. As Stauffer has remarked, "individualized teaching and learning does not mean that it is solitary."[3] Indeed, the importance of each child's relating to and interacting with others in a group setting is of great concern to all elementary school teachers. Group instruction, therefore, does not imply that the instruction within a group is without regard for individual differences. Group learning can be personal to the extent that each pupil is encouraged to respond in an individual manner. In applying the concepts of individualization and level of development to reading, personal relevance and involvement in the learning are foremost considerations. Creative and divergent thinking must be encouraged, and pupils must be given opportunities for reacting personally in many types of reading situations.

INDIVIDUALIZATION WITHIN SPECIFIC INSTRUCTIONAL APPROACHES

With all the knowledge of child development, learning theory, and the reading process and with the extensive array of materials and the variety of approaches available for teaching reading, it should be easier now than in former years to develop instructional programs which provide individualization of instruction. One criterion for evaluating a school's reading program today is the extent to which the program makes effective use of available resources to meet individual differences. Individualization must be an integral part of every approach. Specific efforts must be made to reach pupils as individuals and to go beyond the prescribed content in every standard instructional approach.

Individualization in the Basal Reader Approach

In the basal reader approach, teachers may vary instruction for children of different abilities by adjusting the level of the material and by moving through it at different rates. Alterations in procedures as well as in level and rate must also be made. In all directed reading instruction, teachers can adjust the amount of vocabulary instruction, the degree of depth, the techniques used in background discussion, the types of questions, the extent of discussion of the content read, and the stress on skills and on enrichment activities.

In the vocabulary phase of a basal lesson, the teacher can provide extensive exposure to new words for slower children by first presenting words in context on the board or on a chart and then by using questions such as, "Can you find the word that means _____?" . . . "the phrase that tells _____?" . . . "the word that begins like _____?" . . . "the word that rhymes with _____?" Or, perhaps, "Can you match this word card or phrase with the same word or phrase on the board or on the chart?" For certain children there may be little or no need for this type of vocabulary introduction, while for others it is necessary. For still others, the context type presentation will suffice.

The teacher can extend the background of pupils through the use of pictures, audio-visual materials, and additional discussion of unfamiliar concepts. He alters his questions according to the pupils' needs in comprehension, and he always considers the level of thinking at which different children are operating. As suggested in chapter 8 on comprehension, with slower pupils it is advisable to utilize oral situations to present thinking tasks required in reading.

The amount of time spent on skill development also will vary according to level and need. If the teacher schedules skill periods for groups of pupils each day, he can compose these groups flexibly according to the needs of individual pupils. For example, if the teacher is working on a skill in an average group and a child from a higher group needs that practice, the child can join the group for that particular lesson. For some pupils, additional materials designed specifically for supplemental instruction in skills may be essential.

Teachers will find suggestions in the manuals for encouraging additional independent reading, language activities, or follow-up and enrichment activities very useful in extending the individual competencies of students. Able pupils especially ought to have extensive opportunities for original writing, wide reading, and research projects.

Individualization in the Individualized Approach

In the individualized reading approach, the teacher has an ideal system for individualizing reading instruction through the pupil-teacher conference and the self-selection of material. The encouragement of wide reading on subjects of personal interest and the close pupil-teacher rapport in the conference are excellent means of providing for individual differences in interests and levels. Since all children are reading different materials in their particular spheres of interest, personal motivation is high with a favorable attitude toward learning. The teacher's record-keeping for each child contributes to diagnostic teaching based on knowledge of each child's present strengths and weaknesses. The records of books read, new vocabulary learned, and skills mastered give each individual an indication of his progress and also add to motivation for learning.

Any successful approach to reading must promote positive attitudes toward the self. The individualized approach makes a great contribution in this respect since each child is moving at his own pace and feels no competition from other members of the class. Labels often associated with reading groups are eliminated. For gifted pupils, this approach offers the opportunity to advance rapidly without being held to the rate of a group.

The features of the teacher-pupil conference and wide independent reading are so valuable for the individualization of instruction that they should be incorporated into other approaches. However, since group settings for learning are also important, it is likewise advisable for group activities to be incorporated into the individualized approach.

Individualization in the Language Experience Approach

In the language experience approach, individualization of instruction also is evident. Personal experience stories on topics of high interest provide content of relevance and meaning for the child. The reading and writing vocabularies are personalized because the pupil uses those words which are needed by him for the expression of his thoughts. Pupil-teacher conferences in this approach develop a close personal relationship between both parties. Since children compose their own reading materials, the creative nature of this approach promotes another aspect of individualizing instruction—that of divergent and creative thinking. The advantages of interest, intrinsic motivation, and personal involvement in learning are obvious in the language experience approach. Instruction is adapted for individuals by alteration in the rate vocabulary is added to the word banks, in the amount of time spent on reviewing personal stories for slower pupils, and in opportunities for able pupils to do much independent writing and wide reading. The individual word banks of personally selected words offer a means of relating instruction directly to the needs and interests of individuals. The desirability of having reading materials containing the language patterns of the pupils is a distinct advantage in providing appropriate materials for culturally different pupils. In this approach as in others, record keeping is a necessity for teachers, and flexible groupings for skills as needed is recommended.

Individualization in Other Approaches

Individualization of instruction is also featured in other approaches and with other materials. The *Programmed Reading* materials are based on the philosophy of having pupils progress at their own rate as they go through the sequence of programmed books. The self-learning and self-checking features of these materials require the active involvement of the learner.

The *SRA Reading Laboratories* also provide materials which permit pupils to start at a level commensurate with their level of achievement and to advance at their individual pace. Pupil evaluation and pupil record-keeping inform the students of their progress and help the teacher evaluate learning.

Computer Assisted Instruction (CAI), which was developed by educators at Stanford University and first tried in the Brentwood Elementary School in Palo Alto, California,[4] is being used in some school districts in the United States. Specific reading lessons have been developed for computer presentation. Instruction is planned for individuals according to the content, type of presentation, and sequence of presentation. Materials selected for each child are controlled by his past performance and indicated level. While an average child may complete a lesson in about thirty minutes and a fast pupil in ten minutes, a slow pupil may require three to four presentations of a lesson.

Individually Prescribed Instruction (IPI) also uses computers in its program of sequenced worksheets and lessons developed to permit children to advance at their own pace.[5] IPI was developed at the University of Pittsburgh and the Oakleaf School in Pittsburgh. The computer prescribes a curriculum for each child who then works at his own speed. Content in science and mathematics as well as reading is programmed. Each child receives from the teacher a "prescription sheet" which contains his lesson. The child then completes his assignment independently with the necessary equipment (tape recorder, computer, and other aids). His work is checked by the computer, and subsequent lessons are programmed for him. Much of the beginning reading instruction is based on the *Programmed Reading* materials. Occasional group instruction is also used when a common need is identified or for certain types of activities.

Teachers find that the diagnostic features of CAI and IPI aid greatly in planning and in conducting appropriate instruction on an individual basis. Using these programs, the role of the teacher is that of a diagnostician as well as a presenter of content. One report stated that 70 percent of the teachers surveyed felt that the teacher is more important in the IPI setting than in the traditional classroom.[6]

The presentation of learning in small steps with the systematic sequence of skills is considered advantageous by many teachers. However, many others feel that reading is so complex that not all reading activities can be presented with CAI or IPI programs, and that the computers can only do a part of the reading instruction.

Individualization in Combination Approaches

Although individualization in a number of approaches is possible, as we have seen, no single instructional approach or set of materials can sufficiently meet individual differences. If individualization of instruction means appropriate instruction and opportunities for personal exploration in learning beyond the standard content, it is evident that it does not generally occur when too great or exclusive reliance upon one method exists. The creative teacher will see value in using many adaptations from many approaches as he seeks to fit instruction to the child.

A Classroom Environment for Individualization

The classroom setting fosters individualization of instruction through the atmosphere or tone set by the teacher, the materials available, the scheduling, and the organizational arrangements. The teacher must know his pupils as individuals, stimulate creative and critical thinking, foster an atmosphere in which pupils feel free to respond, and base instruction on careful evaluation of all pupils.

The classroom is best organized so that pupils have access to many materials for independent work. Learning centers are becoming common in elementary schools for the purpose of providing opportunities for independent learning. As teachers work with individuals or sub-groups in a class, other pupils use a number of learning stations for independent activities. Commonly, the learning centers are related to all curriculum areas, and many materials which a teacher formerly had to present to a class personally can be prepared for the centers, to be used and reused as needed.

Among the learning centers often found in a modern classroom are a reading corner, with a vast array of materials for recreational reading; a listening station with a tape recorder, a record player, and head phones for pupils; and a writing center with materials such as pictures, objects, catchy titles, group word banks, dictionaries (picture dictionaries for lower grades, more

"As teachers work with individuals or sub-groups in a class, other pupils use a number of learning stations for independent activities."

advanced ones for higher levels), and suggestions for creative writing. An art center can provide additional experiences in that curriculum area and can be utilized in conjunction with book sharing projects.

Classroom learning centers help combat the dilemma many teachers experience of not having enough time "to get everything in," especially in the creative areas of music, literature, creative writing, art, and drama, while at the same time finding it difficult to provide children with enough to do independently. Learning centers have much to offer in solving this problem. For example, if an art experience with a special medium or technique is introduced to the entire class in a directed lesson, additional experiences with this technique can be provided independently in the art center on following days. If a teacher wishes to present additional literature experiences, tapes of stories can be made available for use in the listening station. After the initial recording, no further teacher-time is required, yet children may listen to their favorite stories again and again. Having pupils prepare tapes also provides a valuable experience in meaningful oral reading. Teacher-prepared tapes of specific skill content are often correlated with work assignments. Commercially developed materials can also be used in centers.

OTHER FACTORS IN INDIVIDUALIZATION

The role of a teacher in individualizing instruction centers around diagnostic teaching and adapting instruction according to the group of individuals in the class. The role of the administration, on the other hand, is to support and facilitate individualization. In addition to the types of individualization within the various reading instructional approaches discussed above, specific practices of a more narrow focus can be implemented.

Key Practices in Individualization

Following are several examples of the most common ways in which to implement individualization.

   ■ If, as a teacher observes individuals during reading lessons, he notes a particular difficulty a child is experiencing with vocabulary, word attack, or comprehension, he may ask the child to remain after the lesson while he repeats the topic to be learned or reteaches some essential prerequisite skill. Practices such as this are extremely important in diagnostic teaching.

■ Many teachers form a small, temporary sub-group for reteaching or for the practice of some skill needed by all pupils in the temporary group.

■ Teachers also keep records on individual children, noting their progress, the content learned, books read, special interests, individual reactions, and other relevant information. They then use this informatoin to plan instruction.

■ Children's reading programs are planned on the basis of careful evaluation of records, standardized and informal tests, teacher observation, and recognition of special interests.

■ Groupings within a class are kept flexible and are modified when pupil performance in reading indicates that a different placement is desirable.

■ In some schools, a team of teachers plans the optimum placement of each child in a group for reading instruction.

■ Attention is also given to wide independent reading in many types of materials which have been personally selected by individual pupils.

■ Similarly, children are given open-ended assignments which can be developed creatively and differently. Writing a different ending, developing one's own stories, answering questions such as, "How would you feel if . . .?" or "What would you have done?" encourage divergent individual responses.

■ Individualization is fostered each time a teacher suggests to an individual, "Here is a book I think you will like. It is about. . . ."

■ Children working independently with some of the commercial materials designed for individual work and differing levels of achievement constitute one part of individualized instruction in reading.

■ Children are encouraged to form temporary and flexible interest groups for a variety of purposes such as sharing independent reading, creative writing, or other individual projects. If children wish to read favorite passages orally, groups can be formed for this purpose.

■ Pupils ought to be free to express themselves in new, personal, and original ways within any art activity, writing experience, or language discussion.

■ Children enjoy working in a buddy system, reading to each other, thereby providing extra practice and a successful experience.

■ Pupils and teachers work together from time to time in individual conferences, the length of which is directly related to the individual's present needs and interests.

■ Use of a recorder to tape their oral reading of favorite stories is immensely popular with children. As individuals evaluate their oral reading, each child can identify personal goals for improving oral reading.

■ The compilation of individual word lists for reading and writing—particularly word banks—is yet another way of individualizing reading instruction.

■ Children can use learning centers within the classroom for independent learning.

■ Effective teachers make special provision for more concrete learning for slower pupils through art media, through audiovisual materials, and through activities such as constructing models.

■ Teachers stimulate able readers to pursue topics of interest in depth through more individual reading and study and less drill.

Sex Differences in Reading

In designing instruction for individual differences, sex differences have to be considered. Until recently, schools tended to neglect the influence of this aspect on reading achievement.

In general, girls tend to surpass boys in reading achievement in the primary grades, although, by the intermediate grades, boys may "catch up." Because successful experience in the early years is of great importance, any difficulty encountered by boys in the primary grades should be acknowledged and examined. Some boys, in fact, never overcome the difficulties experienced in grade one and continue to meet failure in succeeding years. Heilman reports that the percentage of boys in remedial reading situations ranges from 65 to 90.[7]

The biological fact of being a boy does not in itself mean difficulty in reading, for any group of boys will show a wide range in ability and in other traits. Nevertheless, teachers need to be alert to different levels of readiness and to different ways of motivating and teaching those boys who exhibit signs of difficulty in learning.

Factors which may influence boys' poor achievement in reading have been elaborated by a number of writers. One of the chief factors appears to be that reading in this country is frequently regarded as a feminine activity. In the home it is often the mother who reads to the children. Boys are ordinarily encouraged to participate with other boys in active sports rather than in quiet activities such as reading.

Another factor is the fact that the majority of elementary teachers are women. Boys therefore lack male models in the school for identification with the masculine role. In the primary grades, where the discrepancy between the achievement of boys and girls is the greatest, the ratio of female to male teachers is the highest.

It may also be significant that girls tend to be more mature in both physical and linguistic development than boys during the early school years. Thus, girls are more ready for beginning reading instruction, while boys may suffer if formal reading instruction is begun too early or if the instruction offered is not adjusted for individual differences.

In addition, reading materials have tended to contain a preponderance of stories about home and family life which may interest girls more than boys. Authors and publishers today indicate that they are aware of the need to provide materials of interest to boys. Many new materials now meet this criterion.

Girls seem to adjust to the activities of most schools more easily than boys, who may be more active, more restless, and more likely to have a short attention span and to be behavior problems, exhibiting poor attitudes toward learning.

Concerning the question of whether certain instructional

methods may be more effective with one sex than another, the extensive studies of the U.S. Office of Education of instructional approaches in first grade reading are illuminating. This research reported that no single approach was clearly superior to other approaches for boys.[8] In a study of sex differences in first grade reading achievement, Wyatt further supported the view that the lag of boys in reading achievement seems to depend upon something other than the teaching method used.[9]

Clearly, adjustment to sex differences in learning requires adjustment to individual differences. The teacher must approach each boy and girl as an individual at the same time as he must be aware of general factors which bear on boys' motivation and achievement. For particular children, the teacher may well need to select materials with masculine appeal and to vary instructional periods by making them shorter and by interspersing them with more activity. Again, the teacher will need to evaluate readiness for initial instruction carefully and to make the necessary referrals and indicated adjustments in the instructional program.

GROUPING

Individual needs of children can often be handled by grouping children within the classroom, for they learn effectively in group situations when the groups are carefully formed and instruction is carefully planned. Grouping, in fact, is often suggested by the teacher's guides in reading materials.

Two reasons are usually advanced in support of group instruction. First, certain children often have common needs, so that it is more efficient to instruct them at one time than to do it individually. For example, a teacher might note that eight children need help in using initial consonant substitution. He forms a group for that topic and teaches eight children at one time.

A second reason usually given for grouping is that children often learn better in a group than individually. In teams formed for self-instruction and in discussions, they can learn from each other's responses. In fact, it seems reasonable that many children are less pressured and more relaxed in a group setting. As they relate to their peers in the group, they are learning important skills in human relations. As such skills improve, group learning situations become even more useful.

Common Grouping Practices

The two most common grouping practices in reading consist of 1) teaching the entire class at one time and 2) dividing the class into sub-groups—often three in number.

Full class instruction is a useful technique for the numerous instances when it is not feasible to do otherwise. For example, film presentations, a teacher reading to the class, children sharing experiences with one another, and teacher lecture situations tend to require full class instruction unless special physical facilities are available.

Many teachers use full class instruction effectively; however, many also misuse it. There is seldom a justification for all children reading from the same book, and yet this practice persists. When one acknowledges the individual needs and growth patterns of children, one realizes that it would be rare for a group of thirty children to be able to profit from the same reading lesson at the same time.

Dividing the class into groups—usually "fast," "average," and "slow"—helps meet the individual needs of children. Instruction is then designed to meet differences in 1) the reading level of the children, 2) the skill instruction of children, and 3) the speed with which reading material is covered. Typically, the teacher in a third grade classroom allows an hour and a half for reading instruction each morning. He works approximately one half hour with each group in directed activities. As he works directly with one group, the others work independently on activities which the teacher has assigned or on activities of their own choosing.

It is also common for the different groups to work from three different reading books. In the third grade, the fast group may be working with a fourth grade book, the average group with a third book, and the slower group with a second grade book. In the classrooms where there is only one set of books, the teacher commonly has children moving through the material at different rates. The fast group, needing less skill instruction and less preparation for reading, moves rapidly. The slow group, however, receives more detailed instruction and moves more slowly. In either case the children have a decided learning advantage over reading situations employing entire class instruction.

However, the three group technique is not without limitations. First, the children in any given classroom do not fall neatly into three groups. Table 5 shows the reading levels in an actual second grade class of twenty-two pupils. The first half of second grade is indicated by 2-1, the second half of second grade by 2-2, and the fact that the child is operating in the primer, an early book for first grade, by 1-P. Clearly, no system of three groups can be justified in terms of meeting the needs of these children.

TABLE 5   Range of Reading Level—Grade Two

Child	Level	Child	Level
1	1–P	12	1–2
2	1–P	13	1–2
3	1–P	14	2–1
4	1–1	15	2–1
5	1–1	16	2–1
6	1–1	17	2–1
7	1–1	18	2–1
8	1–1	19	2–2
9	1–1	20	2–2
10	1–2	21	3–2
11	1–2	22	4–1

The differences become greater as children move through school. Table 6 shows the authors' findings in an actual third grade class. Notice the increase in the range of scores. In second grade they range from 1-P to 4-1; in third grade from 1-1 to 6-0. If any teacher

TABLE 6   Range of Reading Level—Grade Three

Child	Level	Child	Level
1	1–1	15	3–1
2	2–1	16	3–1
3	2–1	17	3–2
4	2–1	18	3–2
5	2–2	19	3–2
6	2–2	20	3–2
7	2–2	21	3–2
8	2–2	22	4–1
9	2–2	23	5–1
10	2–2	24	5–1
11	2–2	25	5–1
12	3–1	26	5–1
13	3–1	27	6–1
14	3–1		

attempts to group the children shown in either table 5 or table 6 on the basis of one criterion, all of his grouping is doomed to failure.

Another limitation of the three group technique revolves around the self-concept of the children in each group. Teachers who treat the slow group as dull are likely to obtain dull results. If the fast group is treated as elite, relations among the children in the room become strained.

If grouping is determined on the basis of information such as that available in tables 5 and 6, the teacher will need to consider other reading factors, aside from estimates of reading level, important for instruction.

Table 7 shows the phonic skill development of the same children

TABLE 7   Range of Phonic Skill Development—Grade Three

| Child | Reading Level | CONSONANTS | | | Rhyming Words | Vowels |
		Initial	Blends	Digraphs		
1	1–1	S	NS	NS	NS	NS
2	2–1	NS	NS	NS	NS	NS
3	2–1	S	NS	NS	S	NS
4	2–1	S	NS	NS	S	NS
5	2–2	S	NS	S	S	S
6	2–2	S	NS	NS	S	NS
7	2–2	S	S	NS	S	S
8	2–2	S	S	NS	S	S
9	2–2	S	NS	NS	S	S
10	2–2	NS	NS	NS	NS	NS
11	3–1	S	NS	NS	S	S
12	3–1	S	S	NS	S	NS
13	3–1	S	S	NS	S	NS
14	3–1	S	S	NS	S	NS
15	3–1	S	NS	NS	S	NS
16	3–1	S	S	NS	NS	S
17	3–2	S	S	NS	S	S
18	3–2	S	S	S	S	S
19	3–2	S	S	NS	S	S
20	3–2	S	S	NS	NS	S
21	3–2	S	S	NS	S	S
22	4–1	S	S	S	S	S
23	5–1	S	S	S	S	S
24	5–1	S	S	NS	S	S
25	5–1	S	S	NS	S	NS
26	5–1	S	S	NS	S	S
27	6–1	S	NS	NS	S	S

that were the subjects in table 6. In this case their phonic knowledge is evaluated as satisfactory (S) or not satisfactory (NS), based on the Botel Phonics Inventory.

In table 7 the teacher notes that child number 10, like child number 2, has phonic needs in all areas. It is unlikely that they both are reading from the same book, but they might well find themselves in the same group when skills are being taught. Likewise, when consonant blends are being taught, children numbers 1, 2, 3, 4, 5, 6, 9, 10, 11, 15, and 27 can profit from instruction. If all other children have mastered consonant blends, they might better profit from instruction in other content. The table clearly illustrates the need for flexibility in grouping and for consideration of the instructional goals of any group.

General Guidelines for Grouping

In view of the problems inherent in any grouping situation, and in view of the desirability of providing instruction for children in groups, the following guidelines for grouping should prove useful.

First, grouping for reading instruction ought to be viewed as temporary. Groups are to be dissolved when the instructional goals of the group are satisfied, and new ones formed in keeping with new goals. The skills grouping called for in table 7 serves as an illustration. For example, a group could be formed to work with consonants and be dissolved when the skill has been mastered. Temporary grouping serves to motivate the learner and to promote efficiency in the use of instructional time.

Second, grouping of children for reading instruction should always be viewed as flexible. As the needs of a child within a group change, the child is moved from the group to a more appropriate one. If he masters the skills appropriate to the goals of one group, he is removed. Flexible grouping also motivates the child, making it clear to him that his efforts to master the goals are recognized.

Finally, groupings should be handled openly. Children enjoy working in groups when they have some choice in doing so. For example, if a teacher uses a three group method, he may invite any child to read with any group when the child is interested in doing so. Open grouping breaks the above limitation concerning damage to self-concept since a slow reader may occasionally join a fast group when he chooses to do so. The time used in participation with other groups is usually well spent.

Other Grouping Possibilities

At times school-wide grouping can provide for individual needs. At other times grouping can take place within the classroom. A brief study of each type of grouping will be helpful for the teacher's future planning.

Within the School   School staffs often agree to group children for placement with teachers in specific ways. Several of the most common are explained below:

Heterogeneous grouping refers to grouping children at the same grade level on a chance basis. When schools arrange children heterogeneously, children of high and low ability are in the same classroom. Many find such an arrangement most satisfactory for the majority of children, for the teacher has no preconceptions about the makeup of the groups in his classes.

Homogeneous grouping within a school is similar to the three group method of grouping with a classroom. Within a school, however, it relies on decisions concerning which teacher will teach the fast children, which will teach the average, and which will teach the slow. The lack of similarity among groups arranged homogeneously is readily apparent, for no group is truly homogeneous. The major disadvantage is that it is difficult to move a child from one room to another, thus violating the idea of flexibility.

Inter-class skill grouping calls for rearranging teacher assignments when skills in reading and/or language arts are being taught. Teachers may develop particular competencies such as perception, language, vocabulary, or word attack development. When a child needs certain skills, he can be moved from his regular teacher to the one who best teaches these skills. He then spends the remainder of his day in his regular classroom situation.

A special grouping arrangement, the Joplin plan, has received acceptance in many school systems. This arrangement calls for the regrouping of children across grade lines during reading class. If a fifth grade child is reading on the fourth grade level, he is assigned to a teacher who instructs on that level for reading class. Normally he will spend the remainder of his day with children in his regular classroom. Narrowing the range of reading ability with which a single teacher must cope is a major advantage of the Joplin plan. The limitations of this method include the limitations of homogeneous grouping plus the difficulty of coordination of reading with other areas of the curriculum.

Team teaching is another arrangement which capitalizes upon the strengths of individual teachers. There is no one team arrangement; different teams operate in different ways. Usually, team teaching calls for several teachers to plan together for the instruction of children assigned to them. A team might consist of four sixth grade teachers, each responsible for the instruction of children assigned to them, but each assisting the others in planning and teaching. For example, one teacher may be a specialist in the language arts, one in the sciences, another in the fine arts, and so on. The major advantage of team teaching is that while an elementary teacher specializes, he also sees the relationship of his specialty to the entire curriculum and plans and teaches accordingly.

Within the Classroom   Teachers usually have considerable freedom to arrange their classes in a manner suited to their teaching style. Several of the following opportunities can be investigated:

As discussed previously, grouping by reading ability is widespread and commonly accepted. However, it assumes that within a reading group, children's needs are the same. A reexamination of table 7 indicates that such is not the case.

Teachers have found that grouping for reading by reading level and regrouping by skill needs for skill instruction are useful techniques. Through such an arrangement, a teacher provides instruction for children according to their strengths as well as their weaknesses. Skill groupings must of necessity be flexible and temporary.

Through open grouping, also previously discussed, a child can choose to join a group for a series of lessons when 1) he feels that he needs such instruction, and 2) when he feels he has something to add to the group. Naturally, he can also be assigned to a group for a temporary period when the teacher assesses that he needs instruction or that he can contribute to the group.

Finally, interest grouping has been a favorite technique of many teachers. Children with similar interests may choose to work together or be assigned to work together on units. Personal reading and projects can be shared within a group regardless of ability levels. The motivation of the group is based on the interest which the students bring to it.

Whether grouping is arranged between classrooms or within classrooms, all teachers eventually find reasons for instruction in groups. Plans for flexible, temporary, and open grouping arrangements will contribute to a favorable environment for learning.

PROBLEMS IN INDIVIDUALIZATION AND GROUPING

All individualization and grouping have inherent problems, just as any instructional arrangement does. An examination of several of the major challenges, however, will assist the teacher to cope with most of them.

Differences Within Any Group

Regardless of the system for selecting a group for instruction, more differences exist within the group than between groups. Again in table 5, if a teacher made the first ten children his first group, it is obvious that when considering reading levels, child number ten is more like child number eleven than he is like child number one. Likewise, if a teacher groups by reading level alone, all other differences among the children remain. Differences such as ability, specific reading skills, cultural background, sex, age, size, and attitude will be the same only by chance; and the chance is slim.

Grouping children who are alike in reading level is but a substitute for individualization of instruction. In grouping, several of the differences can be accounted for, while the others remain. In tables 5 and 6 the only consideration for similarity of needs is the grade level of reading, not an entirely satisfactory grouping criterion.

Differences in the Rate of Development

It is common knowledge that children learn at different rates. A child assigned to the slow group today might not belong in that group next week or next month because of his rate of development. Teachers must keep their grouping flexible in order to adjust to such developmental changes. Flexible grouping requires the teacher to form groups for temporary needs, then disband them, and move a child from one group to another.

Groff found that although many teachers and authorities advocate flexible grouping, in most classrooms children are assigned to groups and remain in them for extremely long periods of time.[10] Hawkins replicated Groff's study and came to basically the same conclusions.[11] Both researchers found that the higher the grade level, the lower the percentage of changes in reading groups, and both reported that the largest percentage of changes occurred during the first weeks of the school year.

The Learner's Self-Concept

Attitudes of teachers toward the learners in various groups appear to be reflected to some degree in the learners' attitudes. Clearly, if the teacher has little regard for the worth of the learner, such regard is transmitted to the learners. Rosenthal and Jacobson concluded from their research that chldren tend to perform in accordance with the expectations of their teachers.[12] A change in teacher expectancy resulted in a change in the intellectual performance of the children.

It is difficult to estimate precisely the value of a positive teacher attitude or the damage of a negative one; however, the value and damage are real. The teacher must take special precautions to be certain that grouping is not a reflection of his value or sense of worth for a group of students.

Chapter Review

Individualization of instruction has progressed significantly in today's schools, but providing for individual differences will continue to be a major concern of educators. To teach both effectively and efficiently, total group, small group, and individual teaching and learning situations must be utilized. A combination of materials, practices, and classroom organization based on diagnostic teaching are the essentials of individualization of instruction. No easy solution exists for the problem of adapting instruction to the individuals within any group. A pupil's level, not a specified grade level, must be the prime consideration.

NOTES

[1] Robert F. DeHaan and Ronald C. Doll, "Individualization and Human Potential," in *Individualizing Instruction* (Washington, D.C.: Association for Supervision and Curriculum Development, 1964), p. 11.

[2] Ibid., p. 13.

[3] Russell G. Stauffer, "Individualizing Reading Instruction—A Back-

ward Look," in *Readings in Reading: Practice Theory Research*, ed. Delwin G. Schubert (New York: Thomas Y. Crowell, 1968), p. 236.

4 "Those Computers in Palo Alto," *Reading Newsreport* 2 (October 1967): 14–23.

5 "Learning by the Ton," *Reading Newsreport* 2 (November 1967): 15–18, 48.

6 Ibid., p. 19.

7 Arthur W. Heilman, *Principles and Practices of Teaching Reading* (Columbus: Charles E. Merrill, 1967), p. 407.

8 Guy L. Bond and Robert Dykstra, "The Cooperative Research Program in First-Grade Reading Instruction," *Reading Research Quarterly* 2 (Summer 1967): 122.

9 Nita Wyatt, "Sex Differences in Reading Achievement," *Elementary English* 43 (October 1966): 596–600.

10 Patrick J. Groff, "A Survey of Basal Reading Grouping Practices," *The Reading Teacher* 15 (January 1962): 232–235.

11 Michael L. Hawkins, "Mobility of Students in Reading Groups," *The Reading Teacher* 20 (November 1966): 136–140.

12 Robert Rosenthal and Lenore Jacobson, *Pygmalion in the Classroom* (New York: Holt, Rinehart and Winston, 1968).

SUGGESTED ACTIVITIES

1. From the data in tables 5 and 6 try grouping pupils into two groups, into three groups, and into four groups. What is the problem? Discuss it in class.
2. Interview an elementary school teacher and ask how he individualizes instruction. Discuss the comments in class.
3. Observe a lesson being taught to a group of children. List the ways in which you might be able to provide more individual attention to children if you were teaching that lesson. If you can list none, then list the ways in which the teacher individualized his teaching.

SUGGESTED READINGS

Doll, Ronald D., ed. *Individualizing Instruction*. Washington, D.C.: Association for Supervision and Curriculum Development, 1964.

> Presents a philosophy of individualization with the emphasis on releasing human potential through the school setting and curriculum experiences.

Groff, Patrick. "Comparisons of Individualized and Ability-Grouping Approaches as to Reading Achievement." *Elementary English* 40 (March 1963): 258–264.

> An annotated listing of studies relating to grouping procedures, useful as a reference for further study.

Heilman, Arthur H. *Principles and Practices of Teaching Reading.* Columbus: Charles E. Merrill, 1967.

   Chapter 11, devoted to sex differences, presents findings of research, explores causal factors, and recommends practices for educators in meeting the different needs of boys and girls.

Schubert, Delwyn G., ed. *Readings in Reading: Practice Theory Research.* New York: Thomas Y. Crowell, 1968.

   A collection of periodical articles and conference reports on many topics in reading. Chapter 6 on individual differences includes discussion of grouping, individualization, and the needs of slow and able readers.

Shane, Harold G. "Grouping in the Elementary School." *Phi Delta Kappan* 41 (April 1960): 313–319.

   Thirty-three grouping plans are offered as ways in which teachers can provide flexibility in grouping.

CHAPTER THIRTEEN

EVALUATION

Advance Organizer

One of the most exciting concepts in contemporary education is that of evaluation, viewed as a healthy, positive process designed to help a child and a teacher develop the most desirable instructional situation. Emphasis on the negative, punitive nature of testing children is discouraged, while stress is placed upon identification of the strengths and weaknesses of the instruction itself. In reading, evaluation is seen as a daily process in today's schools, in terms both of the specific desired behaviors and global outcomes.

THE CONCEPT OF EVALUATION IN EDUCATION

Too often, at all levels of education, teachers assume that something which has been presented to children has been learned. They often test children to measure learning before they evaluate the effectiveness of the instruction. The terms *evaluation* and *testing* are used differently in this chapter. *Evaluation* refers to those checks which a teacher makes to determine whether or not children have responded appropriately to the learning situation provided. It places the major focus on the effectiveness of the instruction and does not end in a grade for the child. Instead, if through evaluation a teacher realizes that his instructional efforts have been ineffective, he reconstructs them and reteaches *before* he tests.

Testing, in contrast, refers to those checks which a teacher makes to determine the degree to which children have retained information and previously evaluated skills. In testing situations, the child is traditionally graded or marked in some way. Of course, testing can also be used for evaluation purposes, to determine whether reteaching is needed. Evaluation, then, is used to designate instructional effectiveness, while testing is used to determine student mastery.

Evaluation is universally regarded today as something that should be an on-going process—occurring every day, in every lesson. As the teacher presents information, skills, or ideas to children, he evaluates the effectiveness of his instruction before proceeding to advanced levels. If learning has not been effective, he cannot safely move ahead. Testing, on the contrary, does not need to be a daily occurrence. In fact, children may be tested too often, whereas instruction is not evaluated often enough in most elementary school classrooms.

For the most efficient evaluation, a teacher must be able to state clearly the objectives of a given instructional period in terms of the desired student behavior. In so doing, he will be able to evaluate instruction simply by determining whether the children can perform that particular behavior. For example, the objective "To provide instruction in the sounds of initial consonants" is impossible to evaluate and can only serve as a general aim of instruction. It leaves unanswered the question of what specific behavior is expected of the child. However, if the objective is restated "To apply initial consonant substitution of the consonants *b, f,* and *s* to the common endings *at, ake,* and *old,*" the teacher can easily evaluate his effectiveness by determining whether the children can perform specific skills. Modern teachers write instructional objectives in terms of pupil behavior, rather than in terms of teacher performance. In this way, evaluation becomes easier and more meaningful.

Evaluation determines the need for review. When child behavior is appropriate but lacks precision and speed, review may be needed. In the example above, several children may have been able to substitute the consonants only with labored efforts. For those children, review lessons can be constructed.

Evaluation also determines the need for restructuring the learning situation. When confused pupil performance is indicated, the teacher must consider a restructuring of the learning. Confused performance is not the child's fault. The teacher must assume the responsibility and restructure the learning situation so that the child can respond appropriately. Using the above example again, evaluation may reveal that some children need help in a previous learning such as auditory discrimination or letter-sound relationships. The teacher may even realize that he has omitted a key step in the instructional sequence, or that more examples are needed, or more practice under teacher direction. Any such adjustments are the teacher's responsibility; clearly, they are beyond the control of the child.

Evaluation also involves the pupil's awareness of his response. Because evaluation does not call for grading, it can be handled in such a way that the child is aware of it, but not threatened by it. In general, the more aware a child is of his learning, the more effective the learning situation is.

Evaluation, furthermore, is healthy and positive. By calling attention to the successes children have, teachers can keep them informed of their progress and provide motivation for future learning. If teachers will think of evaluation as positive, children will also. For example, if twenty-five children are to complete an assignment, and one child fails to do it, the teacher has the alternative either to focus on the one child or to focus on the other twenty-four. While many teachers prefer the former, it appears that praise for the twenty-four is far more effective. If attention needs to be given to the one unsuccessful child, it should be done privately rather than in front of the group, and it should be constructive.

To take a similar instance: if twenty-five children are working on the behavioral objective previously given and twenty master it, what course of action should the teacher follow? In most instances, he will do better to praise the twenty and construct either a review or a new learning situation so that the five can master the objective and receive praise also.

When viewed as healthy and positive, children will tend to look forward to evaluation sessions and to become more effective with self-evaluation techniques.

Evaluation is conducted along with, or as close as possible to, the time of learning. In theory, it is useful to evaluate every response a child makes at the time he makes it. For example, if a group of children are responding to a question and many have the correct answer, the teacher can make a statement such as, "Yes, *picnic* does have two syllables." He can note which children did not seem to know the correct answer. And more important, he can provide all children with this correct answer. Because the evaluation and correction were adjacent in time, all children have a better chance of responding correctly to the next question. To give children an assignment and not provide evaluation for several days is an all too common practice which loses virtually all the advantages of evaluation as discussed in this chapter.

While the advantages of evaluation in terms of specific behaviors are numerous, the teacher is urged to draw back occasionally and view the total child. Has he responded to the broad goals of the reading program? Has he responded from a *global* view? For still another aspect of evaluation is the total child. Such evaluation helps teachers to avoid the pitfall of seeing the child as a conglomerate of unrelated or related skills.

TECHNIQUES OF EVALUATION

There are several different techniques of evaluation. The teacher may conduct most of the evaluation, the student may evaluate himself, or his peers may evaluate. Regardless of the technique, the concept of evaluation discussed above is applicable.

Evaluation by the Teacher

Teachers can evaluate by using behavioral objectives, observations, skill quizzes, discussions, every-pupil response cards, or tests. For example, if it is desirable to check the ability of children to recall specific details from a selection they have just read, the teacher can give each child *true* and *false* cards. As the teacher makes statements about the details in the chapter, each child can respond by holding up the appropriate card. The teacher makes a mental note of the response, provides the correct response, and goes on to the next statement. Occasionally, rereading might be necessary. At other times, a discussion of the different responses might be needed. Again, the twofold advantage is realized by permitting the teacher to evaluate and the children to become aware of their progress.

The technique just described, and modifications of it, can be effectively used to replace the traditional techniques of using pencil and paper tests or of asking questions to which children volunteer answers by raising their hands.

As children work individually or in groups, the teacher can evaluate the way in which they complete their work. Do they seem to use their time well? If not, how can they be helped? Does the material seem too hard or too easy for them? Is the child under too much pressure? Many questions such as these can be answered when teachers work with children as they read.

Self-Evaluation by Pupils

Children are constantly evaluating their own learning effectiveness. Many teachers have found it useful to help them become better and more positive evaluators. Materials such as the SRA *Reading Laboratories* and the McGraw-Hill *Programmed Reading* have utilized the idea of self-evaluation by permitting the children to have the answers and check their own responses. The children are placed in a flexible evaluation situation, for they may choose to reread the question or the selection, to skim, or to look at the correct answer. In any case, they are actively involved in their own evaluation. They are not threatened, so they need not fear making mistakes. The evaluation techniques used in these materials can easily be adapted to any material the teacher desires to use. Children can become skilled at self-evaluation with such techniques and more actively involved with their own learning. An important secondary benefit of such techniques is that the teacher is free to work instructionally with children who need help.

Another self-evaluation technique can be structured by permitting the children to read orally into a tape recorder and then listen to their own reading. A private situation can be created so that each child can correct his errors without the constant embarrassment of reading poorly in front of his peers. The records a child keeps of individualized reading, new words encountered, comments about books, and skill progress sheets help him focus positively on the progress he is making.

At other times, the teacher may have children work independently with some skill activities. As soon as the children are finished, the teacher provides the correct answers, and each child corrects his own paper. Children who do not understand their errors may consult with the teacher privately.

Learning centers, as described in this text, can also be used for self-correcting reading activities. Answer keys are provided for children as needed, thus diminishing the time between the child's response and reinforcement with the appropriate answer.

Evaluation by Peers

Formerly frowned upon as damaging to the self-concept, today many children are finding peer evaluation less threatening and more helpful than teacher evaluation. When groups of children are working together toward the same objective, peer evaluation is taking place whether it is planned by the teacher or not. Capitalizing upon it might be worthwhile. One type of peer evaluation comes from discussion sessions involving higher levels of comprehension. For example, in critical thinking discussions or debates with other children, a child might be expected to defend his statements. Another type of peer evaluation stems from permitting a skilled reader to work with one who is not so skilled in specifically designed activities. If oral reading practice is desired, the skilled reader can listen to the less skilled, help him with difficult words, and make evaluative comments that are positive and nonthreatening.

While some children cannot perform peer evaluation without insulting or embarrassing the child who is being evaluated, many others can. Teachers should help all children to learn the skills of peer evaluation—for the present and the future.

Other Modes of Evaluation

Teachers have the unique opportunity of observing children over extended periods of time and of making tentative evaluations concerning behaviors that appear to be other than normal. In such cases, the teacher should refer the child to a specialist.

Physical Teachers have responsibilities for evaluation of students in physical as well as instructional areas. Getman claims that teacher observation is superior to most screening tests in attempts to identify vision problems.[1] Symptoms of visual discomfort, hearing disorders, and general physical irregularities should be noted, discussed with the school nurse or doctor, and referred to appropriate agencies. Excessive squinting, holding the book too close to the face, and constant rubbing of the eyes are easily noted symptoms and should result in a visual referral. Tilting of the head, inability to follow directions, and difficulty in learning phonics might well result in a hearing referral. Children who are excessively fatigued, very much overweight, or absent from school an excessive number of days are best referred for a general physical examination. As a rule it seems reasonable for teachers to refer children to specialists when physical discomforts are interfering with their learning.

Psychological   Symptoms of emotional discomfort which appear to consistently interfere with instruction are also justifiable reasons for referral. Awareness that emotional symptoms such as inattentiveness, distractability, and anger are also symptoms of certain physical deficiencies will caution the teacher against jumping to conclusions or making the diagnosis himself. The fact remains that children may be in need of professional help in the emotional area and that the teacher is most likely to see the first signs. Again, referral is made with notations concerning symptoms.

Intellectual   Symptoms of deviation in intellectual functioning should also be noted by the teacher. Exceptionally good or poor memory, reasoning ability, hand-eye coordination, and verbal ability may lead to a referral for an individually administered intelligence test. Knowing that scores on group intelligence tests are extremely unreliable for dull and bright children, for culturally-different children, for emotionally disturbed children, and for children with reading handicaps makes individual testing essential if accurate information concerning intellectual functioning of the child is to be obtained.

Reports from referrals will provide the teacher with information he needs to make instructional adjustments which facilitate learning for the children. For example, a report from a vision specialist might result in shorter periods of visual performance and in adjusted seating in the room. A psychological report might advise that a certain child not be placed in a situation with undue competition. Through evaluation in noneducational areas, the teacher can provide better learning situations for handicapped children.

EVALUATION OF THE READING PROGRAM

All teachers are interested in periodically evaluating the effectiveness of the reading program. Focus on this type of evaluation centers to some extent on general global objectives as opposed to behavioral objectives. Are the children learning to read? Are the best possible techniques being used with the children? Are the materials in use the most appropriate materials available? As answers to such questions emerge, the teacher evaluates and modifies his program. Improvements are implemented, and a spirit of trying to do a better job emerges.

It is possible for teachers to conduct program evaluation without the aid of their peers or supervisors. In such cases, self-evaluation is dependent upon the ability of the teacher to look objectively at his own efforts and to be knowledgeable enough to make improvements. Through reading the literature, attending in-service meetings, and continuing formal education, the teacher can prepare himself for self-evaluation.

Discussion with peers and supervisors yields another form of program evaluation. The suggestions of others can be weighed and used as the teacher finds them appropriate. Many find evaluation in this form preferable to self-evaluation, inasmuch as the factor of bias is somewhat removed.

Most schools conduct periodic testing programs for all children in order to assist teachers and supervisors to evaluate the program through the performance of the children. Such testing can identify weaknesses in certain areas, such as comprehension or word attack, and can help in planning for program improvement. In most schools, testing has been conducted toward the end of the school year. However, many teachers are now asking for school-wide testing to be completed toward the beginning of the year so they can use the information in planning instruction for children with whom they are going to work.

Testing in the Evaluation Program

Testing in the reading program can take the form of teacher-made or standardized tests. Both have a place in the program and deserve consideration.

Teacher-made Tests Children are accustomed to taking tests made by teachers. Because a teacher is interested in determining how effectively the children have learned, such tests usually follow a unit of work. When they are well-constructed, teacher-made tests relate directly to behavioral objectives. Since the objective of a test is to determine student learning, trick and ambiguous questions are not included. Directions for taking the test are clearly stated and ample time is allotted for completion.

Teachers often test informally during reading sessions. When a child is having particular difficulty, it is often useful for the teacher to listen to his reading and attempt to determine his strengths and weaknesses. Oral reading for testing purposes is best done privately with the teacher, rather than in front of an entire group. Materials selected for such reading should be appropriate to the child's instructional reading level—the level at which he can read with some teacher assistance.

When children display difficulty with teacher-made tests, instruction concerning techniques for test-taking is recommended. Many children have actually learned the content that is tested but do not perform successfully on tests constructed to measure that learning.

Standardized Tests Many publishing companies have developed standardized tests for which norms have been set. Tests for oral and silent reading, as well as for word attack, are available in standardized form. Most are easily administered, but it takes considerable experience and study to interpret them properly. A careful study of the teacher's test manual for administration procedures and interpretive information is necessary. Inexperienced teachers do well to seek help from their supervisors concerning the interpretation of test results.

Because single scores and single errors are not reliable, teachers should use all tests to determine *patterns of scores* which indicate the strengths and weaknesses of their children. For example, if a child has difficulty with the word *lake* and calls it *like*, no generalization about his error is made until other mispronunciations of the same type are observed. If, on the other hand, the child consistently confuses vowel sounds in words ending in vowel-consonant-final *e*, instruction can be developed to assist him with such word patterns. The teacher can also conclude that the child does well with initial and final consonants. In this way, both the child's strengths and weaknesses are noted.

One of the serious limitations in the use of standardized tests is the interpretation of scores which are either very high or very low. As a rule, such scores are generally unreliable, and it is advisable not to draw conclusions if the tests do not permit the student to answer a large number of questions and to exhibit difficulty with a large number of items so that errors can be analyzed for patterns.

Therefore, a sixth grade child who is experiencing serious difficulty in reading will not score reliably on a test constructed for sixth graders, but might score reliably on a test constructed for children at his reading level. (Appendix C contains an annotated list of the most available standardized tests.)

Another limitation of standardized tests is the lack of reliability of test scores. Teachers might find these tests a better measure of how a group of children are performing than of how a given child performs. The unreliable nature of test scores suggests that a portion of the score is achieved by way of a chance factor—not a desirable method of evaluating individual performance.

ISSUES IN EVALUATION

Certain questions are presently being explored in the area of evaluation. The teacher's awareness of such issues will assist him in dealing with them when they arise in his own work with children.

What Does Grade Level Mean?

Tests and printed material are often identified by a grade level designation. The grade level as such indicates that the material is useful for the average child assigned to that grade. More specifically, grade levels on tests are determined by the mean score of all children of a particular grade who took the test. Therefore, if 20,000 students take a sixty item test, the raw scores of all children are added and then divided by 20,000. Thus computed, many children will score above the grade level score and many will score below it. However, if a magic reading method were to be introduced and the mean of 20,000 testees were raised by several points, the grade level would change, but many children would continue to score above and many below grade level.

Since grade level is determined by a score, it is difficult to assess its meaning. What does 4.2 mean? How is 4.2 different from 4.7? One can only say that a grade level reflects how a child performs in comparison with other children taking the same standardized test. However, the problem does not end here, for all standardized tests are less than completely reliable. Therefore, if a child scores 4.2 today, he could score differently tomorrow.

It is recommended that teachers focus their attention on what children can and cannot do on tests, not on the grade scores which the test yields. Teachers should also assess attitudes toward learning as an item equal in importance to skill performance.

Should Informal or Standardized Tests Be Used?

The answer, of course, is to use both types of tests. There is no reason to believe that informal tests yield more reliable scores than do standardized tests, but they are useful when carefully designed. As mentioned before, informal tests can be geared to measure specific behavioral objectives, a feature often difficult to measure by the more global nature of standardized tests. Informal tests can include material which the children have been taught and therefore are more appropriate to measure their performances.

Teachers who use both measures to seek patterns of performance will find that informal and standardized tests complement each other and do yield useful information concerning a child's reading performance.

Teacher's often use test scores, whether informal or standardized to place children into reading groups. When other information is not available, such a procedure is practical. The following guidelines may be of help when test scores are used for placement:

- Because of possible error in the score, group placement should be temporary. Remain flexible so that incorrectly placed children can be easily moved.

- Use the obtained scores as the frustration or failing level of the children. Generally, it is unwise to start them in material at the same level as the test. To insure a good start, it is usually advisable to drop starting levels by half a year or more.

- Watch for other strengths and weaknesses. As discussed in chapter 12 (grouping from test scores), there are other factors of equal importance to consider when placing children. Grade level alone called for one type of grouping. When skill proficiencies were added, other groupings were appropriate. Clearly other factors could also be considered—attitude, interest, experiences—which would make grouping by test scores a limited technique.

- Do not prejudge the children to the point of expecting poor performance. Accept each child, his reading level, and his skill development with the attitude that he can and will learn. Such an attitude is essential to success.

Of What Use Are Skills Tests?

Tests which measure specific skill performances are available and their precise nature makes them extremely useful. For example, there are tests which provide information about a child's ability to work with various phonic skills. Scores from such tests can help teachers plan efficient word attack programs. However, these tests usually do not provide information concerning whether a child can use those skills while reading a book. Therefore, the teacher is urged to ascertain through teacher-made tests from books used in the classroom and through planned activities whether the child can apply the skills he indicates knowledge of on a skills test.

Can Interests and Attitudes Be Evaluated?

Certainly interests and attitudes can be evaluated. Teachers who are trained to watch the performance of children become quite skilled in evaluating their interests and attitudes and in observing the extent of personal reading. However, caution must be exercised, for interests and attitudes are ever-changing, causing today's evaluation to be incorrect for the same child next week.

Generally speaking, pencil-paper tests of attitudes and interests are not particularly useful for elementary-age children. They tend to anticipate the "desired" answer and mark the test accordingly. Day-to-day evaluation based on a child's natural performance in school and at play is a more useful technique to measure interests and attitudes. Mager suggests that attitude toward learning can be evaluated by teachers themselves or by peers using the ideas of *approach responses* and *avoidance responses*.[2] This system adds certain types of objectivity to the evaluation of the attitude toward learning.

How Are Children Graded in Reading?

Report cards generally require grades in reading, although many schools are now moving toward parental conferences or check lists of proficiency. The problem is that many children are graded "poor" merely because they are not ready for the instruction provided, or because they do not learn as fast as other children in the group. Each teacher will have to report student performance to parents within the framework of the school's reporting system. However, the following guidelines should be considered:

- If the child is working diligently but slowly, a poor grade cannot be justified. If we are interested in teaching reading and not in pitting one child against another, the grade earned should be a reflection of effort rather than of relative standing in the class.

- Skill accomplishments should be reported. If the reporting system does not allow this practice, notes sent to parents or conferences with parents can report the accomplishments.

- Grades should meet the criteria of evaluation. If they are punitive, a teacher can expect negative reactions.

- Teachers should be honest with themselves and their children. They should not let the grading procedures of others interfere with what they believe to be fair and correct.

Some schools have found it useful to issue two grades for reading. One grade indicates the reading level of the child; the other indicates the child's performance with respect to his ability. Such systems are a compromise with the criteria mentioned above but can be considered as a start toward the more realistic grading of children. Surely the schools will soon abolish the grading of students.

Chapter Review

Instruction based on evaluation is the goal of contemporary education. Evaluation is the process through which the teacher and the children discover their strengths and weaknesses and accordingly improve instruction and learning. Evaluation in reading can be done by the teacher, the peers, or by the child himself. In any case, it helps the child to take a more active part in his learning and to regard the learning as valuable. Only after evaluation and necessary reteaching are accomplished should testing take place.

More and better evaluation tools are being developed. Awareness of them and insight into their usefulness is encouraged for all teachers.

NOTES

[1] G. N. Getman, "Visual Success is Reading Success," *Journal of California Optometric Association* (August–September 1961): 2.

[2] Robert F. Mager, *Developing Attitude Toward Learning* (Palo Alto: Fearon Publishers, 1968).

SUGGESTED ACTIVITIES

1. Examine Appendix C for a list of reading tests. Select one and examine the various subtests. How would you use the results of that test? What limitations do you see in using it?
2. As a class project, collect report cards from many different schools. Discuss how progress in reading is reported and how you would improve it so as to provide accurate, useful information to parents.
3. Have a "brainstorming" session concerning techniques which you might use to evaluate children according to the guidelines in this chapter.

SUGGESTED READINGS

Austin, Mary C. et al. *Reading Evaluation.* New York: The Ronald Press, 1961.

A useful guide for the teacher plagued with evaluation problems. Reading evaluation in the classroom and within the school is discussed in detail.

Barbe, Walter. *An Educator's Guide to Personalized Reading Instruction.* Englewood Cliffs: Prentice-Hall, 1961.

Chapters 7 and 8 present check lists of skills appropriate for various grade levels.

Farr, Roger. *Reading: What Can Be Measured?* Newark, Delaware: International Reading Association, 1970.

A through discussion of the use of tests with children provides the reader with essential background.

Harris, Albert J. *Readings on Reading Instruction.* New York: David McKay, 1963.

See chapter 5 for five selections on measuring reading outcomes. Different points of view concerning several of the issues raised in our chapter are presented.

Wilson, Robert M. *Diagnostic and Remedial Reading For Classroom and Clinic.* Columbus: Charles E. Merrill, 1967.

See chapter 4 for more specific diagnostic techniques appropriate to the classroom.

CHAPTER FOURTEEN

THE ROLE OF THE READING SPECIALIST

Advance Organizer

Serving as a knowledgeable consultant to teachers, parents, and children, the reading specialist is an invaluable member of the school faculty. With children, he undertakes primarily diagnostic and remedial work, although he may also work to increase enrichment opportunities. When teachers invite him to join with them in attacking reading problems, he may observe classes or groups of children and may cooperate with the teacher in planning alternative instruction.

The specialist is also active in total school activities, particularly in in-service education and meetings with parents.

For maximum benefit from the services of a reading specialist, effective communication and rapport must exist between the specialist and the teacher.

Who Is the Reading Specialist?

From one school district to another and from state to state, one hears of *reading supervisors, reading specialists,* or *reading consultants* in reference to individuals fulfilling similar responsibilities.

The International Reading Association Standards[1] for defining professional positions suggest that the term *reading specialist* is most appropriate and most widely used for the service individual who works with children, teachers, and parents to assist in providing each child with learning tasks he can handle successfully and to improve the teaching of reading through teacher-specialist communication.

THE READING SPECIALIST WORKS WITH CHILDREN

The reading specialist's work with children centers around diagnosis and remediation. He serves as a diagnostician to discover why a child has a reading difficulty, and he conducts remediation with individuals or with groups of children. In both these functions, however, the specialist's job does not end in his contact with the children. Rather, it is the interpretation and discussion of diagnostic information and remediation techniques with teachers that is the specialist's primary concern. Teachers must not feel that having a reading specialist on the staff relieves them of all responsibility for reading problems; instead they must understand that a cooperative approach is possible.

Diagnosis

At the request of the teacher, the specialist may test a child to determine not only his reading problem but also the probable cause of the difficulty. Suppose that through classroom diagnosis the teacher is able to determine that a child has a serious word recognition problem but that the teacher has neither the knowledge nor the testing materials to explore the cause and extent of the disability. If the reading specialist can determine the causes, they, rather than the symptoms of the reading problem, can be treated. The possibility exists, of course, that, even after a thorough diagnosis, the reading specialist may be unable to identify all causes of the child's reading problem. Nevertheless, a full diagnostic examination by the specialist may reveal a pattern of symptoms, so that recommendations for an adjusted classroom program in reading can be given to the teacher.

The reading specialist should always be able to discuss a child's problem with the teacher and to make concrete suggestions concerning the best way to adjust the learning situation in order to improve the child's reading skills. Suggestions should be of a nature that allow the classroom teacher to implement them, and the specialist should insure that the necessary techniques and materials are available to and understood by the teacher.

If the specialist's suggestions prove unsuccessful with a particular child, both teacher and specialist must turn elsewhere. A team approach to diagnosis—with teacher, reading specialist, parents, guidance counselor, and other available personnel sharing their knowledge about the child—can be beneficial. It may be necessary to refer the child to a reading clinic for more complete diagnosis. The possibility also exists that the child may need help from other sources, such as a psychologist or a physician, before he can profit from an adjusted reading program.

Teachers also request diagnostic aid when a child in the classroom exhibits outstanding reading ability. They want to know more about the level at which he is reading and how they can help him to continue his reading growth. After working with the child, the reading specialist can help the teacher plan an enrichment program.

Remediation

The reading specialist may be responsible for conducting remediation either with individuals or with groups of students. In some instances, he will use special techniques which cannot be employed by the classroom teacher because of inexperience or time limitations. For example, he can supply kinesthetic reinforcement to a child if necessary in order to learn new vocabulary. When remediation is part of the reading specialist's duties, he can devote the time and individual attention necessary to carry out these techniques.

The specialist may also work with groups of youngsters reading below expectancy. He diagnoses each child's problems, plans a remedial program, and then takes the children from the classroom and works with them. Often, the response of children to the reading specialist is excellent, as a result of the individual attention given them as well as the interest and concern shown them.

When remedial sessions have been completed these children return to the classroom and again interact with youngsters reading at varying levels. In this situation, so very different from the one with the reading specialist, they need the support of the classroom teacher, who must accept them as they are and provide them with meaningful experiences which help them to transfer their new reading skills to the classroom work.

Because of this adjustment problem, it is often advisable to let remedial students remain in their regular classroom environment all along. While the teacher conducts a lesson with the majority of the class, the reading specialist works with a small group of students having difficulty. The children feel that they are still part of the group and that they do not have to be removed from the classroom for special instruction. The teacher gains ideas from observing the reading specialist at work. Thus some of the frustration and failure felt by both teachers and children as a result of reading problems is lessened.

Similarly, there is no reason why the specialist's classroom work with children should be limited to only those pupils experiencing problems with reading. If the teacher works with children experiencing reading problems, while the specialist teaches those who are reading at potential, benefits to both children and teacher can occur. The teacher can observe techniques applicable in instructing the achievers. The children will realize that the reading specialist does not work only with poor readers. And the reading specialist has an opportunity to design instruction for good readers who need an enriched reading program.

THE READING SPECIALIST WORKS WITH TEACHERS

If there is effective communication and rapport between the specialist and the classroom teacher, their combined efforts can be a potent means of improving the reading program. It has been suggested that instead of working primarily with children, the reading specialist can be more influential by working with teachers to improve their teaching. Austin has noted the irony that schools seem to show "more concern over the child who has failed to read adequately than over the teacher who has failed to teach adequately."[2] Many possibilities for teacher-specialist interaction exist. The specialist may participate in observation. He may plan and participate in in-service programs. He may act as a resource person for teachers. And he may consult with teachers when research projects in reading are being conducted.

The Specialist and Observation

Whether observation conducted by the reading specialist is a requirement of his position or an optional act performed at the request of various teachers, the purpose of the observation should always be to improve instruction rather than to evaluate teaching. The specialist who observes for evaluative purposes will certainly be blocked in his efforts to build effective rapport between the teacher and himself. The teacher should view the observation session as a constructive device for improving his teaching rather than as an opportunity for the reading specialist to judge the effectiveness of a particular lesson. The teacher and specialist must be able to communicate freely with each other. The observation of a reading class should not only suggest improvements but should also note strengths which the teacher demonstrates in his work with children.

The specialist observes more than the teaching of a particular lesson to a small group of children; he is concerned with the reading activities of the other children in the classroom. Are they being stimulated in their independent activities? Are they assigned work which has been differentiated so that they can pursue it independently? Do they exhibit an interest in reading by choosing to read in their free time?

The follow-up immediately after the observation greatly affects its potential value. In this discussion with the teacher, problems of teaching and specific suggestions for overcoming weaknesses are treated.

Although a single observation may be a good technique for noting and commenting on a teacher's procedure, it is not the only technique for facilitating change in teacher behavior. Several observations during a short period of time, along with discussions, demonstrations, and practical assistance, are preferable.

Observation of teaching may occur through the use of video-tape to film a short lesson (a micro-lesson). It preserves a full record of the class, and has the additional advantage of providing the teacher with an actual picture of his performance before a class. A micro-lesson can be viewed not only by the teacher alone, for self-evaluation, but by both the teacher and the reading specialist, for analyzing teaching style. The specialist and the teacher can in this way record several behavior patterns which the teacher might change. After several weeks, a lesson can again be taped and analyzed to check on improvements.

Classroom observations may also be structured so as to observe one child in a typical group situation, since the child may react differently in a one-to-one situation with the reading specialist. Although the specialist and the teacher discuss the problems of this child, the teacher may be unable during the course of a normal class period to observe all of the child's significant behavior patterns, either because of lack of experience on the part of the teacher or because of involvement and concern with many children at once. In observing the child as he relates to his teacher and his peers, the reading specialist should be able to notice and evaluate the child's emotional attitude toward learning, his attention span, and his methods of working independently. Observation in classrooms also aids the reading specialist in making recommendations for adjusting the total reading program.

The Specialist and In-service Education

A key service performed by the reading specialist is to assist in planning and conducting in-service programs. Because these programs should be developed around the needs and interests of the teachers, it is essential that teachers as well as specialists be involved in the planning stages. Unless teachers are actively involved in all phases of the in-service meetings, the meetings will not be an effective means of initiating change. If the faculty has a myriad of concerns, a priority should be determined and in-service plans developed accordingly.

Consultants from local universities or from other school districts frequently participate in in-service programs, presenting to teachers the latest ideas concerning the teaching of reading. They also serve as motivational speakers, to "kick off" a particular theme or project of the faculty.

Another method of providing in-service training which specialists find useful is the demonstration lesson. For example, if a school district wishes to improve oral reading, the specialist conducts a reading lesson showing techniques through which children can use oral reading meaningfully. In the process, the specialist may demonstrate materials such as multi-level reading kits or listening stations. All too often, available materials gather dust in the storeroom because the teacher is not quite sure how to fit them into the classroom program.

Demonstration lessons are most effective when the classroom teacher participates in the lesson with the reading specialist. The two plan the lesson, share in the instruction, and evaluate each other's performance. Through participation, the teacher moves from a passive, receiving role to an active, responding one. Most teachers feel more comfortable when they are in charge of the class. This team approach to demonstration lessons has great possibilities for behavioral change in teachers.

Certain limitations of demonstration lessons for both teacher and reading specialist need to be mentioned. In a typical demonstration situation, the demonstrator walks into the classroom knowing he is to teach a word attack lesson to a group of second graders. Although he has his lesson well prepared and his materials gathered, he faces some major disadvantages. He may not know the children whom he will be teaching; he may not even know their previous learnings, or previous experiences which will affect the lesson. Therefore, the learning situation is not a typical one for the children, and often they do not act typically. Teacher reaction many range from enthusiastic comments about the tremendous lesson to skepticism about the practicality of the technique in a real classroom situation. Changes in teacher behavior may not result because teachers view the demonstration as inapplicable to their own classroom. However, teamed demonstrations overcome these usual limitations.

The Specialist As a Resource

Teachers, supervisors, and administrators daily encounter problems which, whether about theory or about actual problems in reading, can and should be discussed with a knowledgeable specialist. With his extensive knowledge of methods and materials in the teaching of reading, the specialist should be able to communicate valuable knowledge to the school staff. He should be able to encourage the faculty to discuss ideas regarding reading in the total school curriculum and the school's effectiveness in meeting the reading needs of children. In this way classroom teachers become involved in the development of curriculum, and their ideas can be continually developed and extended by curriculum specialists.

If a teacher wishes to explore a different type of reading program from that usually followed in the classroom, the reading specialist should not only discuss the pros and cons with the teacher, but should also encourage such efforts to innovate. If it is decided that the program can be put into effect, the specialist can assist the teacher in formulating the program and in obtaining necessary materials. If a teacher were interested in trying individualized reading in his classroom, for example, the specialist would probably first discuss this type of reading with him to determine the extent of his knowledge about the approach. The two might then decide to modify the program to suit the particular children being served. The reading specialist could subsequently work with the teacher in the classroom and assist him in starting the program. He might hold individual conferences with children, or he might teach a skill lesson with some of the children while the teacher conducts an individual conference. Both teacher and specialist then evaluate the on-going program. Because of one teacher's interest, more teachers might well become interested, so that individualized reading would form the topic for an in-service workshop. Soon the program could be extended to additional classrooms.

The reading specialist may also meet with groups of teachers to answer questions. Through such meetings, the specialist may discover that certain areas of the reading program need improvement; he then brings this knowledge to the attention of the administrators and curriculum specialists. For example, if various tests and other objective information reveal that children in the school perform poorly in word attack, the reading specialist may meet with all teachers of reading to discuss this problem and to make plans for improving the teaching of word attack. If a change in the organization, textbooks, or techniques used in the school system is deemed necessary, a committee composed of the reading specialist, teachers, administrators, and supervisors can be formed to study the problem as a group.

In some school districts, a reading committee meets with the reading specialist on a regular basis to examine new materials and methods and to discuss their relevancy to the current and future reading program of the school district.

The Specialist's Role in Research

Whether research involves a small scale project with a small sample of pupils in only one classroom or a massive operation on a school-wide or system-wide basis, the reading specialist plays an important role. He identifies topics needing information from research, explains the purpose of research projects to teachers, and helps teachers realize their contributions to educational research. Involving teachers in research often results in increased interest in instructional methods and in detailed analysis of teaching and learning, leading in turn to many exciting new programs and improved achievement. Research results may also show specific needs in the total school reading program and can thus aid in planning improved programs.

As research activity in education increases, particularly in reading, the role of the reading specialist in assisting with research projects will also broaden.

THE TEACHER'S RESPONSIBILITY TO
THE READING SPECIALIST

The reading specialist who assumes the duties and responsibilities described above will face a challenging task. He cannot carry out these responsibilities successfully without the cooperation of the teacher. For the reading specialist to be fully effective in upgrading and enriching reading instruction, teachers must initiate contacts and ask for his assistance. Teachers can inform him of their concerns about reading and about the reading problems of individual pupils. Observations, demonstrations, and suggestions for alterations in instructional programs for individual children must grow from common concerns of the reading specialist and teachers. In-service education will be more effective if it is an outgrowth of teachers' needs and requests. Teachers must realize too that, after suggestions have been offered by the reading specialist, they should try those suggestions to effect program improvement.

Even in working directly with children, the reading specialist depends greatly upon the teacher. The attitude a teacher has toward a child who is having difficulty is important in determining whether the reading specialist will ever see the child. Some teachers may prefer to handle a child's problem alone and may resent interference by someone who does not work directly with the child in the classroom. All of us react differently when we meet an obstacle; a conscientious teacher with a child who is not learning may consider this solely a fault of his own teaching which he himself ought to be able to remedy. Yet, there are so many causes of learning difficulties that teachers ought willingly to seek aid from another educator. Certainly seeking aid is not an admission of failure, but rather the demonstration of the attitude that all steps should be taken to assure success.

THE READING SPECIALIST AND PARENTS

Teachers are accustomed to hearing questions such as the following from parents:

You've done wonders in getting Johnny interested in learning to read. How can I help at home?

What should I do when Mark asks me to tell him a word? Should he be able to figure words out for himself?

Should I teach my four-year-old the alphabet?

Bernadette is such a good reader. Can you suggest several books which I could buy for her?

Why is Timmy in the "low" group in reading? He can read every word perfectly.

Sometimes teachers can answer such inquiries to the satisfaction of the parents. At other times, however, it is difficult for inexperienced teachers to explain the reading program clearly. Through activities such as group meetings with community people or conferences with individual parents, the reading specialist can assist teachers in promoting effective relationships between the school and the parents.

Group meetings with parents provide an excellent opportunity to explain the reading program—especially why certain materials and techniques are employed. Group meetings can also consider parental concerns about school philosophy and methods. Parents should be given an opportunity to ask questions of the reading specialist and of a group of teachers who might be participating in a panel with the reading specialist. Also, parents may serve as participants in various meetings, as teachers and other parents often profit from listening to their concerned viewpoints. Parents who are specialists in other fields (sociology, medicine, psychology, for example) may be able to share their knowledge and its relationship to education.

A primary objective of such group meetings is to help parents understand their role in helping their child to read. In the past schools have tended to promote the attitude that parents should keep their hands off; teaching is the school's responsibility. Currently, there is increased recognition that parents can contribute greatly to a child's success in school. If the school helps parents to understand and fulfill their roles, children will tend to exhibit improvement in both attitude and achievement.

Although group meetings can be effective, the reading specialist often finds that individual conferences with parents are necessary. Parent-teacher conferences are common, but those between parent and reading specialist or between parents, teacher, and reading specialist are less frequent. At times it may be valuable to invite the child to the conference. Taking the time to talk with a child to ask him why he is having reading difficulties can be very revealing. Glass has discussed the misconceptions that children have concerning their reading problems and has stressed the teacher's responsibility to help pupils understand their reading problems if improvement is to occur.[3]

Conferences can be initiated by the teacher, by parents, or by the reading specialist. It is important that a record be kept of each conference and that any person concerned with the success of the child be informed of information learned from the meeting. (Additional discussion of teacher-parent conferences occurs in chapter 15.)

Chapter Review

In the schools of tomorrow, it will be common to see teachers and reading specialists working together to devise the best possible learning situation for each child. As more individuals are trained to be reading specialists, more schools will have their help in developing dynamic reading programs adapted to the learning needs of individuals and constantly upgraded by the efforts of the total faculty working with the reading specialist.

The key to successful utilization of the reading specialist lies in effective communication between teacher and specialist, with each understanding the other's role in building a better educational program for children.

NOTES

[1] *Minimum Standards for Professional Training of Reading Specialists* (Newark, Delaware: International Reading Association, 1961).

[2] Mary C. Austin and Coleman Morrison, *The First R: The Harvard Report on Reading in the Elementary Schools* (New York: Macmillan, 1963), p. 183.

[3] Gerald G. Glass, "Students' Misconceptions Concerning Their Reading," *The Reading Teacher* 21 (May 1968): 765–768.

SUGGESTED ACTIVITIES

1. Interview a reading specialist, discussing his role in the total school program and how he works with teachers and pupils.
2. Attend an in-service meeting about reading. Was it useful? How did the teachers seem to react?
3. Hold a class discussion concerning the values and limitations of having a reading specialist in your school.

SUGGESTED READINGS

Austin, Mary C. and Morrison, Coleman. *The First R: The Harvard Report on Reading in the Elementary Schools.* New York: Macmillan, 1963.

> Presents research findings reflecting reading practices conducted in school districts throughout our nation. Chapter 7 discusses the role of the administrator, reading specialist, and supervisory personnel.

Cohn, Stella M. and Cohn, Jack. *Teaching the Retarded Reader.* New York: Odyssey Press, 1967.

> Special attention is given to the role of the reading consultant in chapter 6. Discussions about the reading consultant and his work with parents, teachers, and administrators are included.

Robinson, H. Alan and Rauch, Sidney J. *Guiding the Reading Program —A Reading Consultant's Handbook.* Chicago: Science Research Associates, 1965.

> Presents a treatment of the reading consultant and his role in building a successful reading program. Chapter 5 provides suggestions for in-service programs.

Wilson, Robert M. *Diagnostic and Remedial Reading for Classroom and Clinic.* Columbus: Charles E. Merrill, 1967.

> Contains information for both teacher and reading specialist concerning the diagnosis and remediation of reading problems. See chapter 11 for a discussion of the reading specialist and problems which may arise for him.

CHAPTER FIFTEEN

THE ROLE OF PARENTS

Advance Organizer

Learning in reading, like all learning, is affected by the home environment of the learner. Parental support can be a positive force in encouraging a child, while parental pressure, often unintentional or unrecognized, adversely affects both performance and attitude. The educative process can be strengthened through open communication between parents and teachers if each group perceives accurately what it can contribute to the other. In this chapter we examine what the teacher of reading needs to know from the parent as well as how the teacher can help parents work with the school for the benefit of their children.

IMPORTANCE OF HOME-SCHOOL COOPERATION

Most parents want and should be given information about the reading program offered by the school. Similarly, only when the teacher of reading can count upon parents as a source of information about individual children and as supporters of the school program, are conditions for optimum learning possible.

Parents are the child's first teachers. They have known him better and for a longer period of time than anyone else. In both the pre-school years and in the school years, home influence has tremendously far-reaching effects on school performance and adjustment. Parents' education, attitudes toward discipline, socio-economic level, employment, and other characteristics influence their interaction with their children and their interpretation of the school's efforts. The parents' attitude toward learning is also an influential force in a child's success or failure.

In the early school years, parents are likely to be more concerned about a child's achievement in reading than in any other subject. Magazines, newspapers, and television bombard parents with information and advice about reading instruction, much of which varies widely in general value and accuracy. Teachers can help parents evaluate such information and can, in the process, communicate with them about the school's curriculum.

The basic premise of this chapter is that teachers must regard parents' interest as an asset in promoting favorable attitudes toward learning in both the school and the home. Accordingly, we shall explore how the teacher can assist the parent in his relationships with children at home, how the parent can function as a visitor at school, and how communication between home and school can be strengthened.

THE PARENTS AT HOME

Assisting parents to understand how their relationship with children in the home affects school learning is an important responsibility of the teacher. Love, pressure, encouragement, interest, or the lack of it, and expectations of parents, while often unknown by the teacher, influence the response of a child. Most parents appreciate specific suggestions from teachers which contribute to the welfare of their children. When parents ask how to help, they are often thinking of direct instructional assistance. Teachers can help parents to realize, however, that indirect support is extremely important while also guiding them with suggestions for direct help.

Following are several suggestions which teachers may offer when answering the parent's query, "How can I help at home?" The suggestions start with the pre-school stage and include both general and specific contributions parents can make to a child's learning.

Parents Help Pre-schoolers by Providing a Foundation for Later Success in School

If the home environment is a stimulating one, with rich and varied experiences along with encouragement of language development through opportunities for hearing and expressing ideas, the child is given an invaluable foundation for school. Early exposure to books, television, and other people will add to the background for learning to read when he enters school. The child whose parents encourage him to question, discover, and experiment is indeed fortunate. The child who is secure at home and who feels that school is regarded with respect and openness begins with a positive attitude.

Parents of pre-school children may wish to begin to instruct their children in reading before kindergarten or first grade. If a child is interested and wants to learn, his curiosity should certainly be encouraged. Although educators disagree on the value of teaching young children to read, there is little disagreement on the importance of parents' spending time with a child in activities in which he is interested. Some children learn nursery rhymes and songs easily and show an early interest in letters and printed words seen on television, on food packages, and in other daily situations. If a child wants to know a word, or asks for help in writing his name and other words, parents should be encouraged to help. If, however, a parent has to force his child to sit and look at a book, to learn the alphabet, or to write letters or his name, such learning can be of negative value to the unmotivated child.

Parents Help by Reading to Children

Children who enter school after having had pleasant experiences with books and reading are more likely to be motivated to learn to read than those who have not been read to in the home. Children who are exposed to books have an early advantage in vocabulary and other aspects of language development, general knowledge background, and imaginative thinking. Even after children have learned to read, the enjoyment of reading in a family situation has many values.

Frequently parents ask teachers to recommend books to be read at home. The reference list in Appendix A provides a helpful resource in this regard, as do the Suggested Readings at the end of chapter 10.

Parents Help by Being Readers Themselves

A parent who reads and enjoys reading communicates through his actions more than his words that reading is a valued activity. Parents who provide books for their children but who do not use their own leisure time for reading may be unaware of the significance of their model. The model of reading parents is valuable in the pre-school years as children first realize that meaning comes from the printed page, although the model of parents enjoying reading both with and independent of children should continue through the school years. Of particular importance to boys is that the father who reads demonstrates that reading can be a masculine pursuit. In a reading home, children can read to each other for practice and pleasure in a setting with an interested audience.

Parents who are library users will probably have children who are also library customers. Teachers would do well to point out to parents the importance of encouraging children to obtain library cards and to frequently use the public library. Parents who take their children to the library, who read to them, and who listen to them read demonstrate that reading is a valued activity.

Parents Help by Taking an Interest in Children's School Experiences

By letting children take home books which they can read easily, teachers encourage children to share their school success with parents. Children can take home booklets of their language experience stories, creative writing, samples of other written work, and special projects. Parents, meanwhile, should be urged to comment on the positive features of the work a child brings home instead of focusing on any errors or shortcomings. If parents are worried about the child's performance in any way, because of the materials he brings home, they should feel comfortable about requesting a conference with his teacher.

Parents Help by Assisting with Reading Instruction at Home

Home instruction by parents should not place the child in an uncomfortable or frustrating learning situation in a manner that is not consistent with the school's approach. Parental help with reading is a fact. A recent survey has shown that almost all parents in the survey offered help when asked to do so, and that parents of slow readers were asked to help more frequently than the parents of average and good readers.[1]

Teachers who enlist parents' assistance have a responsibility to educate parents to recognize situations in which direct instructional help is desirable and situations in which it may be detrimental. Providing parents with specific suggestions should facilitate the learning which occurs at home and can result in correlation, instead of conflict, with the efforts of the school.

One common situation is the moment when a child, reading at home, does not know a word. The parent may wonder if he should tell the child the word or if he should require the child to use phonics to arrive at the pronunciation. The teacher can explain to the parent why he should tell the child the word so that undue discouragement or frustration will not result and so that the meaning of the sentence or story will not be lost because of diverting attention to word analysis. The teacher may explain too that the school's approach to phonics may be different from the parent's and that the child may be confused by the differing approaches. The teacher can also inform parents about the level of the material being used and the rate of the child's progress, so that the parent's expectations of performance are commensurate with the child's ability.

Another common situation that may occur in the home is the occasion in which a child is asked to read at sight material he has never seen before. Parents need to know that children should have a chance to read material silently before being asked to read it aloud. Naturally, there will be times when a child will take home a book which he has read in class, and which he can read orally to his parents without silent reading first. If a child takes home a library book or is given a new book, however, the parents must remember that it should be read silently first unless the child feels it is so easy that he wants to read it orally immediately.

Parents need not ask children to read aloud every book brought home or to read all of a single book. Often, having the child read the part he liked best, or the most exciting section, will be enough to provide a situation in which the parent's interest is conveyed and the child's reading progress assessed. One parent reported that his son who was reluctant to read aloud at home did so eagerly when given his personal tape recorder. The parents did not press the child to play the tapes for them; however, after a few tapes were made, the boy played them proudly for his parents.

Children may feel that reading to their parents involves only the saying of the words but not the understanding of ideas. While parents need not ask questions about every minute detail of a story, and should not expect paraphrasing of a complete story, they should be encouraged by the teacher to talk informally with children about the incidents in the stories they read.

Parents Help by Promoting Good Study Habits

One duty of the teacher is to alert parents to the importance of a quiet, well-lighted study area away from the distractions of the other activities of the home. Setting a time aside for study and reading activities is recommended. Study time at home is ideally balanced by other types of activities. It is also helpful for the homework policies of the school to be clearly articulated to parents. These policies should not be so rigid or punitive that a child is required to spend an excessive amount of time studying. Also, a teacher must be certain that the reading work required of a child at home is worthwhile, that it is needed, that it is on a level where he can be successful, and that it enhances instead of detracts from the child's attitude toward reading and learning.

The teacher may recommend that parents be available for assistance when asked, but that they see their job as one of setting conditions for effective study rather than making home study a tense situation.

A teacher must realize too that for many children the conditions described above are not possible. Requiring homework for these children may be asking something which is impossible regardless of their desire to comply. In such cases, study time at school should be provided if the independent study is essential to school success.

Parents Help by Supporting the School

The confidence of a child in his parents will affect his attitude toward learning. If the parents respect the school, the child will be more likely to do so. When children go home occasionally with misunderstandings about school, it is important that parents, instead of being critical of the school, discuss their questions with the teacher or other school officials. Parents show their support both by their informal comments to children and by their attendance at meetings, conferences, and other school functions.

Parents Help by Providing a Healthy Emotional Atmosphere for Children

A healthy emotional atmosphere is probably the most important contribution of parents to children's well-being and learning. Excessive emphasis on school performance can damage a child's self-image, and parents must be aware of the effect of their expectations on a child's reactions and feelings about himself.

Praise from a parent is a marvelous motivation for a child. When sincerely given, it can result in continued effort by the child. Comparison of a child's achievement or ability with his siblings and peers should be scrupulously avoided. Reasonable expectations, genuine encouragement, and positive guidance help a child to develop a healthy self-concept and sense of self-worth.

THE PARENT AT SCHOOL

Today's schools should be open to parents as visitors and as partners in their children's education. With the exception of a child's comments about school, the communication which occurs in these contacts will be the parents' major source of information about the school's program.

Parents come to school for scheduled activities such as parent-teacher meetings, special programs, and conferences. They may also visit the school informally in the course of transporting children. Parents who feel welcome in both the planned meetings and the informal encounters will have better attitudes toward the school, as well as a greater understanding about the school's program.

Some parents even work directly with the school as aides, as resource people, and as members of school committees such as curriculum revision study groups. The use of para-professionals to assist with nonteaching tasks is becoming an accepted practice. Head Start and other federally funded programs have popularized the use of parent aides who perform clerical tasks, correct papers,

The use of para-professionals—parents and others—to assist with nonteaching tasks is becoming an increasingly widespread practice.

duplicate materials, and assume other duties which detract from a teacher's instruction time. The aide does not normally assume the responsibilities of instruction but can offer some individual help under the guidance of an experienced teacher. Occasionally, a mother who is a trained teacher will volunteer her services as an aide. Such a person can offer valuable help with instruction under the direction of the teacher. Many mothers welcome the opportunity to participate, feeling that they have something to contribute and that they are truly helping.

Drawing upon parents as resource people enriches both the school program and parents' reactions to that program. Many of today's parents have traveled widely and have much to offer in certain facets of curriculum study. Parents of all professions and vocations can profitably discuss or demonstrate their special competencies or interests in relation to children's studies. In some communities parents have helped construct needed materials in work sessions. Occasionally, there may be a parent who is an author of children's books and would like to talk to children about his books and about the way in which they came into being.

In addition to being directly involved in classroom activities with children, parents can contribute by serving on committees which study curriculum or other concerns of the school. If a school district is interested in "nongrading" the elementary schools, for example, it is extremely wise to involve and inform parents and to listen to their feelings about such actions. By incorporating parents in the consideration of adaptations, changes, and additions in school programs and policies, schools will be more likely to enlist parental support.

COMMUNICATING WITH PARENTS

All the above suggestions imply communication between teachers and parents. Channels of communication need to be fostered in specific, deliberate ways, as discussed below.

Reporting

Efforts must be made to give parents information about both the total school reading program and their own child's reading performance. These efforts can be both oral and written, such as communication through report cards, conferences, parent-teacher meetings, newsletters, bulletins, and other means.

The teacher must, of course, report student performance to parents within the context of the school's reporting system. The two most common means of doing so are parent-teacher conferences and report cards. We have already stated guidelines for evaluating children's reading achievement (see chapter 13). The points made were that a report should reflect the child's effort instead of his relative standing in the class, that specific accomplishments in reading skills should be reported, and that evaluation should be honest, fair, and accurate. The purpose of reporting to parents is to inform them, not to present judgmental ratings.

In reporting a student's performance in reading, therefore, the teacher must consider what the parents want to know in addition to what the teacher feels the parents should know. It has long been accepted that "parents want concrete evidence of the status, progress, and development of their children, whether by report cards, by letters, or by conferences."[2]

In addition to information about achievement and adjustment, parents should be given background about reasons and specific recommendations. If a parent is told that his child could do better work in school, for example, he should also be informed why the teacher thinks the child is not working up to his potential. Even more important, specific ideas should be exchanged on how the teacher plans to help the child and how the parent can assist.

Formal reporting is traditionally communicated through some

type of written report. In some instances, the school policy will require grading on achievement only. In other instances, schools permit grades which reflect the child's effort. Teachers have known for some time that grades as such do not serve an effective communication function. Many schools today are looking for a better system to report formally to parents. Check lists of accomplishments are beginning to receive wide use. Such lists do not grade the child, but do indicate which instructional objectives the child is working on and mastering. Other schools are insisting on meeting the parents face-to-face for verbal explanations of the child's progress. In other cases, conferences are used to supplement written reports.

Most educators today sense that grading as it has been traditionally practiced is an unsatisfactory communication system. At times it is even dangerous. Every effort should be made to develop a reporting system which focuses in a positive manner upon what a child has accomplished. The child should understand such a system, and the parents soon should learn to value it. The progress report should be viewed as a bridge to communication between the school and the home.

Conferences

Individual conferences with parents are becoming more widely used in public schools for reporting pupil progress. These can be very influential in building effective home-school communication. In conferring with parents, teachers will find that many of the suggestions given above for eliciting parental help with reading will be welcomed.

The teacher should view a conference not only as an informative session for parents, but as a learning situation for himself. Teachers who listen responsively to parents' concerns are more likely to promote good communication which will work for the welfare of the child than those who treat parental comments lightly. Even when the teacher feels a parent has no basis for his anxiety about a child, that anxious parent does need reassurance that the child has no serious problem.

Parent-teacher interaction involves obligations on both sides. Parents should be encouraged to report symptoms of poor reactions toward reading and toward school. Children may convey to parents certain feelings and fears about school which a teacher may not realize. Discussion between parent and teacher can reveal whether a child is shy or uncomfortable about participating in certain activities and may even uncover the reasons causing certain behavior.

Parents also have an obligation to provide the school with information in regard to health problems so that the teacher can make all possible adjustments in the classroom to compensate for or alleviate any learning problems stemming from the physical problem. A teacher ignorant of a health problem may expect a child to perform in a way in which he cannot possibly succeed. It is also the parent's obligation to follow through on referrals when the school recommends that children receive visual, auditory, psychological, or other evaluations from specialists. It is the teacher's responsibility, in turn, to follow up to determine what action was taken.

Conferences are often most successful when focused on behavioral objectives. The conversation then revolves not around the subjective views of the parent or teacher but on what a child should be able to do after instruction has been given. For example, if the behavioral objective is to be able to pronounce words using initial consonant substitution, the objective can be demonstrated with the child and understood by the parents. Suggestions given to parents may follow this pattern of explaining content in relation to tasks a child should be able to perform.

Examples of the child's work in reading and other objective evidence of his strengths and weaknesses should be available for the conference. Records of the conference should be kept so that future teachers or other school personnel may be aware of teacher suggestions and parental reactions. Generally, these summaries should be written up only after the conference is completed so that parents are not constrained by the teacher's taking notes. An outcome of the conference should be the mutual impression of both parent and teacher that the other is working cooperatively for the benefit of the child.

Meetings

Following a survey of school practices concerned with reading instruction, Austin and Morrison stated: "Apart from reporting pupil progress, school systems make little or no effort to inform parents about the goals of the reading program and the means used by teachers to attain the objectives."[3] This comment points up the significance of communicating with parents in addition to reporting children's achievement. However, many schools are now changing to correct this situation.

A major way of reaching parents to convey information about the school's reading program is through open meetings sponsored by the school. Reading programs are often discussed at PTA meetings with teachers, administrators, and consultants participating as speakers or on panels. Occasionally, a demonstration with children can be presented. Open question and answer sessions between teachers and parents can help eliminate misconceptions or fears parents have about reading instruction. A group meeting is an excellent means for presenting information about how the parents can help both at home and at school.

The demonstration of media such as films, filmstrips, and video tapes helps show specific techniques and materials in use. The materials presently being developed locally by many school systems, with the assistance of their educational technology staffs, are usually fascinating to parents.

Exhibits of many kinds can increase the parents' awareness of what children are doing. Samples of children's work related to reading can be displayed. Also, copies of materials used in the reading program can be placed on exhibition for parental examination. A visit to classrooms should also provide evidence of reading activities.

Printed pamphlets published by the school may be sent home to keep parents informed. Although local pamphlets may be more relevant and meaningful, schools can also purchase pamphlets from various organizations and publishing companies for distribution to parents. For example, the National Education Association prints a small pamphlet entitled, *"Your Child and Reading."* Another helpful booklet is *Ways You Can Help Your Child with Reading.* (See Suggested Readings.)

PROBLEMS IN WORKING WITH PARENTS

In working with parents, as in all phases of the teaching of reading, problems will occur. Some of the most widely discussed are treated here.

The Occasional Disgruntled Parent

Complaints about grouping, methods, and grading may be expressed by parents. If the teacher can convince the parents of his interest in their child, hopefully he will find himself working with the parents for the best interest of the child. Parents should be invited to visit a class to observe instruction and their child's response to the instruction. After an observation session, the parents and teacher analyze the learning situation so that parents can realize the teacher's objectives and have a realistic view of the child's performance at school. The teacher must be open to parents' comments and questions, and he should try to respond to these positively without becoming defensive. The teacher must be able to express clearly his philosophy of learning and his approach to instruction.

The Parent of the Unsuccessful Child

The worried parents of the child who is experiencing difficulty in reading must be given special attention. They usually evidence great concern which in turn affects the child. The poorer a child's achievement, the greater the parental anxiety. If involved diagnosis and remediation are in order, then the parent will need to talk with the reading specialist and others involved in the evaluation of a child's status.

Parents often are not aware of the special services available for problem situations. The teacher needs to explain how specialists can help the child. Recommendations to parents are featured in any written report or case study, but oral interpretation of these recommendations is advised, preferably in the form of a conference including the teacher, the parents, and the specialists involved.

For the child with serious reading problems it is especially important that the specific course of parental action be clearly stated, considering the individual characteristics of the situation.

Parental help with direct instruction should be regarded with caution for those children who have experienced repeated failure and frustration with reading. Only if the teacher is certain that the extra reinforcement offered by the parent will add to, rather than detract from, a child's response to reading should such instruction at home be advised. In a report of neurological and psychological evaluations in a clinic for dyslexic children, Worden and Snyder have stated that "home tutoring leads to anger, frustration, friction, negativism, loss of motivation and considerable family disorganization and conflict."[4] They report that such tutoring failed to result in improvement of reading skill and had undesirable side effects. However, it is possible to guide parents to understand how to assist children so the latter do receive positive help without conflict or frustration. For some children, however, parents should be urged not to give instruction until the severity of the problem has lessened and until the attitude of the child has improved. Advising parents of children with reading problems is always an individual matter.

The Child from a Nonreading Home

Children from homes with few of the opportunities normally associated with reading success need to be identified by each classroom teacher. He should be aware that the home situation may provide little chance for oral communication and that it may also be lacking in books and other materials which would encourage interest in learning. When the teacher becomes aware of experiential limitations, he should attempt to adjust the school experiences to the special needs of the child. In many communities efforts are being made to bring children from such homes to school earlier than kindergarten or first grade so that compensatory education can be offered.

Head-Start programs have involved parents actively in the educational effort. In many urban areas intensive efforts have been made to enlist parental help and to communicate with parents about the school's concern for their children.

Chapter Review

Parents greatly affect the learning situation offered to their children both at home and at school. At home they are responsible for the availability of books and other reading materials. They may be able to provide a quiet area for study. They can take an active interest in homework, in reading to their children, and in discussing books and learning. Even their personal reading habits and attitudes influence their children's view of reading. In conjunction with school, parents can also be of tremendous help in fostering good reading habits. Parent-teacher conferences, group conferences, and observations of lessons all aid in comprehending the specific problems of children and the reading program in general.

The resources of parents add to the total environment for learning. The goal for the future will be improved cooperative efforts of parents and teachers for quality education. Effective learning of the communication skills of reading is facilitated through open communication between parents and teachers.

NOTES

[1] Robert M. Wilson and Donald W. Pfau, "Parents Can Help!" *The Reading Teacher* 21 (May 1968): 758–761.

[2] Gaither McConnell, "What Do Parents Want To Know?" *The Elementary School Journal* 53 (November 1957): 88–90.

[3] Mary Austin and Coleman Morrison, *The First R: The Harvard Report on Reading in Elementary Schools* (New York: Macmillan, 1963), p. 162.

[4] Don K. Worden and Russell D. Snyder, "Parental Tutoring in Childhood Dyslexia," *Journal of Learning Disabilities* 2 (September 1969): 52.

SUGGESTED ACTIVITIES

1. Ask several parents in your community how they are involved in school activities.
2. Attend a PTA meeting. What happened? How many teachers were there? Was there any teacher-parent interaction?
3. Ask parents how reading is taught in their children's classrooms and how the school informs them about reading instruction.

SUGGESTED READINGS

For the Teacher:

Gans, Roma. *Common Sense in Teaching Reading.* New York: Bobbs-Merrill, 1963.

> Presents specific suggestions for developing effective teacher-parent communication.

Smith, Nila B. *Reading Instruction for Today's Children.* Englewood Cliffs: Prentice-Hall, 1963.

> See chapters 19 and 20 for a discussion of techniques and materials for developing parent-teacher communication. Constructive suggestions concerning the role of the parent in the reading process are also included.

Wilson, Robert M. *Diagnostic and Remedial Reading for Classroom and Clinic.* Columbus: Charles E. Merrill, 1967.

> Chapter 10 treats the parental role in diagnosis and remediation.

Suggestions are given to help parents prevent reading problems from developing.

For the Parent:

Casey, Sally. *Ways You Can Help Your Child With Reading.* Evanston, Illinois: Row, Peterson and Company, 1950.

This small pamphlet provides the parent with suggestions for helping his child with reading.

Larrick, Nancy. *A Parent's Guide to Children's Reading.* New York: Doubleday, 1958.

Provides lists of books which parents can obtain for their children and suggests criteria by which books can be selected.

Russell, David H., et al. *Your Child and Reading.* Washington, D.C.: National Education Association.

Contains articles written by reading authorities to help parents develop an awareness of the complexity of reading and to present facts about the effectiveness of reading as it is taught today.

CHAPTER SIXTEEN

FUTURE READING INSTRUCTION

Advance Organizer

Men and women presently entering the elementary teaching profession are doing so at a time of tremendous upheaval in our schools and our society. This is an exciting time to be teaching any subject, and reading is no exception.

This chapter provides a look into the not-too-distant future of the teaching of reading. It illustrates the necessity for viewing education as an ever-changing process. Young people starting their teaching careers will find this discussion helpful in anticipating the future of their profession. They will also note that much of what we consider futuristic is presently in the preliminary stages of development.

To speculate about the future is always difficult. However, the glimpse this chapter provides should help the reader become aware of the fact that the situation as it exists today will not be the same in a few years.

Reading instruction today and tomorrow will be a dynamic, developing field. Innovation is the order of the day. Regardless of our present development, new insights, problems, conceptions, and misconceptions will force us into positions necessitating change. In addition to changes in theory and policy, changes will occur in society as a whole, in public attitudes, in professional preparation, and in school design.

PRESENT AND FUTURE SETTINGS

Reading as it is today is far from being a final product, finished and polished. The reading process, reading instruction, materials for the classroom, and teacher education are always changing—hopefully for the best.

Classifying children's learning by grade level will be increasingly less important. Programmed materials will be used to teach certain types of skills systematically and efficiently through self-pacing, self-correcting techniques. More time will be spent developing the individual as a person who relates effectively to other individuals.

The design of school buildings will reflect teachers' philosophies of how children learn. Buildings will contain large open areas in which several teachers work together to meet children's individual needs. Individualized learning centers will be featured in which children study according to their needs. Small group learning centers will stress activities to promote skill in human relations. In large group learning centers master teachers will present programs appropriate for large groups—programs including features such as lectures, films, and demonstrations.

Financial support for education will be considerably more substantial than it is today, with educational needs at all levels—federal, state, and local—receiving top priority. With increased financial support will come increased responsibility for educators to place all children in effective learning situations. Educators will be held accountable for the education of children. Mediocre teaching, inefficient techniques, and the wasting of student potential and time will not be tolerated. Educators will need to provide evidence of increased efficiency in order to encourage the continued and increased support which is needed.

School systems will provide teachers with resource personnel to assist teachers in implementing the latest research, techniques, and materials. Private organizations not controlled by the schools will bid for opportunities to assist teachers by developing specific programs. Schools will be able to select those programs which fit their needs and purchase them on a contractual basis.

THE TEACHER OF READING

As a closer relationship develops between the schools and colleges, a more meaningful teacher education program will evolve.

Public schools will work with colleges to provide pre-service and in-service experiences. All prospective teacher education students will have extensive field experiences with children as well as pre-service study in the teaching of reading. Teacher education will focus on helping students develop the knowledge and competencies needed to be a skillful teacher.

The graduate will begin his teaching as a member of a team which will include experienced master teachers. He will work closely with other teachers rather than in a self-contained classroom with thirty children dependant upon him alone for all their instruction. Learning from others as a team member will result in continuous professional development. Change, based on new theories and research, should reach the teacher more quickly in team situations.

Not only will teachers work in teams but the full resource potential of the community will be a part of the educational program. Para-professionals, paid aides, volunteer aides, and community resource personnel will find useful roles in the education of the

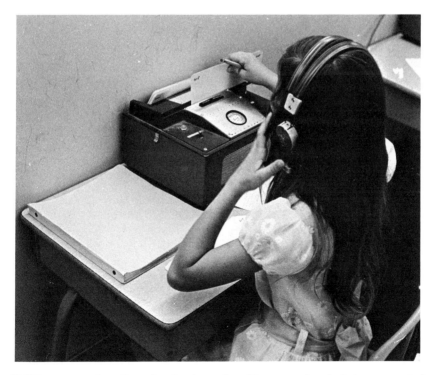

Skill lessons, such as those in phonics and spelling, are already being presented through highly interesting, programmed techniques.

children in their community. The utilization of community resources will enrich the program and also provide teachers with more time to devote to instructional and guidance activities.

Teaching skills for reading will include competency in such areas as diagnosis, programming, questioning, and facilitating human relations. Skill lessons, such as those in phonics and spelling, will be presented through highly interesting, programmed techniques. Teachers will thereby be freed to use their time to direct children toward programs most suited to their previous learnings and their potential. Much of the child's work will be self-correcting—the child will have more opportunities to choose his own areas of work and evaluate his own progress. Children's progress will also be evaluated via the computer which will feed information about the child's performance directly to the teacher. The teacher's time allotted to reading activities will be used to work with small groups of children featuring problem-solving projects related to creative and critical responses to reading materials. Time will be available for individualized attention to any child who needs it.

Training in the area of human relations will be required of all teachers. As the nation's population continues to grow and people continue to live in centralized areas, the problems of getting along with others will become even more demanding than they are today. School situations will be created in which children learn to respect the rights of others, work well together, and understand the behavior of others. Reading lessons will feature literature designed to illustrate many of the problems of human relations in lifelike settings. Stories such as *Stevie,* for younger children, and *Waiting for the Man,* for older children, will replace the types of stories traditionally used as reading material.

THE FUTURE OF REMEDIAL READING INSTRUCTION

Remedial reading as it is now known will no longer exist. Most children will be learning on their own specially identified developmental tracks. As a result, experts in reading will find their attention focused upon diagnostic techniques, programming, research, interpretation, materials evaluation, and instructional strategies. They will be working with teacher teams as resource personnel.

Children with complicated learning disorders may continue to be taught in specialized learning situations. Specially trained teachers will work with these children using the best educational programs.

Most children, however, will be receiving instruction on a developmental track, permitting success and stimulating them through challenge. Children with minor learning problems will be taught in regular classrooms which reflect the philosophy of this book.

READING RESEARCH AS AN ON-GOING ACTIVITY

Because it is a complex process, reading will continue to be studied. The thinking and research from fields such as psychology and linguistics will have far-reaching effects upon reading. A hierarchy of factors in the reading process will be developed with the relationship of reading to language and thinking clearly established.

Research in reading will become more sophisticated. Groups of researchers will combine their talents for more meaningful results —as occurred in the first grade studies of the 1960s. The results of the research will be made available to all educators without the delay of traditional publications. The time gap between the findings of a research project and its implementation in the schools will be lessened considerably. ERIC (Educational Resources Information Center) systems will span the country, providing school personnel with information and new ideas as they are made available.

The reading teacher will be able to conduct research on what he is doing in the classroom. Research assistants will be available to advise and provide technical assistance. Teachers will also find themselves working on local, state, and national research projects, and because of this involvement, will have improved attitudes toward research findings.

Research in reading will be concerned with a better understanding of diagnostic techniques and teaching. Children's strengths and weaknesses will be identified early, and programs will be developed to provide optimal learning situations for all children.

EMERGING READING MATERIALS

Hopefully, publishers will print all educational materials planned for classroom use in experimental editions. Field trials and field tests will determine whether a given material should be mass produced for use in the schools. Such materials will have stated behavioral objectives and will be evaluated according to the objectives. Effects of these materials will also be evaluated as they relate to the attitudes of children toward their learnings.

Technicians, creative professionals, and subject area specialists will be hired by publishing companies as teams to develop high quality books and programs, using exciting combinations of auditory and visual stimuli.

Once tested, materials will be made available to teachers upon request. Computerized centers will store many materials and make them instantly available by a simple dialing procedure. If the material is appropriate for the child, his responses will be recorded and immediately given to the teacher. If the material is not appropriate, the teacher will be informed and a new program selected.

Schools will provide released time for the teacher to act in a professional role in materials selection and program planning. A total program designed to meet the abilities all of the children will need to be carefully planned and will include a selection from many materials.

Instructional Materials Centers

The library will include a wide variety of instructional materials, thus changing its function as a unit used solely for housing and distributing books. In instructional materials centers, any book in print will be available through systems of microfilming and computerized selection. The same will be true for records, films strips, motion pictures, television film clips, and other audio-visual aids.

The instructional materials center will command a central location and consume considerable building space. Children will use the center for recreational reading, studying in areas of interest, and conducting research. The center will be staffed by experts in media to assist children and teachers in locating appropriate material.

Many centers will be open twenty-four hours a day as service centers for the community. Adults as well as children will find the instructional materials useful as they further their studies. Specially trained teachers will staff the centers to provide guidance and assistance.

A great deal more is in the future of reading instruction. And while you live it, you will contribute to it, conduct research in it, make new changes in it, and become a part of it. We hope you will not lose sight of the fact that the children you teach are more important than the specific practices you employ.

SUGGESTED ACTIVITIES

1. Discuss with your fellow-students the "ideal" reading program of the future. What elements of current programs would you include? What new features?
2. Prepare a list of the materials you would order for an ideally equipped classroom.
3. Describe the type of teacher needed for improving the teaching of reading in the future.
4. Visit the most modern elementary school which you can find. How does it compare to the one in which you were taught?

APPENDIX A

CHILDREN'S BOOK LISTS

The following references and book lists are valuable aids in selecting books for children. These materials are available in most public and school libraries.

American Library Association. *Books for Children 1968–1969.* Chicago: The Association, 1970.

> Intended as a book selection aid for librarians and teachers, this publication lists numerous titles by subject and appropriate grade level. The original edition covers the period from 1960 to 1965 and thereafter yearly supplements are published.

—————. *Notable Children's Books 1949–1959.* Chicago: The Association, Children's Service Division, 1966.

> This edition includes books from 1949 to 1959 which have been popular for a minimum of five years. Supplements are published annually.

Arbuthnot, May Hill; Clark, Margaret; and Long, Harriet, eds. *Children's Books Too Good To Miss.* 5th ed. Cleveland: Western Reserve University Press, 1966.

> This illustrated publication lists older books which should not be overlooked because of the abundance of new books and which the editors feel "should be salvaged because of their rich significance for children today." The 200 books included with well-written annotations are for children ages six to fourteen.

Baker, Augusta, ed. *Books about Negro Life for Children.* New York: New York Public Library, 1963.

> Titles with prices and publishers are listed according to subject topics for different age levels.

Child Study Association of America. *Books of the Year for Children.* New York: The Association.

> This inexpensive, annual publication is a good resource for keeping informed about new books.

Crosby, Muriel, ed. *Reading Ladders for Human Relations.* 4th ed. Washington, D.C.: American Council on Education, 1966.

The annotations of over 1,000 books are grouped around six themes dealing with human values and growing up in American society. Within each of the six categories, the listings are arranged in order of difficulty from primary, intermediate, junior, and senior, to mature readers. This publication also contains suggestions for using the books to develop understanding of the themes.

Eakin, Mary K., ed. *Good Books for Children.* 3rd ed. Chicago: Phoenix Books, University of Chicago Press, 1966.

This edition includes reviews of 1,391 outstanding books published from 1950 to 1965. The books range from the pre-school level through high school, although the majority are for ages four to nine.

Growing up with Books. New York: R. R. Bowker.

This brief and inexpensive publication, revised annually, is recommended for parents and lists popular and high quality books.

Growing up with Science Books. New York: R. R. Bowker.

This small, inexpensive, annually revised pamphlet lists 200 of the best science information books.

Guilfuile, Elizabeth, ed. *Adventuring with Books.* New York: The New American Library, Signet, 1966.

This edition contains a listing of 1,250 books for children from ages three to fourteen. Evaluative comments, subject categories, and suggested age levels are given for each book.

——————. *Books for Beginning Readers.* Champaign, Illinois: National Council of Teachers of English, 1962.

An explanatory section provides information on the characteristics, uses, and values of the "easy-to-read" books. Listed with their respective reading levels are 320 books.

Hall, Elvajean, ed. *Personal Problems of Children.* Boston: Campbell and Hall.

Especially helpful for teachers interested in bibliotherapy, this publication lists books in categories of children's problems and classifies them as appropriate for easy, middle, and upper reading levels.

Haviland, Virginia. *Children's Books.* Washington, D.C.: Library of Congress, 1970.

This annual publication gives annotations of books for children from the pre-school stage through junior high school.

Shor, Rachel and Fidell, Estelle A., eds. *Children's Catalog.* 11th ed. New York: H. W. Wilson, 1966.

This comprehensive source of several thousand titles includes a brief statement of content for each entry. Only those books which meet certain standards are listed.

Smollar, Eleanor, ed. *Guide to Book Selection.* Washington, D.C.: National Reading Is Fundamental Program, 1970.

This publication lists paperbacks and other inexpensive books for the elementary grades. It also includes a list of books for ethnic groups: black elementary, teenage, and adult; Indian elementary, teenage, and adult; and Spanish-speaking elementary, teenage, and adult. Each entry states the reading and interest levels.

Solomon, Doris, comp. *Best Books for Children.* New York: R. R. Bowker, 1970.

A paperback publication, this catalog lists 4,000 popular and highly recommended titles by age level in three categories: pre-school—third grade, fourth—sixth grade, and seventh—twelfth grade.

Spache, George D. *Good Reading for the Disadvantaged Reader.* Champaign, Illinois: Garrard, 1970.

This book suggests multi-ethnic resources of interest to minority groups.

—————. *Good Reading for Poor Readers.* Champaign, Illinois: Garrard, 1970.

The emphasis in the annotated bibliographies in chapters 5 through 9 is on materials of high interest but easy reading levels for children who have difficulty reading. Readability levels are given for each listing.

Sunderlin, Sylvia, ed. *Bibliography of Books for Children.* Washington, D.C.: Association for Childhood Education International, 1971.

This bulletin, revised every two years, provides a list of recommended books for children ages two to twelve. Books are classified by topics and each annotation states the age level.

—————. *Children's Books for $1.50 or Less.* Washington, D.C.: Association for Childhood Education International, 1969.

This brief listing, revised every two years, divides inexpensive children's books into eighteen categories with very short annotations for each title. Reading levels are indicated in some instances.

APPENDIX B

BASAL AND
SUPPLEMENTARY
READING
MATERIALS

This appendix is divided into three sections: Section 1 lists basal materials including publishers' names; Section 2, supplementary materials such as books, workbooks, programmed materials, multi-level reading materials, and kits; and Section 3, games and puzzles.

SECTION 1—BASAL MATERIALS

The Alice and Jerry Basic Reading Program
Harper & Row

The Bank Street Readers
Macmillan

Basic Reading Series
Science Research Assocates

Be a Better Reader
Prentice-Hall

The Best in Children's Literature
Bobbs-Merrill

Betts Basic Readers
American Book

The Bookmark Reading Program
Harcourt Brace Jovanovich

Breakthrough Series
Allyn and Bacon

Chandler Language Experience Readers
Chandler

The Creative Reading Program
Harper & Row

The Developmental Reading Series, Basic Reading Program
Lyons and Carnahan

Early-to-Read i/t/a Program
i/t/a Publications

The Ginn Basic Readers
Ginn

The Houghton Mifflin Reading Program
Houghton Mifflin

Instant Readers
Holt, Rinehart and Winston

Language Experiences in Reading
Encyclopaedia Brittanica Press

Let's Read
Clarence L. Barnhardt

Lippincott's Basic Reading
J. B. Lippincott

The Macmillan Reading Program
Macmillan

Merrill Linguistic Readers
Charles E. Merrill

The New Basic Readers
Scott, Foresman

Open Court Basic Readers
Open Court Publishing

Palo Alto Reading Program
Harcourt Brace Jovanovich

Phonetic Keys to Reading, Keys to
Independence in Reading
Economy Press

Programmed Reading
McGraw-Hill, Webster Division

THE READ SYSTEM
American Book

Reading 360
Ginn/Xerox

Reading for Concepts
McGraw-Hill, Webster Division

Reading for Meaning
Houghton Mifflin

Scott, Foresman Reading Systems
Scott, Foresman

The Sheldon Basic Reading Series
Allyn and Bacon

TMI Programmed Primer
Teaching Materials Corporation

Winston Basic Readers
Holt, Rinehart and Winston

SECTION 2—SUPPLEMENTARY MATERIALS

Books, workbooks, and programmed materials provide those supplementary materials more commonly found in classrooms today. Kits and multi-level materials include supplementary materials packaged for use in elementary classrooms.

Books, Workbooks, Programmed Materials

Barnell Loft Series
Barnell Loft

Building Reading Skills
McCormick-Mathers

The Challenge Reader Series
McCormick-Mathers

The Developmental Program in
Visual Perception
Follett

Garrard Poetry Books
Garrard

Gates-Peardon Practice Exercises in
Reading
Teachers College Press

Go Ahead Books
McCormick-Mathers

Ideas, Images and I
American Book

Learning to Read Through Creative
Movement
Kimbo Records

The Macmillan Reading Spectrum
Macmillan

The New Phonics Skilltexts
Charles E. Merrill

The New Reading Skilltext Series
Charles E. Merrill

Phonics We Use
Lyons and Carnahan

Phonovisual
Phonovisual Products

Readiness and Language Arts
Program
Behavioral Research Lab

Reading for Meaning
J. B. Lippincott

The Reading Round Table Series
American Book

Reading Skill Builders
Reader's Digest

Rebus
American Guidance Service

Sounds of Language
Holt, Rinehart and Winston

Specific Skills Series
Barnell Loft

Standard Test Lessons in Reading
Teacher's College Press, Columbia University

Visual-Lingual Reading Program
Tweedy Transparencies

Webster New Practice Readers
McGraw-Hill, Webster Division

Weekly Reader Practice Books
American Education Publications

Word Clue Series
Educational Developmental Laboratories

Words in Color
Ginn Xerox

Multi-level Reading Materials and Kits

Building Reading Power
Charles E. Merrill

Classroom Library Packet
Economy Company

EDL Study Skills Library
Educational Developmental Laboratories

Language Kit A
Ginn

Peabody Language Development Kits
American Guidance Service

Phonics Practice Program
Harcourt Brace Jovanovich

THE READ SYSTEM, READ ROUNDUP KITS Levels A, B, C
American Book

Reading Pacemakers
Random House

Speech to Print Phonics
Harcourt Brace Jovanovich
SRA Labs and Kits
  Organizing and Reporting Skills
  Pilot Library
  Reading for Understanding
  Reading Labs Ia, Ib, Ic,
    IIa, IIb, IIc,
    IIIa, IV
  Word Games Lab I
Science Research Associates

Tactics in Reading I, II, III
Scott, Foresman

Webster Classroom Reading Clinic
McGraw-Hill, Webster Division

Word Growth Program
Curriculum Associates

SECTION 3—GAMES AND PUZZLES

Dolch Letter and Word Games
  Basic Sight Cards
  Consonant Lotto
  Group Word Teaching Game
  Match
  Picture Word Cards
  Popper Words
  The Syllable Game
  Take
  What the Letters Say
  Vowel Lotto

Garrard

Flash Words
Milton Bradley

Milton Bradley Games
Milton Bradley

My Blue Puzzle Book
My Green Puzzle Book
My Red Puzzle Book
McCormick-Mathers

New Puzzle Pages 1–4
McCormick-Mathers

Picture Word Builder

Phonics Crossword Puzzles, Books A, B, C
McCormick-Mathers

Phonics We Use, Learning Game Kit
Lyons and Carnahan

Puzzle Fun
McCormick-Mathers

The Rolling Reader
Scott, Foresman

Space Carnival
McCormick-Mathers

Word-Roll
McCormick-Mathers

Words that Go Together
Milton Bradley

APPENDIX C

STANDARDIZED
READING TESTS

This appendix contains a listing of reading tests commonly available to classroom teachers. Section 1 treats reading readiness tests; Section 2, group reading tests for elementary grade levels; and Section 3, individual reading tests for elementary grade levels.

All of the tests mentioned have manuals of instruction and interpretation for the teacher's use.

SECTION 1—READING READINESS TESTS

Clymer-Barrett Prereading Battery. Princeton: Personnel Press, 1966–1967.

> Subtests: Visual, auditory, and visual-motor discrimination.

Gates-MacGinitie Reading Tests. New York: Columbia University, 1968.

> Subtests: Listening comprehension; auditory and visual discrimination, following directions, letter recognition, visual-motor coordination, auditory blending, word recognition.

The Harrison-Stroud Reading Readiness Profiles. Boston: Houghton Mifflin, 1956.

> Subtests: Using symbols, making visual and auditory discriminations, using context, using context and auditory clues, naming letters.

Lee-Clark Reading Readiness Test. Monterey: California Test Bureau, 1962.

> Subtests: Matching, cross-outs, total vocabulary, following instructions, and identification of letters and words.

Metropolitan Readiness Tests. New York: Harcourt Brace Jovanovich, 1964.

> Subtests: Word meaning, listening, matching, alphabet, numbers, and copying.

Murphy-Durrell Reading Readiness Analysis. New York: Harcourt Brace Jovanovich 1965.

> Subtests: Phonemes, letter names, and learning rate.

SECTION 2—GROUP READING TESTS

The Botel Reading Inventory.** Chicago: Follett, 1966. Grades 1-6.

Subtests: Word opposites (reading), phonics mastery.

California Reading Tests.* Monterey: California Test Bureau, 1957. Norms revised 1963. Grades 1-2, 2-3-4, 4-5-6.**

Subtests: Reading vocabulary (mathematics, science, social studies, and general) and reading comprehension (following directions, reference skills, and interpretation of material).

Gates-McGinitie Reading Tests. New York: Columbia University, 1965. Grades 1, 2, 3, 2-3, 4-6.**

Subtests: Vocabulary, comprehension, speed, and accuracy.

Iowa Tests of Basic Skills.* Boston: Houghton Mifflin, 1956. Grades 3-6.**

Subtests: Vocabulary and reading comprehension.

Metropolitan Reading Tests. New York: Harcourt Brace Jovanovich, 1959. Grades 2, 3-4, 5-6.**

Subtests: Word knowledge and reading.

Stanford Achievement Tests.* New York: Harcourt Brace Jovanovich, 1964. Grades 4.0-5.4, 5.4-6.9.

Subtests: Vocabulary and comprehension.

SECTION 3—INDIVIDUAL READING TESTS

Botel Reading Inventory. Chicago: Follett, 1966. Grades 1-6.

Subtest: Word recognition.

Gilmore Oral Reading Tests. New York: Harcourt Brace Jovanovich, 1952. Grades 1-6.

Subtests: Oral reading accuracy, comprehension, and speed.

Gray Oral Reading Tests. Indianapolis: Bobbs-Merrill, 1963. Grades 1-6.

Subtests: Oral reading errors, speed, and comprehension.

For further information on tests listed and for information concerning other tests in reading see:

Austin, Mary C., et al. *Reading Evaluation.* New York: Ronald Press, 1961.

---

*Part of an Achievement Test Battery.
**Advance levels also available.

Buros, Oscar K. *The Sixth Mental Measurements Yearbook.* Highland Park, New Jersey: Gryphon Press, 1965.

—————. *Reading Tests and Reviews.* Highland Park, New Jersey: Gryphon Press, 1968.

Dechant, Emerald. *Diagnosis and Remediation of Reading Disabilities.* West Nyack: Parker Publishing, 1968.

Wilson, Robert M. *Diagnostic and Remedial Reading.* Columbus: Charles E. Merrill, 1967.

INDEX